Kitchen Conundrums

ROBERT J STORDY

Published by New Generation Publishing in 2018

Copyright © Robert J Stordy 2018

Second Edition

The author asserts the moral right under the Copyright, Designs and Patents Act 1988 to be identified as the author of this work.

All Rights reserved. No part of this publication may be reproduced, stored in a retrieval system or transmitted, in any form or by any means without the prior consent of the author, nor be otherwise circulated in any form of binding or cover other than that which it is published and without a similar condition being imposed on the subsequent purchaser.

www.newgeneration-publishing.com

Contents

Introduction 1

Part 1: METHODS OF COOKING 5

  Chapter 1 7

    DRY METHODS OF COOKERY 7

      Shallow frying 7

      Grilling (broiling) 17

      Roasting 18

      Baking 34

      Microwave cookery 35

  Chapter 2 37

    MOIST METHODS OF COOKING 37

      Braising and stewing 37

      Boiling, poaching and pressure cooking 45

      Steaming 52

  Chapter 3 53

    STOCKS, SOUPS AND SAUCES (Including dressings) 53

  Chapter 4 80

    FRUIT AND VEGETABLES 80

  Chapter 5 100

    DESSERTS and PUDDINGS 100

  Chapter 6 119

    PASTRY AND BAKED GOODS 119

PART 2 135

  Chapter 7 136

    Heat transfer *(kinetic energy)* and cooking 136

  Chapter 8 141

    COOKING PROCESSES 141

Chapter 9 154
    FOOD PRESERVATION 154

Chapter 10 169
    FATS, CARBOHYDRATES AND PROTEINS – AN OVERVIEW 169

Chapter 11 177
    KITCHEN EQUIPMENT, UTENSILS AND GADGETS 177

Chapter 12 185
    Food safety and hygiene 185

RECIPES 193
    Basic stock 193
    Consommé (basic recipe) 195
    Potato and watercress soup (basic recipe) 196
    Cured and pan fried mackerel, apple and fennel salad, cucumber mayonnaise 197
    Open seafood lasagne, English asparagus, Prosecco and dill sauce 198
    Tagliatelli Aribiata 200
    Paella 201
    Steak with Thai green risotto, shitake mushrooms 202
    Strawberry parfait 203
    Amaretto panna cotta, mixed berry compote 204
    Basic Ice cream recipe – vanilla 205
    Lemon curd ice cream: 206
    Short crust pastry: 207
    Sugar (sweet) paste 208
    Choux pastry 209
    Nut brittle 209
    Caramels 210
    Fudge 211

Chocolate brownie	212
Fondue	213
Passion fruit curd	214
Basic Cold set vanilla cheese cake recipe	215
Orange marmalade	217
Resources and useful contacts	219
GLOSSARY	222
BIBLIOGRAPHY	232
INDEX	234

KITCHEN CONUNDRUMS – WHAT WENT WRONG?

Introduction

My first induction in cookery was at the age of eleven, when I asked my mother if I could help to make the Sunday lunch. In those days our family lunch always consisted of a roast meat with the usual vegetable and potato accompaniments and on this occasion, as I remember, it was leg of lamb. I don't know why I volunteered my help, but I do know that this experience was the first of many to launch me onto a career in the Catering Industry. After a two year stint at catering college, I joined the industry as a commis chef and for over forty years continued my career as a chef. This book is therefore a culmination of my time as a chef, chef manager and a college and university lecturer.

Why 'Kitchen Conundrums'? I wanted a title that would best represent the theme of the book. Whilst not a cookery book based on recipes, it attempts to address the problems which all too often arise when cooking or baking.

The intention of this book is to provide the reader with easy to understand information about a broad range of food and cooking issues, including some secrets and tips of the trade along the way. It also sets out to explore many of the fundamentals of cookery whilst explaining, in simple terms, some of the science behind it.

I wrote this book with the intention of making it both informative and of interest to as many people as possible, from the person who occasionally dabbles in the kitchen to the serious amateur or professional cook and chef. I also believe that it makes a useful reference book for those who would like to broaden their understanding of food and cooking.

When cooking does go wrong, it can be extremely frustrating, at times annoying and on rare occurrences, it can evoke a self imposed vow to never set foot in a kitchen ever again.

After the disappointment has subsided, and the large glass of wine or beer has taken effect, the best policy, I believe, is to deal with mistakes or failures by adopting a constructive and pragmatic approach. After all cookery is very much a practical subject.

Cookery is a huge subject. It is continually evolving with the introduction of new ingredients, flavour combinations, ever changing trends and innovations. Nevertheless, the fact remains that the basic principles of cookery are unchanged, regardless of this diversity. The overriding principle, the real essence of cooking lies in the control of heat and the length of time that food is subjected to it.

To the beginner, cooking can seem daunting. My advice for those starting off from scratch or with very little knowledge or experience in the kitchen, is to start with simple recipes and strive to prepare the food to a good standard before moving on to more complex ones. Assess and review what you have made, identify the good and the bad points of the dish. How can you improve on it next time, what would you do differently? Once you can answer such questions then you will become a more accomplished cook and your self confidence will continue to grow.

How to use this book:

This book consists of two halves. The first part is the 'Instructive' and the second half, the 'Informative'. In the first section I have provided information on aspects of the different cookery methods, and hopefully in a way that allows for quick access to answers on a particular topic. The second half is a mix of subject chapters ranging from what happens to food during cooking, the ins and outs of kitchen equipment, food safety in the home and food preservation techniques.

Also included is a glossary which provides definitions and explanations of food and cookery terms used throughout the book.

Although this was never intended as a cookery book in the true sense, I have supplied a number of recipes with the intention of illustrating the use of various ingredients and cookery methods.

A word of caution about recipes on the internet. There are thousands upon thousands of them, and just because they are in the public domain does not mean that they are trustworthy. Many I have found to be either confusing or inaccurate and at the very worst, do not work at all. My advice is, use recipes that have been written by accomplished food and cookery writers. Cookery and bakery institutes and associations are also good sources of recipes, advice and tips.

Finally, if you have been inspired, intrigued or just want to find out more about a particular topic or subject in this book, I have provided a list of trustworthy resources. This again can be found towards the end of the book.

My ten top tips for successful and enjoyable cooking:
1. Put time aside to cook, trying to fit other activities around are a distraction (easier said than done, I know).
2. Plan what you are going to cook: read the recipe and make sure that you have ALL the ingredients and equipment to hand.

3. Prepare and organise the work area, weigh out ingredients, pre-heat oven where applicable, prepare cooking equipment; line cake tins etc.
4. Follow the recipe and don't cut corners.
5. Keep a watchful eye over pans on hobs and food in the oven to ensure they are not getting to much heat i.e. simmering and not boiling, lightly browning not burning in the oven.
6. Use a digital temperature probe to test 'doneness' when cooking meat.
7. Always taste the dishes that you are cooking, they may need additional ingredients such as seasoning, herbs or cream. It is important to remember this if you are cooking for others and not just yourself.
8. Make a note of any changes that you have made to a recipe or method. If it was successful you will more than likely want to make it again sometime.
9. Accept constructive criticism, it may help you improve the dish for next time.
10. Wash up as you work, soak any equipment with stubborn cooked on food in warm soapy water; it leaves less to do at the end.

I hope you find this book informative and stimulating, Happy Cooking.

Part 1

METHODS OF COOKING

INTRODUCTION

When food is cooked, the method or methods that are used form an integral part of the recipe; in many circumstances, it is the only way the food or dish is cooked. Throughout the process of cooking food, one or a combination of methods is used, and this ultimately depends upon the complexity of the dish or meal.

This is particularly so, where there is a need for differing levels of heat; for example, in the preparation of braised steak; prior to braising, the meat is shallow fried quickly to give it colour.

Tender, choice cuts of beef such as steaks are never stewed or braised, but grilled or pan-fried. In contrast, tougher cuts, such as shin or brisket, would never be pan-fried or grilled but necessitate being cooked by slower, moist methods of cooking.

The amount of heat and time required varies considerably from one cooking method to the other. At extremes, a traditional grill (a broiler in USA) can reach temperatures in excess of 400°C, whilst poaching employs more gentle temperatures of around 70-85°C. Cooking times can be as little as a few seconds, for a steak served bleu (very underdone), or many hours for a slowly braised oxtail.

Categorised into dry and moist methods, each method is chosen for its suitability to cook a varied range of ingredients in order to produce a desired food item or dish:

METHODS OF COOKING

Moist	Dry
Boiling	Frying (shallow and deep)
Poaching	Grilling/broiling
Stewing	Baking
Braising	Roasting
Steaming	Microwaving

Chapter 1

DRY METHODS OF COOKERY

Dry cooking involves the transfer of heat to foods without the presence of an aqueous liquid, such as water. Differing forms of heat transfer are involved. During baking, convection currents in the oven transfer heat to the food. Conducted heat is transferred through contact with metal utensils (i.e. pots and pans) as used in shallow frying. Radiation is a process of cooking food with radiated infrared heat as for grilling. Finally, microwaving cooks food in a similar way to grilling but uses a different type of radiation.

Temperatures involved in dry cookery methods are generally much higher than those used in moist methods.

Certain chemical reactions cannot take place unless there is sufficient heat; caramelisation and Maillard reactions namely require temperatures in excess of boiling (100∘C) before reactions can occur, therefore the colouring of foods (such as meats, fish, vegetables and starch foods) is only possible with the application of dry heat.

Many foods, especially meat, fish, fruit and vegetables, contain large amounts of water and, during the application of dry heat; this moisture is driven or evaporated off from the foods surface in the form of steam by the high temperatures reached.

Not all foods, though, are suited to these methods of cooking; many foods need a certain amount of liquid in the cooking process to achieve the desired outcome, in particular where lower temperatures of cooking are used such as in stewing or braising.

For further details about heat transfer please go to Chapter 7.

Shallow frying

This term can also include griddling, pan-frying, stir-frying, sautéing and sealing or searing, although there are subtle differences in their method and application. These methods of cookery use high temperatures for short periods to cook a range of food types, which are generally portion size. Steaks, bacon, chops and cutlets, fish fillets, chicken pieces, eggs, stir-fries, diced or sliced vegetables, pancakes, are all examples of foods cooked by one of these forms of shallow frying.

METHOD

Food is fried quickly and at high temperature, this ensures that the food cooks and colours within a short time. Frying temperatures usually range between 170 and 190°C, and with the exception of dry-frying, various oils or clarified butter (ghee) is used. During the frying process the fat acts as a cooking medium and conducts heat from the pan to the surface of the food. In the case of sealing or searing, the outer surface of the food is subjected to high heat for a matter of seconds. Treating food this way adds colour and produces new flavour compounds, in the way that frying a steak not only adds colour, but gives the meat that mouth-watering beefy, umami flavour.

HEAT TRANSFER: Conduction.

The heat is conducted from the pan through the fat onto the surface of the food, where it is conducted through the food. No other forms of heat transfer are involved, unless a further method of cooking is applied.

PROCESS

Many foods that are shallow fried contain varying levels of moisture, both internally and on the surface. When foods are placed into a hot pan, the surface moisture is vaporised immediately, but over a period of time, the foods internal moisture seeps out, and if this is allowed to collect in the pan, the food can boil rather than fry. When shallow frying meat, this is a particular concern as meat juices can collect in the pan and cause the meat to boil, resulting in a toughened piece of meat. It is therefore vital that the pan is heated to a high temperature at the onset, and maintained during the frying process, so that any moisture seepage is driven off immediately. Secondly if the pan becomes too cool, the Maillard and caramelisation reactions will stop, halting further colouration and the creation of new flavour molecules. Finally, excessive oil or fat can be absorbed by certain foods, resulting in an overly greasy mouth feel.

    The choice of pan is important in shallow frying, especially if using an electric ring, plate or ceramic hob. The pan base must be flat to ensure good contact with the cooking surface. If the base is uneven, then the opportunity for gaining maximum heat is lost. This is not a concern with gas ring hobs as the heat from the gas is in direct contact with the total area of the pan base. Heavier, thicker pans made from cast iron or stainless steel conduct the heat more evenly along the pan base and hold the heat longer than that of a thin aluminium pan.

    Traditional tinned copper pans, whilst look fantastic when polished, are impractical for the domestic kitchen. Though very good at conducting heat, they are very heavy and are not suited to high temperature cooking, such as stir- frying, because of the low melting point (232°C) of the tin lining.

A good heavy, non-stick coated stainless steel or aluminium pan is ideal for most shallow frying needs.

For further information on sauce and frying pans, please see Chapter 11 Kitchen Equipment and Utensils.

SHALLOW FRYING TIPS:

1) Ensure the food that is intended for frying is not wet, this is important, where foods have been washed or rinsed, such as raw vegetables, or meats that have been marinated; failure to do so will cause the hot fat to spit and at a high enough temperature has the potential to catch fire.
2) Cut all raw meat and vegetables uniformly, so they cook through evenly. Remember also that some ingredients cook quicker than others, so add these towards the end of the frying process, especially green vegetables.
3) If food is to be seasoned, this can be done prior to frying or by adding seasoning to the food in the pan. In either case, the seasoning should be minimal, particularly with inherently salty food.

   NOTE: if the intention is to use the pan juices from the food as a base for the sauce then even minimum seasoning of the food could ultimately result in a finished sauce which is too salty.

4) Heat the frying pan with a little fat (oil or clarified butter or both) until hot before adding food items. For cuts of meat, such as chops, culets and steaks, it is essential to heat the pan before adding the food. This will sear the surface of the meat and quickly evaporate or burn off the water content from the exuding juices; if the temperature is too low the meat will begin to boil in its own juices, resulting in toughened meat.
   NOTE, frying meat such as steaks or chops in hot fat does NOT seal in the juices; the purpose of placing meat into a hot frying pan is to initiate the Maillard reaction thereby creating surface colour, and development of numerous new flavour and aroma molecules.
5) Place the ingredients carefully into the pan, away from you to avoid splashes of hot fat. A safer way is to oil meats prior to frying, rather than pouring oil into the frying pan. Do not overload, as this will lower the temperature of the pan and promote water seepage from the food. This can also result in soggy food. Keep the food on the heat to maintain a high temperature, and keep it moving continually to cook and colour evenly.

6) During the frying process, adjust the heat according to the doneness and colour of the food. If an item has reached the desired colour, but requires further cooking, then continue cooking in a moderate oven. This way, the food will be cooked thoroughly without colouring further.
7) When shallow frying multiple portions of bread crumbed food, clean the pan out between batches. Breadcrumbs, because of their dryness, burn quickly and, if not removed, will stick to the next batch as unsightly small black particles.
8) Remember to rest all shallow fried meats for about 5 mins. before serving to allow muscle proteins to relax and maintain as much moisture content as possible.
9) NOTE: shallow frying with butter adds a wonderful flavour to foods; however, because butter contains small amounts of solids, it colours and burns easily at a lower temperature than ghee or oils. By compromising and adding a small amount of butter to oil, food can be fried without the butter becoming too brown but still result in the food taking on a buttery flavour.

Steaks for frying (or grilling)

While prime steaks such as fillet, rump and sirloin are still the most popular, lesser known cuts are becoming more available in butchers shops and on supermarket counters.

These steaks are cut from large primal joints, which originally would be used for stewing or braising meat. Modern butchery techniques, such as seam cutting has enabled the removal of these single muscle meat cuts.

Bavette or sirloin flap steak
A thin long, flat cut of beef from the lower part of the sirloin. The meaty is quite fatty but has plenty of flavour.

Flank steak or London broil
Cut from the abdominal muscles (flank) and has very coarse long meat fibres, has plenty of flavour but can be tough, marinades well and should be sliced thinly.

Flat iron or butlers
Is a steak cut from the feather muscle from the shoulder. It contains a large connective tissue membrane which can make the meat tough if not removed, these cuts are both flavour full and tender.

Onglet (hanger or butchers steak in UK)
Is a flat cut of meat from the diaphragm of the animal. It has a loose grain but can be tough if cooked more than rare.

Picanha (Portuguese for cap of rump)
A steak cut from the rump cap. It has a lean texture with a thin layer of surface fat.

Rib eye steak
A cut from the rib section with bones removed. It contains good levels of fat marbling which adds flavour and keeps the meat fibres moist during cooking.

The thumb rule for cooking these steaks is to grill or pan fry at high temperature for short periods. They should be served rare to medium rare, further cooking tends to make the meat tough. Because the muscle fibres in these cuts are quite course, it is important to slice/ carve the steaks 'across the grain'

Fish

Most types of fish lend themselves well to being cooked by shallow-frying. But as with other cookery methods, shallow frying fish has its own challenges. Fish can be easily over cooked, and because of its structure, becomes delicate to handle and breaks apart easily.

In cookery parlance the term *meunière* (translated: millers style) is the traditional way in which fish is dredged with flour, shallow fried and served with lemon, parsley and nut brown butter (beurre noisette).

The process of shallow frying fish is therefore the same, although many recipes do not coat the fish in flour before frying and many dispense with the butter sauce.

Shallow frying is a suitable method for cooking small whole fish and fillets; plaice, sole, sardines, trout, herring, mackerel, sea bass; small cuts from large fillets; cod, pollock, salmon; some shell fish, prawns, squid and scallops. The cook also has the option of leaving or removing the skin prior to cooking.

TIPS:
1. Use a frying pan, preferably non-stick and one that makes good contact with the heat source.
2. Some recipes suggest lightly flouring the fish; this helps the delicate flesh hold together during frying. Flour also helps to give the fish an even golden brown colour.
3. Pans must be sufficiently hot enough to start the frying process immediately. Failure to do so can quickly result in breaking up of the delicate flesh.
4. Fish fillets should be placed presentation side (the surface next to the bone) down in the pan, so when turned over and cooked on the reverse side, they are ready to be transferred to the serving dish.
5. Searing small fish cuts such as fillets to crisp the skin and barely cook the fish requires a very hot pan with a very small amount of oil which should be almost at smoke point before placing the fish in. The fish must be placed skin side down first, and it is also usually necessary to hold it down initially, as it has a tendency to curl inwards; this ensures searing of the total skin surface.
6. It should not be necessary to turn fish over in the pan more than once.
7. After frying thick cuts of fish and fish on the bone, they may need further cooking in the oven; this will ensure that the fish is thoroughly cooked.

Pancakes and crêpes (sweet or savoury)

There is very little difference between the two; pancakes are traditionally British, while crêpes have French origins; it can also be argued that crêpes are normally made thinner than the traditional British pancake.

The three key considerations when making either of these batter - based preparations are: the pan, the viscosity (consistency) of the batter, and the technique involved.

TIPS:
1. Use a good non stick frying pan. Omelette pans are also a good alternative as they usually have a non-stick coated surface.
2. The batter should be similar to the consistency of whipping cream: if it is too thick it will not spread out thinly on the base of the pan, resulting in a thick stodgy pancake; if it is too thin, then the pancake will form holes, be more likely to stick to the pan and be too delicate to turn over.
3. It is important to strain batter through a sieve before using to remove any lumps.
4. A good technique requires pouring the batter into the pan and, at the

same time, swilling it around to cover the pan base. Any excess batter can be poured off before returning the pan to the heat. If the pan has a good non-stick surface then oiling/greasing between pancakes should not be necessary.
5. Whist tossing pancakes may be fun, it can be wasteful, a palette knife to turn over the pancakes makes the task easier and more reliable. When the pancake begins to brown at the edge, this is the time to turn it over onto the other side.
6. It is important not to stack hot pancakes on top of each other as they will stick together; separate them with Clingfilm or pieces of greaseproof paper.
7. If perfectly uniform, round pancakes are desired, trim around the edges using a large pastry cutter or up turned plate.
8. Crêpes and pancakes can be made well in advance and kept refrigerated or frozen until ready for use.

Sauté

Translated from French means to jump and shares the same principles to those of shallow frying and stir-frying. Sautéing is usually done in a shallow pan; the food item is tossed (sautéed) during cooking to ensure even cooking and colour. Some meats, vegetables and potatoes can be cooked by sautéing. When meats are sautéed, the dish is often finished by deglazing (swilling) the pan's residue with stock, wine or vinegar, which then forms the base of the sauce. Many classical sauté dishes can be found in older cook books, but one that is still popular today is poulet (chicken) sauté chasseur: sautéed chicken pieces in a white wine, tomato, and mushroom and tarragon sauce.

Sweat – to sweat or sweat off

Onions, shallots and garlic in particular are said to be sweated off when shallow-fried without colour. Other root vegetables are also sweated off, usually in butter or oil. The purpose of this process is to partially or totally cook the vegetable, which by softening the cell walls, releases flavour and aroma molecules and, also makes them softer to the bite. It is important that low heat is applied in conjunction with regular stirring to avoid adding colour to the vegetable in question.

Stir-frying

This is an extremely quick method of shallow frying food that is synonymous with oriental cuisines. Stir-frying is not easily done well, especially without the correct cooking equipment. Stir frying demands high temperatures to cook and colour food items within very short time periods and some cooking appliances struggle to deliver such intense heat. The main problem lies with the heat source; consider a commercial wok burner, it is basically a large open gas burner that produces intense heat; it also requires a highly effective extraction system, something the customary home kitchen does not possess.

Stir frying can be achieved successfully in the home if the cooker has a gas top burner, the pan can be moved around and tossed whilst still in a position over the heat; it also allows the use of a wok rather than a frying pan, whereas this is almost impossible with an electric or ceramic hob. If using an electric ring, plate or ceramic hob, use a flat bottomed frying pan and make sure that it has good contact with the heat source.

STIR-FRYING TIPS:

1. Because it is such a fast method of cooking, it is important to make sure that all elements of the dish are prepared and ready to add to the pan. Having to interrupt the stir frying process to prepare a further ingredient, means removing the pan from the heat source. This inevitably results in heat loss, which in turn will allow the food to boil rather than fry
2. Ensure all vegetables are cut into even thickness of slices, dice or strips. This will help to cook them evenly.
3. Meat and fish should also be uniform in thickness;, bear in mind, the thinner the cut the quicker they will cook through. Make sure any marinades are wiped off so that the meat or fish is dry, excess liquid will cause undue spitting, cool the pan down and may cause the food to boil instead of fry.
4. It may be necessary not to season the food before stir-frying, especially if the dish is to be finished with a salty sauce, such as soya, teriyaki, oyster or black bean.
5. Make sure the correct oil is used; canola,(rapeseed), groundnut sesame, soybean, or peanut oils, are ideal as they have a high smoke point. Olive oil (not virgin which has a low smoke point) can also be used for stir frying but like peanut impart, their own distinctive flavours.
6. Pre-heat the pan before adding the oil: it needs to be very hot. Use your own judgment about the amount of oil; this will depend upon

the amount of food to be stir fried; too little and the food will stick to the pan and burn, too much and the food will be greasy. Control of heat is the essence, in conjunction with continuous movement of the pan, to effect even cooking and browning. The object is to cook the food items, such as raw meat and fish, until they are just done, whilst vegetables remain crisp with their natural vibrant colours. Some light browning may also be desirable.
7. Add any sauces towards or at the end of the stir fry process.

Velveting is a process used in oriental cookery where meat, particularly chicken and pork is coated with a mixture of egg white and corn flour, prior to further cooking. Strips or small pieces of meat are soaked in a mixture of egg white and corn flour and in some recipes; rice wine and soy sauce are also added. The meat is then dipped in simmering water or hot oil for a matter of a few seconds before being finished by stir-frying. The egg and corn flour mix gives the meat a protective coating, allowing juices to be retained and at the same time, acting as a heat buffer to prevent the meat from becoming over cooked.

Deep-frying

METHOD: Food is totally immersed in hot fat; usually at temperatures between 175°C and 190°C, although the temperature for blanching potatoes (cooking without colour) is usually about 120°C. The frying medium or cooking oils used today are all derived from plants. They, not only have higher smoke points than animal fats, such as lard or butter, but are considered healthier; they are also chosen for their neutral flavour.

HEAT TRANSFER: Convection currents in the oil heat the surface of the food, heat is conducted from the surface through to the centre of the food.

PROCESS:
When food is added to hot oil, it begins to form bubbles. These bubbles are pockets of water that are quickly turned to steam and escape as vapour through the oil and to the surface. The hotter the oil and the higher the moisture content of the food, the more vigorous the bubbles are. During this stage the internal moisture of the food transforms into steam and has already began the process of cooking the food. The food surface becomes crisp as it dehydrates. When the excess moisture has been driven off, the bubbles then subside. At these temperatures, Maillard and caramelisation reactions take place, giving the food surface or crust its golden brown colour, distinct flavour and aroma profiles.

With starchy fried foods, as in chips, the heat causes starch granules to gelatinize. In foods such as fish and poultry, the proteins denature and in the case of vegetable, cellulose structures soften.

Maintaining the correct oil temperature during frying is crucial. If the temperature drops too low, when frying breaded or batter coated food items, the outer crust forms slowly and the food is at risk of breaking up. If the oil becomes too hot, the food burns on the surface before it has time to cook through. Continued frying of foods at too low temperatures, leads to greater absorption of fats, making the food taste greasy.

DEEP – FRYING TIPS:
1. Set the fryer to the correct temperature before placing food in. If unsure, consult the fryer's instructions or the relevant recipe. Foods requiring blanching(cooking without colour), such as chips/French fries, will need a cooler temperature of about 120°C
2. Ensure food is not fragile and likely to fall into pieces.
3. When deep-frying foods that are coated in breadcrumbs, press the breadcrumb coating to the food and shake off any excess; loose breadcrumbs which fall off food will shorten the shelf life and quality of the oil. If the oil is often used to fry breaded food, then it should be strained regularly to remove coating particles.
4. When frying -food items in batter do not use the basket; the combination of heat and the batter make a perfect glue and will 'weld' the food item to the basket.
5. Make sure ALL food items are dry, placing wet items into hot fat not only reduces the life of the oil, it is exceptionally dangerous, and can result in serious burns and kitchen fires.
6. Don't overload the fryer with items to be fried; this will lower the temperature of the fat, causing delicate foods to break up before a rigid protective coating can be formed.
7. Thick food or foods being deep fried from frozen will require additional cooking times. In these circumstances, food items should be deep-fried initially until crisp and golden then placed in a moderate to hot oven to continue cooking until thoroughly cooked. The use of a temperature probe will help establish that the food is cooked to the correct core temperature.(72-75°C for meat and fish).
8. Remove fried foods immediately from the oil and allow to drain briefly before serving.

Deep-frying oil shelf life

All fats and oils break down over a period of time. This is inevitable, but steps can be taken to maintain the quality of these ingredients for as long as possible:

I. Fats and oils do not like heat, light, or water and it is these factors which cause rancidity, often developing unpleasant off tastes and odours.

II. In general, store all oils in a cool place away from heat and light sources; a fridge is a good place or a cool cupboard. Keep containers covered with lids, caps etc. to exclude air/oxygen. Opened bottles of oil will continue to degrade in quality, so storage for long periods is not advisable.

III. Deep- frying oils should be strained regularly through a cheese cloth or similar and should be topped up with about 25% of fresh oil occasionally. With continual or heavy use, the oil will at sometime need replacing totally. If the fryer is not used for long periods, empty the oil into a suitable airtight container for later use.

Oils with high smoke point:
Safflower oil 260°C
Refined Olive oil 240°C
Soybean, peanut oils 240°C
Vegetable oil 210-230°C
Sunflower oil 220°C
Canola (rapeseed) 230°C
Grape seed oil 215°C

PLEASE NOTE: These temperatures are approximate and will vary according to the manufacturer and seasonal fluctuations of the raw materials.

Grilling (broiling)

Cooking by intense radiant heat, where the food is positioned below the heat source; in the United States this is termed 'broiling'. Control of heat is either by moving the food item nearer or further away from the heat source or reducing its intensity. There are no timing controls on grill appliances so grilled foods have to be watched carefully.

Grilling is a healthy method of cooking because the fat content of certain foods (especially meats and meat products), renders (melts) under the intense heat and it drips off and is no longer in contact with the food.

GRILLING TIPS:
1. Grill foods that are even in thickness, this will ensure even cooking throughout. NOTE: because the heat is so intense, the outer surface of the food will cook very quickly while internally the food can be still quite raw. Thick cuts of grilled meat and poultry that need to be cooked thoroughly should be transferred to the oven to finish cooking. This is essential with cuts of poultry, which must be cooked thoroughly to the centre or core.
2. Most foods need lightly oiling before grilling, especially those that are free of natural fats such as vegetables. Foods should also be seasoned lightly before grilling.
3. Pre-heat the grill 2 to 3 minutes before use, by doing this the food will start to cook as soon as it is placed under the heat source.
4. Ensure food is not placed too close to heat source as this may either burn the item or colour too quickly before the heat has had time to penetrate and cook.
5. Cover parts of foods that are likely to burn, such as rib bones and fish fins with foil.
6. When the side uppermost to the heat is of the desired colour, turn the food item over. It shouldn't be necessary to keep turning the food over and over.
7. ALL grilled meats should be rested for about 5 to 8 minutes before serving, to retain as much of the juices as possible.

Roasting

Is a method of cooking that uses dry indirect, diffused heat and is used to cook fish, meat, poultry, game, vegetables and some fruits.

Poultry
Whole chickens and turkeys are, by their very shape, difficult to cook evenly. When roasting a chicken, the first part to be cooked is the tip of the breast and, last of all, the thigh, in particular the part between the inside of the leg and the breast. So by the time the brown leg meat is cooked thoroughly the white meat has become overcooked and dry.

In the professional kitchen, chefs remove the legs from poultry and often bone and roll them, leaving the breast as a crown (both breasts attached to the carcass), and sometimes the legs are filled with a suitable stuffing then wrapped and secured within the skin. The reformed legs are then usually cooked separately. By doing this, although a little time consuming and requiring some know how, the end result leads to better portion control, a reduction in wastage and an easier to cut portion of meat for the diner. The whole operation produces a superior end product as cooking times and temperatures can be more precise. Similar methods are applied to duckling and game birds, where the breast may be roasted independently and the legs are treated to different methods of preparation and cooking.

Regardless, of the type of bird, it is always advisable to remove the wishbone (furcula), before cooking. This inverted 'v' shaped bone lies either side of the neck, a little under the surface of the breast meat and is loosely attached to the breast bone at one end while articulating with the shoulders at the other. Removal of the wishbone ultimately makes the carving of the breast meat much easier and, thereby reducing waste. However by doing this, the joy of making a wish while pulling the bone with little fingers until it snaps, is not possible.

ROASTING WHOLE POULTRY TIPS
(chicken, turkey and duck)

TIPs:
1. Frozen poultry should be defrosted in the refrigerator on the lowest shelf to prevent dripping onto other foods; this is the safest way but can take some time, and this also depends upon the size of the bird. Birds can be defrosted in a sink of cold running water, but this is wasteful of water and ties up a sink which may be needed for other uses. It is important to make sure all frozen poultry is totally defrosted with no signs of ice before cooking.
2. Remove all poultry from the fridge and allow to reach room temperature before roasting. This can take between 30mins and 2 hours depending upon the size of the bird.
3. Remember to remove the plastic bag which contains the neck, gizzard, liver and stomach (this is already split and cleaned out) from the cavity, these can be placed in the roasting tin with the bird and will add flavour to the gravy.
4. DO NOT wash poultry before cooking; it spreads bacteria contaminated water around the sink area and work surfaces and can contaminate dish cloths and utensils.
5. Always pre-heat the oven so the cooking process starts immediately. Begin with it set on about 210°C gas mark 6/7.
6. Lightly grease the skin of the bird with oil or melted butter. Butter can also be inserted between the skin and breast; this melts and bastes the breast as it cooks. Streaky bacon rashers can also be laid across the breasts (barding), which will help to moisten the meat during roasting. This is not necessary, however, for duck as it has large fat reserves underneath the skin that will help baste the meat as it roasts.

7. Season well, inside and outside. If not already trussed (most usually are) some advise trussing the bird, but this is not essential. The purpose is only to ensure the bird keeps its shape whilst roasting.
8. Start by roasting the bird on one side for about 10-15mins, then turning onto other side for a further 10-15mins. Turn the bird onto its breast, again for about 10-15mins, then finally onto its back for the remainder of the cooking time.

NOTE these times are for an average weight of bird of 1½kg.

9. Try not to stab or puncture the meat during turning, this causes loss of moisture. Placing the bird on a bed of chopped root vegetables prevents the surface of the bird from being in direct contact with the roasting dish and will provide further flavour to the roast gravy.
10. Allow about ten minutes for the bird to rest before carving. This will help to retain the bird's natural juices.
11. It is now thought that basting a bird does not help retain moisture during roasting, although it does attribute to the brown colour of the skin.

How to tell when the bird is cooked.

There are two ways of making certain that the bird is cooked. The first is to slightly raise and tilt the bird at an angle so that the juices can run from the cavity. If the juices are clear and there is no blood present then the bird is cooked. A more accurate method is to use a temperature probe. If the probe indicates the correct core temperature has been reached in the thickest part of the meat (the thigh), then it can be assumed that the rest of the bird is cooked.

NOTE: a temperature probe is not to be confused with a meat thermometer. A probe is used to establish the core temperature of foods during and nearing the end of the cooking process; the probe is inserted, read and then removed. A meat thermometer is inserted into the meat at the beginning of the cooking process and left in the meat so that the internal temperature can be seen at any time.

Modern temperature probes are inexpensive, easy to use and provide highly instant, accurate readings. Care should be taken not to reintroduce bacterial contamination from the probe into the food. Probes should be sanitised before and after use.

Food Standards Agency (FSA) guidelines recommend that the final core temperatures for cooked poultry should be :

75°C or

70°C held for 2mins. or

65°C held for 10mins. or
60°C for 40mins.

However at 75°C poultry is already loosing moisture and becoming dry and overcooked. For a perfect roast, the ideal core temperature is 65°C held for 10mins

The best way to achieve this is to, aim for a core temperature of 62°C, turn the oven off and allow to cool down by leaving the door open for about 10mins, then remove the bird. The residual heat within the meat will continue to cook the bird.

NOTE: Whilst temperatures for roasting chicken and turkey remain the same, roasting times vary depending on the size/weight of the bird and whether the bird has been boned and rolled or stuffed.

Poultry stuffing

The practice of stuffing poultry dates back to Roman times and has been ever-popular since then. Stuffing the large cavity of a bird is not advisable, although the smaller neck cavity may be. The problem arising with this process has no doubt been experienced by many a cook; when the roast meat has reached the correct temperature, the internal stuffing can still be undercooked or not reached a sufficiently high enough temperature to kill bacteria. This is particularly a concern where raw ingredients such as sausage meat are used. However, by ensuring the stuffing has reached a safe temperature, it is likely that the meat will be overcooked. In order to ensure both elements are cooked perfectly it seems prudent to roast them separately.

Game birds

Wild game birds (not frozen) are only procurable during certain times of the year or what is more commonly known as the 'game season'. Farmed game birds however are available all the year round.

The game season commences on 12th August (glorious twelfth) with grouse shooting and February 1st marking its end.

Grouse, partridge, pheasant pigeon, plover, snipe, wild duck and woodcock are all shot during this period. Outside of this, during 'close season', it is illegal to shoot these game birds.

Roasting a game bird whole is still probably the most popular way of cooking it, although many chefs nowadays separate the legs from the breast meat. The legs are boned and stuffed or prepared as a confit, whilst the breast is quickly roasted or pan fried. Whatever method is adopted, game bird meat can become very dry with just a little over cooking, so observing minimum cooking times is paramount, if the flesh is to remain succulent.

TIPS:
1. Game birds are usually bought ready plucked and drawn (removal of the innards); though some may still have a few hairs attached which can be removed by singeing.
2. The wishbone should be removed, (see above: removing a chicken wishbone) this makes carving of the breast easier.
3. It is not advisable to stuff whole game birds; their brief roasting time prevents the stuffing from becoming sufficiently cooked.
4. The legs can be removed and cooked separately; confit is one way to treat the leg meat. Some recipes suggest blanching the crown in boiling water for a couple of minutes and then roasted for a short time.
5. Butter may be inserted under the skin; this will melt during roasting and helps to keep the game meat moist. Barding the breasts with bacon or pork fat also helps maintain moisture.
6. Always roast game birds underdone, over- cooking dries out their meat very quickly.
7. Allow to rest before carving.

Roasting meat (pork, beef and lamb)

To what degree should meats be roasted? This is clearly subjective and, is very much down to individual preference. However there is a generally accepted principle which exemplifies the stage at which a particular meat is considered cooked. This principle suggests that when meat is cooked to the 'right' degree it is at its best, that is, in terms of succulence and flavour. Outside of this, the meat is either under or over cooked.

So when is a meat 'done'? Very few will disagree that beef in general, should be cooked and served at degrees ranging from very rare to medium. This doctrine also applies to the degree at which steaks, and certain other cuts are cooked i.e. calves liver. Lamb is usually cooked pink or rosé, but similarly the definition of pink can be down to the interpretation of the cook or diner. Pork, traditionally, was always cooked thoroughly, this was partly due to the belief that undercooked pork was the cause of trichinosis; a disease transmitted by a small parasitic worm embedded in the meat. However, because of improvements in pig husbandry, the likelihood of this occurring is low. It has also been established that a temperature of 58°C during cooking, is sufficient to kill any parasites that may be present in the meat, thus safely allowing pork to be served slightly under done or pink.

Choosing the joint

Why prime cuts? Prime cuts of meat are not to be confused with 'primal cuts' which are the large joints of meat produced during butchery of a carcass and contain a number of smaller joints or sub primal cuts. 'Prime cut' is a rather loose term to describe those joints of meat that are of the best quality and therefore demand a higher price than poorer, usually tougher, cuts. The term also refers to cuts that are lean, with a minimum amount of fat and contain less connective tissue, contributing to a more tender quality of meat. Such cuts, therefore, are usually cooked by dry methods; grilling, frying or roasting, where there is not the necessity to subject the meat to prolonged moist cooking in order to achieve tenderness.

There are a number of factors that affect the tenderness of a joint of meat; primarily, this depends upon what part of the animal it comes from and, secondly, what usage the muscles of the joint have undergone during the animals life. The shin, a bundle of muscles surrounding the bones of the lower leg, is subjected to the stress and strains of supporting the animal's weight as well as movement, such as walking and, in some instances, running. It is such activities that develop large amounts of connective tissue (collagen and elastin) within the muscle, causing the meat to be tough.

Joints chosen for their suitability for roasting, therefore, must be tender, moist and flavour some when cooked. Joints with less connective tissue (collagen and elastin) make better roasts because of this factor. Meat with high levels of connective tissue are generically tougher, so are best cooked by slower moist methods such as braising and stewing.

The following are some tips on what to look for in a joint of meat or steak, especially beef:

- ✓ the meat has a fine grain i.e. doesn't look coarse; meat fibres are very fine and all run in the same direction.
- ✓ there are only one or two muscle groups within the cut, although there can be more than three muscles in a large cut.
- ✓ there is little connective tissue (this is not a consideration if meat is for braising/stewing)
- ✓ minimum fat content (intra-muscular or marbling) but this can also be down to personal choice)

Suitable roasting joints:

BEEF
Meat obtained from bulls (up to three years), steers (castrated bulls) and heifers

Fillet (aka tenderloin):
A prime piece of meat, weighing about 3kg whole; the most expensive of all cuts. There is very little connective tissue or fat and therefore trimming weight is negligible. It consists of three parts; chateaubriand or head (the thickest end which sits next to the sirloin and rump), the tail which is the thin end or filet mignon and lies just past the end of the ribs.

The head is usually roasted and served as chateaubriand producing two portions. The middle, thicker part of the fillet is used for fillet steaks and tornedos; the tail end or filet mignon for stroganoff and the whole fillet for beef wellington.

The uneven thickness of a whole fillet means it does not lend itself well to even cooking, when the thick end or chateaubriand is done, the middle and tail end are overdone.

When preparing a whole fillet for roasting or beef wellington, about 10-12cm of the tail end should be removed, although it is possible to tuck the tail under, giving the body of the fillet a more even thickness.

Trimming: a thin tough layer of 'silver skin' connective tissue runs along one side of the fillet and this must be removed before cooking. Along the side and loosely attached to the fillet is the 'chain', a piece of meat which also has a high fat and connective tissue content. This should also be removed, although it is likely that shop bought fillet steak will still have the chain and connective tissue still attached.

Fillet should always be served very rare and because of the characteristics of the meat, in particular its lack of fat, can easily be overdone in a matter of a few minutes.

TIPS: season well, sear all over in hot fat before roasting; baste with fat (dripping) or butter or both.

Topside:
A second class roast weighing about 10kg usually cut into smaller joints for roasting; 2.5kg being ideal for carving purposes. Because this is a lean cut, a layer of fat covering on the outside surface helps to baste the meat, keeping it moist.

Topside can be served from rare through to well done, though it can be very dry when roasted well done. Topside also lends itself well to pot roasting.

Silverside:
This cut weighs about 14kg. It can be roasted, but is better suited to pot-roasting or boiling. Brined, boiled silverside of beef was once a popular dish in Britain.

TIP: season well, turn and baste regularly

Sirloin (aka strip loin, contrefilet):
A prime cut of beef from the back of the animal weighing about 9kg. Sirloin can be roasted as a joint or cut into steaks (entrecôte). When a sirloin is trimmed, about 1/3 of the fat layer along the length of the sirloin is cut away, this is done to enable the removal of the 'silver skin' connective tissue which lies between the fat and the meat. Without removing this tough tissue the meat will cook unevenly, and because the meat is roasted for a brief period, the tough tissue will not soften sufficiently.

Ribs (wing, fore, middle and chuck or short ribs):
All are suitable for roasting; however the fore ribs are considered the best. There are two good reasons for roasting meat joints on the bone. One, the bones act as a trivet (i.e. they act as a support for the meat), so the surface of the meat in contact with the roasting tray does not become overcooked and dry. Secondly, the meat between the ribs (intercostal) is very sweet and tender. Carving a rib joint with bones intact, can be tricky, especially if part of the back or chine bone is still connected. If the meat is to be roasted on the bone, the alternative is to totally remove all the bones, and then secure only the rib bones back onto the meat.

Top rump (aka thick flank):
Weighs about 12kg and although suitable for roasting but is better cooked by stewing or braising.

No beef offal is suitable for roasting because of its texture; it is therefore cooked by moist methods.

Portion sizes vary according to cut of meat, method of cooking and personal choice, but guidelines for average weights are:
   Steak: fillet - 165-180g, rump and sirloin – 225g
   Beef on the bone – 340g
   Beef boneless – 225g

VEAL
Meat obtained from cattle calves which are usually male. There are variant types of calf veal. Bob veal is from calves which are slaughtered at about

one month old. Formula and non-formula fed claves are slaughtered usually between eighteen and twenty-six weeks, though no later than twenty six. Rose or high-welfare veal (not restricted to low iron diet therefore the meat is pink in colour) has recently found a place on some restaurant menus.

However, veal has never reached the popularity in Britain as other domesticated animal meats and so many shops and butchers find it impracticable to stock veal meat because of this.

For this reason I have limited the information with regards to cooking veal, and have merely given a cursory look at those cuts suitable for roasting.

Legs:
These are broken down into three boneless cuts: cushion or nut, under cushion and thick flank

These cuts can be roasted, but because they are very lean require some form of additional moisture such as from basting or larding.

Loin and best end
Both of these cuts are suitable for roasting, on or off the bone.

Breast:
Usually boned and rolled with a stuffing prior to roasting.

LAMB
Meat obtained from sheep up to one year old. Over twelve months old the sheep is known as a hogget. Hogget (sheep between one and two years old) meat is slightly darker in colour and stronger in flavour than lamb, but not such a fuller flavour as mutton.

Legs (gigots):
The epitome of a lamb roasting joint, either on the bone or boned and rolled (and stuffed). Legs weigh on average about 3-4kg (bone-in) yielding approximately six to eight portions.

Loin and best end:
Both are prime cuts and make the best roasting joints.

Loins contain half of the backbone (chine bone) and 4-5 rib bones. Because the shape of these bones makes carving and portioning difficult, loins are better boned and rolled before roasting. The main muscle in the loin is also referred to as the 'eye' meat and when this is trimmed and cut into lengths it is known as canons.

Best ends normally have 6-7 rib bones and part of the back bone (chine bone) attached. Traditional butchery involves removing the chine bone whilst leaving the rib bones attached to the meat. The meat and fat surrounding about half the length of the rib is removed, thereby exposing the bones for presentation purposes. This joint is the most expensive cut and can be portioned into lamb cutlets (six- usually three per serving), or left whole as rack of lamb, crown or guard of honour.

Shoulder:
Shoulder joints are always boned prior to roasting because by leaving them intact, their shape makes carving exceptionally difficult. Whole shoulders (about 3kg) are also usually cut into two and after boning, can be filled with various stuffing. Because of the nature of the joint, it lends itself better to slow roasting.

Breast:
A long, thin cut of meat weighing about 1.5kg that can be sometimes quite fatty, they are usually stuffed and rolled and slow roasted.

Saddle:
A large joint of meat (about 3kg on the bone) consisting of both loins and backbone. It can be roasted on the bone, but boning and rolling before roasting provides for easier carving and portioning.

MUTTON
Is a meat from a sheep that is over 2 years old. It has never reached the same popularity in this country as lamb. It has a stronger flavour and darker coloured meat than its younger counter part. Because of its age, mutton meat is somewhat tougher than that of lamb and nearly all joints require methods of cooking more suited to tougher meats; mutton benefits from long, slow, moist cooking. If you are interested in learning more about mutton go to:

<u>www.muttonrenaissance.org.uk/index.php</u>

PORK
Meat obtained from the domestic pig (swine), reared to slaughter weight of about 70kg (hog 100kg) Suckling pigs are slaughtered between six weeks and two months and for pork and bacon, between four months and one year old, depending on the breed.

Legs:
This is a large joint weighing in at about 5.5kg bone in, but is usually cut into smaller cuts and sold as roasting joints.

Loin:
Weighing in at about 6kg this is a prime cut of meat. It can be roasted on the bone or boned as a whole joint or cut into small roasting joints.

Fillet (tenderloin):
This is a very lean piece of meat and is comparative in shape and structure as beef fillet, though somewhat smaller at about 0.5kg. Because of its leanness, tenderloin can become dry if over cooked. Many recipes call for the meat to be coated in some type of herb crust or wrapped in thin slices of cured ham.

Shoulder:
One of the largest joints on a pork carcass (5-6kg) and because of the complexity of the bone content is usually de-boned and cut into smaller roasting joints.

Spare rib:
About 1.5kg in weight, much of which consists of rib bones. Spare ribs are used extensively in Asian and oriental cuisines and are treated with various ingredients such as herbs, spices and condiments prior to roasting.

Offal:
Very little pig offal is eaten in the UK. Pigs' cheeks have become popular and pigs trotters are a delicacy in some European countries.

Suckling pig:
A piglet which is slaughtered between the ages of two and six weeks and weighing anything between 8 and 12kgs. It can be roasted whole or boned and stuffed. It makes an ideal meat for barbecues.

Illustration showing the main cuts of meat and poultry (courtesy 'Counterfeit_ua' istock)

Clearly the nature of the dish being prepared will determine which cut of meat should be used and, in many cases, is quite specific; for example, when preparing beef stroganoff, the tail (filet mignon) or middle of the fillet is used, although sirloin and rump are also suitable. The meat is cut into strips and pan fried for only a few minutes, cooking for any length of time would result in dry meat. Because fillet has small connective tissue content, it is ideally suited to being cooked by this method.

Prime cuts have always been inherently more expensive than their tougher counterparts, and this is based on demand from both domestic and commercial markets. In recent years though, less commonly known, cheaper cuts of meat have become more popular and this has been partly due to their more frequent inclusion on restaurant menus.

The study of meat is a highly complex subject and involves knowledge and understanding at every stage from the animals' conformation and development in the field through to the meat on the plate.

Meat fat

The fat content of meat can vary from as little as 5% to as much as 40%, dependent upon the type of animal, age, breed, diet (such as grass or animal feeds), and activity during its life.

There are two types of fat found in meat, triglycerides; the visible fat, which is high in saturates and can be seen around the outside of cuts and within the meat itself (commonly referred to as marbling). The second is the phospholipids, which are found in the cell membrane, and it is these invisible phospholipids that give meats their flavours.

Fat is essential to meat flavour and texture. At about 50°C fat begins to melt and, by doing so, lubricates the muscle fibres. Unlike meat juices, a percentage of which are driven off during cooking, fat does not evaporate and, therefore continues to keep meat moist as the fibres begin to dry out and toughen. Meat gets much of its flavour from fat by absorbing flavour molecules from the animal's diet and these become more pronounced as the animal ages, which is why mutton has a stronger flavour than lamb.

Meat juices

Most of the liquid in meat is water. The reddish colour that appears in meat juices is not in fact blood but a mixture of water, myoglobin and other substances.

Myoglobin is the protein pigment that gives meat its colour and is found only in animal muscle/meat, not in the blood. Haemoglobin is responsible for the red colour of blood. When raw meat is exposed to, heat, air/oxygen for any length of time, it turns grey/black, this is caused by the oxidation of the pigment and, during chemical changes, forms metmyoglobin. This reaction does not render the meat unusable but it is a sign that meat is not freshly butchered; aging of meat to make it tenderer and concentrate flavour also has the same effect on meat colour.

ROASTING MEAT JOINT TIPS:
BEEF
1. Always preheat the oven before roasting; an initial temperature of about 220°C quickly dehydrates the meat surface, killing most bacteria present and, when high enough, Maillard reactions begin to denature and transform the proteins. After about 10-20mins, reduce the temperature down to about 170-180°C. This is important, as continued high temperature roasting with dehydrate the meat, causing unnecessary shrinkage through excess loss of moisture.
2. Most roasting joints have a layer of fat on the outside of the meat and, if good quality meat, this should not be in excess. If there is a need to trim off some fat, it is advisable to leave at least a thin layer of surface fat, this helps to self baste the meat whilst roasting.
3. Season the meat well, applying a thin layer of oil first helps the

seasoning to stick to the surface. It is interesting to note that seasonings sprinkled over meat joints don't actually permeate far beyond the surface, what makes a roasted joint taste seasoned is that the carving process mixes the carved surface meat with the internal meat.

Note: some of the salt added to a roast will eventually end up in the pan juices, so heavy salting of a joint can result in salty gravy when made from the meats juices and sediment.

4. The use of a trivet of roughly chopped vegetables or bones as a bed to rest the meat on during roasting, this helps to stop the surface of the meat in contact with the roasting dish from over cooking and becoming dry. Both the bones and vegetables will also add further flavours to the gravy..
5. When turning a joint in the oven, resist the temptation to stab the meat with a fork or similar utensil, this unfortunately lets some of the meat juices escape which can lead to drier meat. Use a pair or tongues or two spoons to move the meat around.
6. Baste the meat regularly by spooning over the meat juices and fat in the roasting tray. Some chefs and cooks like to add water to the roast; the water forms steam thereby adding moisture to the roasting environment.
7. Rest ALL meats after roasting and prior to carving. For small joints up to 1.5k about 10-15mins, and over 1.5k about 20mins.
8. Roasting meat very rare (beef) is quite acceptable and poses no food safety concerns, however prolonged roasting makes the meat drier and gives an impression of toughness.
Please see the temperature roasting chart below.
9. It is useful to bear in mind that as a rule, meat roasted on the bone takes less time to cook than meat off the bone.

LAMB

Most of the tips relating to roasting beef are applicable to lamb.

PORK

Most of the tips relating to roasting beef are applicable to pork

Pork crackling:

Countless methods and techniques abound about how to make the perfect pork crackling.

I have used the following method and it always produces a good quality crackling:

a. Score the rind (crackling to be)with a very sharp knife; a 'Stanley' type is ideal

Make the cuts about 2-3cm apart and 3-4mm deep, too deep and the meat will be cut
   b. Ensure the rind is dry, use disposable kitchen paper to remove any moisture
   c. Rub liberally with salt
   d. Pre-heat an oven to about 230°C and roast for about 15mins, reducing the temperature to about 160-170°C for the remainder of the cooking period
   e. How it works: by drying the rind before roasting and subjecting the joint to intense heat the moisture content is reduced. This allows the rind to crisp up. The scoring allows the heat to penetrate and renders the fat layers under the rind, which automatically bastes the meat.

Core temperatures for roasted, pan fried and grilled meats
BEEF and LAMB:
RARE: 48 to 52°C - after about 15mins resting: 55 to 60°C
MEDIUM RARE: 55 to 59°C - after about 15mins resting: 61 to 65°C
MEDIUM: 60 to 66°C - after about 15mins resting: 66 to 70°C
WELLDONE: 67 to 71°C - after about 15mins resting: 71 to75°C

PORK:
MEDIUM: 60 to 65°C C - after about 15mins resting: 68 to 70°C
WELL DONE: 70 to 73°C – after about 15mins resting: 77 to 80°C

CHICKEN and TURKEY:
COOKED: 62°C - after about 15mins resting 68°C
NOTE: Rested temperatures vary according to thickness of joint or steak and whether on the bone or boned and rolled

VENSION
Is the meat of the deer. While wild deer are killed for sport, culling purposes and for their meat, farmed deer are specifically bred for the table. The main species of deer are Roe, Red, Fallow, Sika and Muntjac and in the British Isles, their populations vary from area to area and therefore the availability of their meat.

In terms of eating quality, each has its own particular flavour; though many believe the venison from the Roe deer (chevreuil) is the best.

Having had a more varied diet and active lifestyle than farmed deer, wild deer venison meat has a firmer texture and a more distinctive flavour. Venison, like all game meats is very lean and while this may make it a healthier option, the lack of fat does mean that it has a tendency to become dry quickly during cooking.

The haunch or hind legs and loin are the only cuts suited to roasting. Both cuts can be roasted on or off the bone.

Carving meat

For those of you who are new to this task or have some experience in carving, but still wonder if you are doing it right, here is some advice:

Carving techniques vary and is very much dependent upon the cut of meat being carved. As a rule cutting or carving meat on the bone is more difficult, because the contours of the bone can impede the ability to cut good sized slices; there can also be some loss of meat, which remains attached to the bone. Carving of most meat joints is much easier if the bones have been removed before cooking.

Before commencing carving, make sure any butchers string or webbing has been removed. It is important to use a sharp knife with a reasonably long blade; serrated edge knives are not suitable as they have a tendency to tear the meat.

Lamb leg: begin carving at the lower, narrower end of the leg. Carve at an angle of about 45° to the bone, removing each cut slice and turning the leg from side to side.

Lamb and pork loins can be carved between the rib bones when intact.

Poultry: there are two types of meat muscle, the breast and the legs. The breast or white meat is usually carved by slicing along the length of the breast, working inwards to the ribcage. Removing the leg from poultry gives access to the whole pieces and makes them easier to carve.

A good thumb rule to remember is always to cut across the grain of the meat, as you would a piece of rope or string, this ensures that slices of meat consist of short fibres and therefore give the meat a more tender texture.

Yorkshire pudding

Whilst on the subject of roast beef it seemed pertinent to discuss the problems sometimes faced by cooks when preparing this traditional accompaniment.

Some recipes use self-raising flour, others plain, I have always had success with plain flour, relying upon the eggs in the batter to provide aeration.

TIPS FOR MAKING PERFECT YORKSHIRE PUDDINGS:
1. Pour a little oil, dripping or lard into the tin used for the puddings and place in a very hot oven, at least 230°C until smoking hot.
2. Carefully remove from the oven, fill with batter and place back into the oven immediately.
3. Depending upon the size, the puddings should start to rise within 10 to 15mins.
4. Once they have risen and started to colour, reduce the oven temperature to about 170°C and allow to bake for a further 20 to 30mins. During this time the puddings will form a crisp outer shell which will prevent them from collapsing when removed from the oven.
5. If the puddings are taken out too soon, they will not have had time to crisp up and will collapse, the longer they are left in the oven the drier and crisper they will become.

Baking

HEAT TRANSFER:
A dry method of cooking which involves conduction, convection and radiant heat transfer. In a conventional oven, heat is transferred by natural convection currents caused by temperature differences (hot rising to the top, cold falling to take its place); in a convection oven, heat is transferred by convective heat. Heat is also transferred by radiation from the oven walls.

During my working life as a chef, I have had the experience of using many different makes and types of ovens: conventional gas, electric and solid fuel fired ovens; convection and combination ovens; and the one thing I have learnt is that no two ovens are the same. It takes time and trial and error getting to know an oven's little foibles, but it is time well spent if one is hoping to achieve a consistently good quality end product.

Convection ovens are by far the most efficient and have now superseded the conventional oven; most new cookers are now fan assisted. The advantage of fan assisted heat is that the temperature throughout the oven remains constant, unlike the conventional oven where there are hot and cold spots (i.e. areas of uneven temperatures culminating in a cooler oven lower down and hotter at the top).

It is worthwhile investing in an oven thermometer to help check oven temperatures from time to time. If the oven is a year or two old or older it may be that it is not operating efficiently; just because the oven thermostat regulator (regulo) is set to a certain temperature, it doesn't' necessarily mean that it is actually operating at that temperature, by using an oven thermometer you can measure the actual temperature of the oven and adjust the 'regulo' accordingly.

Oven calibration

It is useful to check that the oven is functioning effectively and this should be done about every twelve months, it is commonly assumed that because the oven regulo/thermostat is set at a specific temperature it is actually operating at that temperature, surprisingly it may not be!

Preheat the oven to 170°C, place an oven thermometer in the centre of the oven so that the temperature can be read through the glass in the door without opening the oven. Allow the thermometer to reach the maximum temperature. Move the thermometer to different areas in the oven - by doing this, you will be able to identify hot and cold spots and, whilst little can be done to remove these, you will have a better understanding of how your oven performs.

A tolerance of between 5 and 10 degrees +/- of an ovens operating temperature is normal according to the International Electrotechnical Commission (IEC), if the difference is greater than this then the oven should be calibrated. With some ovens it is possible to calibrate the oven yourself by following the instructions in the users' handbook or search for the information online.

Please see Chapter 7 where you will find information about a range of pastries and baked goods.

Microwave cookery

The microwave cooker is now used for many cooking and reheating tasks, more so than the traditional oven and hob. Numerous recipes have been created particularly for this purpose and these include anything from baked goods, snacks, to roasted meats. Although it is not possible to cook every type of food in a microwave, it is none the less a very useful piece of cooking equipment.

Microwave ovens are manufactured with a range of power or output options. Less powerful ovens operate on an output rating of 700w, but more powerful and therefore faster operating microwaves have outputs in excess of 1,000w.

TIPS for using a microwave
1. Do not use traditional metals cook ware or utensils in the microwave; it can damage or even ruin it. There are some metal type pots and pans which are designed to be microwave safe.
2. Arrange food evenly on the cooking plate or dish with thicker parts such as stalks facing out. Leave the centre empty.
3. Cover dishes to prevent splattering. Covering with film also traps in steam, helping to cook or reheat food quicker. There is normally a build up of steam, so care must be taken when removing film from micro-waved food.
4. As microwaves vary in their power rating (this is not to be confused with power settings), it is important that you are familiar with the power rating as this impacts the cooking times of food.
5. Remove food frequently to stir or rotate, this will ensure even distribution of microwaves.
6. Pierce any foods that could explode during cooking; sausages and jacket potatoes for example.
7. Always use defrost settings for thawing frozen foods.

Chapter 2

MOIST METHODS OF COOKING

Braising, boiling, poaching, steaming, stewing, (pot-roasting), sous-vide

All share similarities in that they involve cooking food at boiling point (with the exception of pressure cooking or steaming which cook at temperatures above this) or below and in varying amounts of liquid. Certain methods of moist cooking, such as braising and stewing, are done at lower temperatures and, in many cases this is done over a long period of time. These two methods are particularly effective in cooking meat dishes, where meat fibres and connective tissue need to be softened in order to make the meat tender.

Poaching, a more gentle method of cooking food at lower temperatures is ideal for foods that are delicate in structure and would otherwise break or fall apart if subjected to more turbulent methods such as boiling; eggs, fruits and fish can be cooked by this method.

Boiling is quite an aggressive method where firm textured foods are cooked so as to soften tissue structures, making them more tender and easier to eat; root vegetables for example. Swede and carrots are made up of a strong cellulose structure, so these require vigorous boiling to soften the vegetable. Boiling is also used in many cookery applications, from very brief blanching of vegetables to lengthy cooking of whole hams and tougher cuts of meat such as brisket and shin.

Braising and stewing

A braise, also known as a casserole, daub or fricassée, can be defined as tough cuts of meat (or vegetables) slowly cooked in a stock or cooking liquid in a closed container. The meats can be in small pieces, portion sized or large cuts, depending on the dish. The stock or liquid develops during the cooking period; it absorbs flavours and releases aromas from the various ingredients culminating in a rich flavoursome sauce.

The term 'pot-roast' is also interchangeable with the word 'braise', though in terms of preparation, this differs slightly from a braise or stew in that less liquid is used in the cooking process. The Cambridge dictionary gives the definition of a pot roast as:
"A piece of beef that is cooked slowly in a covered dish with a small amount of liquid and sometimes vegetables".

A casserole is a generic term for a stew or braise cooked in an enclosed dish. It can also refer to the dish in which the food is cooked. Historically, a 'Dutch oven' is a type of cooking container made from cast-iron or earthenware, usually with a lid. The more colourful and now more popular 'French oven', differs only in that it is coated with an enamel finish – 'Le Creuset' range is a good example of this type of cooking utensil.

An interesting term found in French culinary repertoires is étuvée. Depending on the source of the definition, it means 'sweated' or 'steamed' and whilst this may seem confusing it actually makes sense.

Étuvée, vegetables, some game, and poultry in particular, are cooked in a closed or sealed container, either with a small amount of liquid, sauce or butter. The food is cooked, therefore, by steam produced from the foods natural moisture content plus the addition of any liquids.

A stew, similar to a braise, again uses tough cuts of meat with the addition of vegetables, aromats and other ingredients, is slowly cooked in a stock or liquid. Some argue that a stew is cooked on the hob whilst a braise is cooked in the oven.

Some fruits and vegetables are also stewed. Apples, plums and rhubarb are stewed in preparation for pies and tarts. Piperade and ratatouille are examples of vegetable stews.

Irish stew, Lancashire hot pot or hotchpot, carbonnade and goulash are all example of meat stews.

The resulting cooking liquor or sauce of a braise or stew varies in viscosity from recipe to recipe. In some stews, the consistency of the liquid is quite thin because no thickeners are used, as in the case of Irish stew, although the potato starch content gives the liquid some consistency. Brown stews, like navarin of lamb and beef ragout, are thickened with flour and provide the final liquor/sauce with a rich and velvety texture. The brown colour of a stew or braise is brought about by frying the meat and vegetables, a brown stock also contributes further colour. One way to achieve a really dark brown sauce or gravy is to cheat and add a little gravy browning. Gravy browning is made from caramel, molasses and spices and was popular in the first half of the twentieth century, but is not widely used today. The Savoy hotel in London once used gravy browning to correct the colour of some of their brown sauces; I hasten to add this was some time ago.

Braising and stewing TIPS
1. Choose a dish with a tight fitting lid; this is to insure that loss of moisture is minimal during cooking. In order to achieve a really hermetic seal, make a thick paste of flour and water and apply it to the gap between the lid and the dish.

2. Trim all meat well, removing excess fat and sinews, keeping pieces consistent in size to ensure even cooking, but remember; the larger the pieces of meat, the longer the cooking time.
3. For brown braises: Flour the meat; for every 500g of meat, use 25g plain flour, shake off excess and fry quickly in a little oil until golden brown all over. The remainder of the flour can be added to fat after frying the vegetables; this will form the roux thickening for the cooking sauce.
4. If vegetables are to be added for the purpose of adding flavour only, and are consequently removed at the end of the cooking process, then these should be kept in large pieces which will make them easier to remove later. Fry the vegetables in a little oil until brown, removing them from the oil afterwards

   This stage is crucial if a rich brown flavoursome braise or stew is to be achieved. The caramelising of the sugars and proteins in the meat and vegetables is so important as they add colour, aromatic flavour and aromas to the finished dish.

   Vegetables intended to be served with the cooked stew should be added about 30mins (depending upon the type and thickness of the vegetable) before the end of the cooking period so that they are cooked but not mushy. This is particularly important when adding green vegetables which soon lose their colour if cooked too long.
5. For white stews, such as Irish stew and hotpots, the intended meat once trimmed should be blanched first. This is done by covering the meat with cold water, bringing it up to the boil, discarding the water and removing any scum from the meat. The meat is now ready for use.
6. Cook in a low oven so that the braise or stew maintains a temperature between 82°C and 88°C. Depending on the type, cut, size and quality of the meat, this can generally take anything from between 1 and 8 hours.
7. Checking for meat tenderness during cooking is essential to check if the meat is still tough. Experience will tell at what stage of tenderness the meat is at, and how much further cooking is required. When checking meat, especially diced meat, for tenderness, sample two or three pieces to ensure all the meat is cooked, bearing in mind that the diced meat will have come from different meat muscles and therefore vary in texture.

Slow cooking

Though the term may appear somewhat ambiguous when attempting to use it to describe a particular method of cooking, it actually implies cooking food for prolonged periods at lower temperatures than, for example, roasting. The definition therefore can be extended to include the practices of braising and stewing. The 'slow cooker' or generically known as the 'crock-pot' is used to facilitate this method of cooking food. These slow cooking pots achieved popularity in the United States in the early 1970s, when cooked meals could be started in the morning, and cooked throughout the day ready for dinner in the evening. They are thermostatically controlled to operate at low cooking temperatures (a range usually between 88°C and 98°C), some have different settings (high, medium and low), but in many cases this is just the difference between the length of time taken to reach the maximum temperature (e.g. low setting - 4 hours, high setting - 2 hours). Some cookers also have built in timers that stop the cooking process at a preset time. Slow cookers still continue to be popular today and are available in different sizes and price range.

Regardless of the ambiguities of the name, slow cookers cook by stewing or braising. It is still necessary therefore, in order to achieve a good quality dish, that all the necessary preparation requirements for making stews and braises are observed when using a slow cooker.

An interesting question about when should vegetables and potatoes be added to a meat dish made in a slow cooker? The answer to this is in contradiction to the practice of adding the vegetables towards the end of the cooking period using traditional methods, (i.e. braising in the oven).

Certain vegetables and fruits remain firm when subjected to low temperature cooking for a period of time. These vegetables contain an enzyme in their cell walls, which is activated at a temperature of about 50°C (above 70°C, the enzyme is deactivated). The active enzyme helps to strengthen the structure of the vegetables, making them more resilient to high temperatures and resistant to breaking down during prolonged cooking.

During the early stages of slow cooking (in a slow cooker), temperature rise is very slow, especially if the process is started using cold ingredients. It is likely therefore that because of the very gradual increase in temperature, the food is held for sufficient time at the enzyme activation temperature. This therefore facilitates the strengthening process of the vegetable structures.

Acids also act to keep vegetables firm during prolonged cooking, the addition of tomatoes in a recipe will act to maintain firmness of texture of other vegetable ingredients.

Choice of meat for braising, stewing
The cook has two options when it comes to choosing suitable cuts of meat for slow cooking. Ready diced stewing and braising meat of beef, lamb and pork is widely available and requires little additional preparation, apart

from some final trimming of excess sinew and fat. The meat used in pre-prepared diced meat can come from any part of the animal, but usually from less expensive tougher cuts. Because more than one muscle bundle is used, there will be difference in the tenderness of some pieces of meat. Choosing a specific cut of meat suitable for stewing/braising will ensure greater consistency of tenderness, the use of a slow cooker will also produce more evenly cooked meat.

Suitable cuts for stewing and braising/slow cooking

BEEF
Topside:
Very lean meat, requiring minimal trimming; can be portioned into steaks or diced for braising, although this is rather too good a cut of meat for stewing purposes, beef Bourguignon is a classical French dish of beef braised in red wine with mushroom and bacon lardons.

Silverside:
Traditionally this joint was brined; soaked and injected with a solution of water, saltpetre (potassium or sodium nitrate) and spices and then boiled; the saltpetre giving the meat a reddish-pink colour. Many modern recipes omit saltpetre because of its toxicity and concerns as a potential cancer causing agent. Boiled beef and dumplings is a traditional British dish.

Thick flank (knuckle):
Is a medium sized cut of beef cut from the hind quarter and weighs about 6kg. This joint can be fatty, but has plenty of flavour and is ideal for stews and braises.

Chuck:
A large cut weighing about 12kg. By seem cutting the joint, several smaller pieces are produced;
  Chuck roll, blade and feather are ideal for slow cooking.

Shin (shank):
Is a highly worked set of muscles and contain large amounts of collagen and because of this is more suited to uses such as mince, stews and stocks. It is ideal for making consommé because of its rich flavours.

Beef/ox cheeks:
These are the facial cheek muscles and because they are continually used in chewing, contain large amounts of connective tissue. Slow moist methods of cooking are the only way to cook these. One cheek weighs

about 500g. Cheeks have become extremely popular in recent years because of their flavour and gelatinous texture.

Liver and kidney:
Ox liver is usually sliced thinly and braised, kidneys are trimmed and diced and used in steak and kidney mixes for puddings and pies. Neither offal is suited to dry methods of cooking.

In contrast calves liver is highly prised and expensive. It is usually sliced thinly and pan fried or grilled quickly and served under done.

Oxtail:
Oxtails weight between 1 and 1.5kgs but a large proportion of this is bone content. Because of the nature of this offal it is always braised or stewed and for making ox-tail soup

Heart:
Hearts consist of extremely tough, though lean cardiac muscle and therefore require prolonged slow cooking such as braising. Hearts can be filled with various stuffing prior to cooking .

Tongue:
An average ox-tongue weighs about 1.5kg. It has a high fat content and is normally boiled for at least 2 hours. It has a very rough skin which must be removed after cooking. Traditional cold tongues were placed in a press with some jellied stock, left to cool, and then turned out. Braised ox-tongue with Madeira sauce is a classic dish.

Tripe:
There are three types of tripe, depending upon which part or chamber (stomach) of the cows' abdomen they are taken from:

Smooth tripe (blanket or paunch tripe) from the rumen or first chamber. Honeycomb (pocket tripe) comes from the reticulum or second chamber; this is considered to be the better quality. Book/bible or leaf tripe from the omasum or third chamber; this is less common and inferior in quality to honeycomb and book tripe. Tripe can be stewed, braised or boiled, tripe and onions was a popular dish in the UK in the mid 1900's

LAMB
Leg *(gigot):*
Both lamb legs are from the hind part of the animal and perhaps too good a joint of meat for stewing or braising, they can however be cut into steaks and braised. The hind shanks (bottom cut of the leg) can be braised.

The fore shanks (attached to the shoulder) are tough cuts and therefore are usually braised or stewed, they are also popularly known as lamb Henry.

Shoulder:
This joint contributes the largest percentage of stewing meat from a carcass of lamb. It can be quite fatty, and therefore requires trimming, but when cooked produces a very flavoursome stew. It is ideal for curries and lamb stews; navarin is a rich dark brown lamb stew.

Breast:
This joint is a flat, triangular and elongated in shape, no more than 2-3cm in thickness. It usually has the lower ends of the rib bones attached, which are removed to facilitate rolling. It can be pot-roasted or braised. It can be quite fatty, so needs some trimming before cooking.

Middle neck:
Like the breast, the middle neck is a flavoursome yet inexpensive cut of meat. It lends itself well to stewing e.g. Irish stew; it can also be braised as chops. The neck fillet is quite tender and is better roasted, grilled or pan-fried.

Scrag end:
Is a primal cut consisting of a high percentage of bone. This joint is usually cut into steaks on the bone and can be stewed or braised or used in soups.

Offal:
Lambs kidneys and liver are best pan-fried or grilled. Lamb tongues can be treated in the same way as ox-tongue. Sweetbreads are usually braised and for some recipes, bread crumbed and fried.

Hearts are always stuffed and braised.

PORK
Cheeks (jowl):
These are treated in the same way as ox-cheeks, slow braising breaks down the connective tissue producing a succulent and flavoursome meat.

Shoulder:
A large joint, providing a large percentage of stewing and mince meat from a pig carcass.

Belly:
A very popular cut of pork weighing about 2kg. Belly pork contains a large amount of fat. It is best cooked slowly, either pot-roasted or braised.

Trotters:
Popular on the continent, these are usually boned and stuffed and boiled or braised.

Offal:
Pigs kidneys and liver are not widely cooked, as the meat has a somewhat strong flavour. Liver can be pan-fried or braised and kidneys can be used as a substitute for ox kidney in steak and kidney pie and pudding filling.

VEAL:
Lean diced veal is suitable for stewing and braising, veal and ham pie and fricassee of veal are two good examples.

Osso bucco is the classic Milanese dish of veal shin steaks (bone in) braised with white wine, tomatoes, garlic and vegetables.

SOUS VIDE
Sous vide means 'under vacuum' and is a method of cooking that has risen to prominence in the last few years, being adopted, in particular, by high – end restaurants and Michelin star chefs.

The essence of this method of cookery is that foods are cooked at constant temperatures, lower than those used in traditional cookery methods.

The process was developed in the 1970's by George Pralus for cooking foie gras; further experimentation by Bruno Gassault saw the establishment of parameters of cooking times and temperatures for a whole range of food types. During this era, it wasn't readily accepted by chefs in the UK and many looked upon the whole idea as 'boil in the bag' cooking so it never really took off.

It has since gained in popularity in the domestic sector by amateur cooks. There is now considerable information on websites and a number of cookery books have been produced for those interested in sous vide cookery. Sous vide equipment; thermostatically controlled water baths and vacuum packing machines designed for home use are available from one or two manufacturers and suppliers in the UK; 'SousVide Supreme' stocked at Lakeland www.lakeland.co.uk/15918/SousVide-Supreme-Demi

The basic principles of sous vide are:
- food is cooked in sealed plastic air-tight bags or pouches
- Food items are (usually) pre-portioned before cooking with flavourings added to pouch

- Cooked at exact temperatures for the desired amount of time
- Food is not subjected to very high temperatures
- Some foods are blanched to destroy bacteria (before cooking)
- Meats and fish are seared to give colour (before or after cooking)

The advantages of such a process are many but, suffice to say, it facilitates cooking food at specific temperatures and therefore reduces the chance of overcooking. Food is cooked evenly, with minimal loss in terms of flavour, nutrients and moisture. Timing, in some cases, is also less critical because of lower temperatures concerned, although as cooking times are correlated with temperatures, minimum specified times must be adhered to.

However, there are still concerns about the temperatures involved in this process and, understandably so, as much of the cooking is done at temperatures within the 'danger zone' (see Chapter 12 on Food Safety) In the catering industry a rigid control system: 'Hazard Analysis Critical Control Point' (HACCP), is operated to ensure that all steps of the process are followed correctly, with monitoring being carried out regularly to maintain its effectiveness, guaranteeing the safety of food and that it is totally compliant with government Food Safety regulations.

Further information can be found at:
www.cuisinesolutions.com/about-sous-vide/
www.amazingfoodmadeeasy.com

Boiling, poaching and pressure cooking

I have already discussed in some detail, aspects regarding the cooking (Boiling and Poaching) of Stocks, Soups and Sauces and fruits and vegetables), in Chapters 3 and 4. But I thought it appropriate to discuss the general principles of boiling, pressure cooking and poaching foods here. A simple definition of the term 'boiling point' (of water) or 'saturation temperature' is when the temperature of the vapour (steam) is equal to the pressure of the atmosphere on the liquid and this is equal to 100°C at sea level. This varies, however, upon the atmospheric pressure present: the higher above sea level, the lower the air pressure and, correspondingly, the lower the boiling point. So, it would take longer to boil an egg on the top of Everest than at ground level.

Poaching, a gentler and cooler moist method of cooking relies on temperatures ranging from about 70°C to 82°C.

In both methods of cookery, heat is transferred by way of conduction from the cooking utensil to the liquid contents and then, through this, by conduction and convection currents, and, by conduction from the liquid through the food item immersed in the liquid.

The term 'never let the pot come off the boil' is quite apt. Because vigorously boiling water (rolling boil) is more turbulent than water one or two degrees cooler, it conducts heat to the food much faster. With this in mind, it therefore makes sense to place vegetables of small batches into large amounts of vigorously boiling water to retain the maximum temperature during blanching/cooking processes, thus facilitating shorter cooking times.

As discussed in Chapter 4, blanching green vegetables by plunging into boiling water for a short period deactivates plant enzymes allowing colour fixing (to retain their natural colour).

Pressure cooking

Pressure cookers were very popular up until the 1970's but disappeared out of favour, probably due to the invention of the microwave oven and changes in domestic cooking regimes. Lately, however, there has been resurgence in their use and this has been due in part, to their appearance in television cookery shows used by celebrity chefs and the like.

Up to about 40% reduction in cooking time can be made by using a pressure cooker, this also means a reduction in the amount of energy (gas and electricity) usage.

They work by raising the temperature of boiling water to around 120°C, thereby speeding up the cooking time. Once the lid is sealed and heat is applied, the steam pressure rises to 15 psi (pounds per square inch), and it is this increase in temperature that cooks food faster. All pressure cookers are fitted with a safety devise to allow excess pressure to escape, making them totally safe.

Pressure cooking is ideal for making stocks and soups, producing good strengths of flavour which are developed in a reduced cooking period. Stocks however can be slightly cloudy and therefore, this method of cooking is unsuitable for making clear soups such as consommé.

Boiling TIPS (General)
1. Choose the right size and type of pan for the job. Whilst a thin pan may be fine for boiling vegetables, it will not be suitable for boiling a jam or a thick sauce.
2. Don't use caste iron, aluminium or chipped enamel coated pans for boiling liquids with an acid (e.g. vinegar, lemon juice or wine) content as this reacts with the metal.
3. When filling the pan with water, and prior to heating, always make allowance for the food being boiled in the water. Add salt appropriately.
4. Always ensure that the food item to be boiled is totally immersed in the cooking liquid, otherwise uneven cooking will occur.

5. Ensure that the water is boiling rapidly before placing in food. This is particularly important with green vegetables; root vegetables should also be started from boiling.
6. During prolonged boiling, cover the pan with a lid; this reduces evaporation of the cooking liquid which would otherwise need replacing regularly. This will also help save on energy.
7. Where simmering is required, turn down the heat source, less agitation of the liquid will prevent breakup of the food item being cooked. Again, this will also help reduce energy use.
8. Check food regularly for doneness. Especially when the cooking time is short.
9. Where appropriate, utilise the cooking liquor for a soup or gravy.

Rice and pasta
Rice grains

Long grain rice, such as Patna and basmati in particular, contain higher amounts of amylose, more so than other rice grains. This characteristic allows the grains to remain separate during and after cooking, which makes them ideal for boiled and pilaf dishes.

Short rice grains differ in that they are made up of a higher amount of amylopectin and about 5-10% less amylose than long grain varieties. Arborio, Carnaroli and Bomba are good examples of this type of rice and these characteristics are necessary for providing the creamy consistency found in risottos.

Choosing the right grain of rice for the dish is all important; long grain rice varieties, for example Patna or basmati, are inappropriate for risottos because of their starch profiles (they would not form the moist creamy texture that are characteristic of risotto rice grains). Arborio or Carnaroli, just the same, would not make a good pilaf or braised rice, where the rice grains should be separate, fluffy and dry.

Risotto

TIPS for making risotto
1. Carnaroli, arborio, vialone nero and calriso rice produce good quality risottos, though each one performs slightly differently during cooking, giving the finished dish its singular qualities in terms of texture and consistency.
2. The importance of the quality of the liquid used in a risotto cannot be over stated. It is the intrinsic qualities of the stock which will ultimately provide the strong or subtle flavour notes in the final dish. Ideally, freshly made stock should be used, allowing seasoning to be controlled more carefully, which is not always possible with convenience stocks.

3. Sweating the ingredients first (as with shallots, onions, garlic or herbs) is important. It softens the plants cells allowing flavour molecules to be released, reducing their pungency and fosters a more subtle taste.
4. Add the liquid (stock), which must be hot, a little at a time, stirring constantly until most of the liquid has been absorbed before adding more. It is useful to try a few rice grains occasionally to determine what stage they are at, the ideal texture should be slightly firm to the bite in the centre (al dente), overcooking results in mushy rice grains. Stirring is all important, it removes the outer surface of the grain, allowing the starch granules to swell and absorb the liquid as it cooks with the heat.
5. There are differing views on what the ideal risotto should be, in terms of consistency, but the general view is that the finished dish should be moist, almost sloppy and with a creamy mouth feel.
6. Further ingredients should be added when appropriate so that they are cooked at the same time as the rice, they may be overcooked if added too soon or still undercooked if added too late. Continued heating of a risotto to cook ingredients that have been added too late will ultimately lead to overcooked rice.

Plain boiled rice and pasta

1. Cook in plenty of boiling, salted water, stirring at the start to prevent the rice or pasta sticking together.
2. Adding oil to the water does NOT prevent pasta from sticking together.
3. Dried pasta can be cooked al dente. However, it is not possible to cook fresh pasta this way.
4. When cooked, refresh in cold water until cold, strain and drain to remove excess water.
5. Store cooked rice dry in a container under refrigeration until needed and reheat well.
6. To store cooked pasta, add a little oil and mix through the pasta, don't store in cold water, the pasta will continue to absorb water making it too soft.
7. Cooked rice reheats well in a microwave in a covered container; ensure that it is reheated thoroughly. Cooked rice should not be reheated more than once after cooking, any left-over should be discarded.
8. Cooked pasta also reheats well in a microwave and can also be reheated in a pan with butter or a sauce, such as tomato or Bolognese.

Pasta

Pasta dough recipes vary: some are enriched with whole eggs or egg yolk, while others simply consist of strong or pasta flour, salt and water, and in some case with the addition of oil.

The choice of flour is not crucial, however flour with the necessary protein (potential gluten) content is, and this varies from flour to flour. Italian grade '00' flour is recommended for making fresh pasta, although the '00' grade refers to the fineness of the flour and not its protein strength. Strong or bread flours (usually milled from durum wheat) are equally as good for pasta making. In terms of preparation, nearly all methods for making pasta are based on same principles.

Pasta TIPS
1. Flours always vary a little in the amount of moisture they will absorb, so it is useful to be aware of this when adding the liquid.
2. If using egg and water, mix both together before adding to the flour. This will allow the liquid to mix in more evenly.
3. Kneading is all important; it develops the gluten in the flour and gives the pasta its strength, elasticity and plasticity.
4. Texture is also crucial; too wet and it will stick to working surfaces and the pasta machine; too dry and it will be very hard to handle, roll out and can break up. It is easier to add more flour to slightly sticky dough than to add liquid to hard, dry dough.
5. The texture of the pasta dough should be smooth, firm and elastic when stretched. It should feel silky to touch, with no signs of stickiness.
6. Once the dough is made, it must be allowed to relax before rolling and shaping. The dough should be wrapped in film and placed in a cool place for about 30mins. If left uncovered, it will form a dry outer crust.
7. Handle pasta dough in small amounts. Even 100g will go along way when rolled thin, so keep the remainder covered until ready for use.
8. Prepared pasta, like spaghetti or tagliatelle, will stick together into a tangled mass if left on the work surface, even for a short time. Sheets rolled out for lasagne or ravioli can also dry out quickly if left. It is important then to cook the pasta as soon as possible or keep it from sticking together by separating it with a further dusting of flour, greaseproof paper or film until ready for use.
9. Always plunge into boiling salted water and stir with a fork regularly for the first two or three minutes, to prevent it sticking together.
10. NOTE: Fresh pasta cooks much quicker than dried, so requires less cooking time.

11. If cooked pasta is to be stored before use, it should be refreshed in cold water, drained and coated with a little oil to prevent is from sticking together. Do not leave soaking in water.

Eggs

Many chefs and food scientists have argued, wrangled and debated about the correct cooking time and temperatures necessary to produce the perfect soft boiled egg. At the end of the day it is down to personal preference, some preferring very set egg whites and yolks whilst others prefer them to be of a softer underdone texture. Whilst all of this is subjective, one fact that has been determined is that eggs do not need to be boiled in order to cook them.

Poaching

This is a moist heat method of cooking foods, similar to boiling, though the process is gentler and cooks food in a temperature range between 70 and 82°C. Foods are also poached using minimum amounts of liquid; milk, stock, syrup, water, and wine are all used as poaching mediums.

Poached eggs

The traditional way of poaching an egg is to use a pan of simmering water, with the addition of salt and vinegar. The purpose of the salt and vinegar is to speed up the coagulation of the egg proteins. This, in turn, sets or solidifies the outer surface of the egg white which protects the yolk from damage. Cooked for the right amount of time, the egg white becomes opaque and is able to loosely support the egg shape, while the enclosed yolk remains runny. If the egg is over cooked or hard-boiled, the yolk becomes firm and crumbly, and the white, rubbery in texture.

The practice of using vinegar, however, has diminished as this resulted in an egg with a slightly acidic flavour, however salt can still be added to the water.

TIPS for poaching eggs
It is important to use very fresh eggs for poaching. During storage, the egg white (albumen) proteins, in particular, ovomucin begins to break down and this contributes to a thinner, less viscous or runny white. When a stale egg is poached, the white does not set around the yolk, but spreads out in the poaching water in an unappetising, straggly white mass. With a fresh egg, the white holds its shape, tightly surrounding the yolk.
1. If using the traditional method crack the egg into a slotted spoon and allow any runny egg white to pour off, this can be discarded.
2. Gently place the egg into the water, which should be at about 82 to 87°C, make sure the egg is totally submersed in the water. The

cooking time will depend on the size of egg and temperature of the water, but on average between 4 and 5mins.
3. The perfect egg will be one with a set egg white and a soft runny yolk. Take care when removing from the pan as poached eggs can break easily.

A further method of poaching eggs:
i. Take a piece of plastic cling film about 15cmx15cm, lay it out on the work surface and grease lightly with a little oil.
ii. Drape the film over a medium sized ramekin or something similar, wetting the inside of the dish helps the film to fall in. Crack the egg into the film- lined ramekin, gather the corners and twist tightly to form a small bag, making sure the film does not unravel.
iii. Place the egg bag into the hot water, ensuring it is totally submerged.
iv. Allow to simmer for about 4 to 5 minutes, again this depends upon the temperature of the water and size of egg. When cooked, remove with a slotted spoon and carefully unravel the bag or cut the twisted end off.

Poached eggs can be made in advance and kept in cold water in the refrigerator for up to three days.

Poached fruits
There are some fruits that do not poach well; raspberries and strawberries are too delicate and even the most gentle of heat does nothing to improve their flavour, texture or appearance. Hard fruits such as apples and pears generally poach well and, in some cases where the fruit is hard or under ripe, the texture and flavour is greatly improved.

Cooking liquors for fruits are usually based upon some type of sugar syrup or wine with the addition of herbs and spices. Sweet and dry white wines are good for poaching fruits, where the natural colour of the fruit is desired. Red wines are also suitable, and can add colour to fruits, giving them an appealing deep reddish-mauve colour.

Recommended fruit cooking times and temperatures
Apples and Pears: 85°C for 40 to 60 mins.
Plums, peaches, nectarines and rhubarb: 75°C for 30 to 60 mins.
Pineapple: 80°C for about 90 mins.

NOTE: these cooking times are dependent upon the size and ripeness of the fruit

Please see further details on poaching fruit in Chapter4 Fruit and Vegetables.

Steaming

When water boils, it produces vapour or steam and, when it comes into contact with the cooler surfaces of food, it condenses (is transformed into water). During this phase change, the energy stored in the steam is released (latent heat of condensation) and the heat cooks the food. Steaming has always been considered a healthy way of cooking; although slower than boiling, it is gentler on food items and helps vegetables, especially, retain natural sugars, nutrients and colour pigments.

TIPS on Steaming

Vegetables: cut all vegetables to a similar thickness, this will ensure even cooking.

Do not pack the food to be steamed too tightly; the steam needs to be able to circulate around all the food, this will insure more even cooking.

Steamed vegetables take the same length of time as boiling, and in both methods of cooking there is loss of nutrients, but to varying degrees.

When steaming a mix of vegetables, add green such as peas and beans a few minutes before the end of the cooking period in order to keep their bright green colour.

Refresh vegetables immediately in cold water, if not being served straight away.

When steaming fish, ensure that the fish is placed on a greased surface to prevent it from sticking. It is also important to covering with foil or film with a few pierced holes will help prevent a build up of water around the fish as the steam condenses.

Steam -blanching of vegetables is an alternative to blanching by boiling (see cooking vegetables Chapter 4)

'En papilotte' (in a paper/parchment parcel)

This method of cooking actually involves baking and steaming, however, I have chosen to discuss it here under steaming, because, although the food parcel is usually baked in an oven, the food is actually cooked by steam. Where steaming equipment is not available, cooking food en papilotte is the ideal alternative. This method is suited to foods which require short cooking times such as fish, shellfish and delicate vegetables, however, by choosing ingredients that have similar cooking times, there is no reason why an entire dish cannot be cooked using this method.

One of the principal aims of 'en papilotte' is to present the cooked parcel in front of the diner. The parcel is then quickly opened, thus allowing the escaping aromas to be enjoyed.

Chapter 3

STOCKS, SOUPS AND SAUCES (Including dressings)

STOCKS

The making and usage of fresh stocks, both in restaurants and in the domestic domain, has declined in recent years. This steady move away from the tradition of preparing stocks for cooking is due mainly to time and effort that is necessary for their preparation. Ready made products are undoubtedly convenient; they are cheap to buy, come in a range of flavours, are easy to use and have a long shelf life. Although shop bought stock products are without doubt labour saving, there are concerns among cooks and chefs about the amount of salt that they contain. In some brands, salt represents as much as 25% of the total ingredients in stock powders or paste. Why so much salt? Mainly to act as a preservative; thus allowing the product to be stored at ambient temperatures for long periods. However, there are now manufacturers who are producing reduced and salt free stock products.

It is a recognised fact that excess salt cannot be removed from cooking, so it is important that the cook has some knowledge about which convenience stock brands contain salt and how much.

In my view, there is no comparison between a well made fresh stock and a stock cube, gel or powder. The flavours of a well prepared stock are fresh and natural, and mirror the true taste of the ingredients used; convenience stocks tend to have unnatural flavours, some having a plethora of additives such as stabilisers, emulsifiers, flavour enhancers, colorants and of course, preservatives in the form of salt. There are, however, some supermarkets that sell fresh stocks in vacuum packs, but my experience is that many are lacking in flavour and expensive to buy.

Stocks (fresh)

Also sometimes known as fumets or bouillons, a stock can best be described as a flavorful liquid made by gently simmering bones and/or vegetables and aromats in a liquid (usually water) to extract their flavors, aromas, color, body and nutrients. By observing the basic rules, there is no reason why a good quality stock cannot be produced, and at a minimum cost. If stocks are made in sufficient quantity, they can be frozen in smaller amounts for later use. This also does away with the necessity to make them on a regular basis.

Ultimately, the purpose of stock is for it to act as the base for many dishes; soups, sauces and stews for example, so it is important that the intended flavor of the stock is apparent and not disguised or over powered with other strong flavors, such as herbs or vegetables with strong flavours.

Stock flavor and colour:
   White Stock: chicken, beef, lamb, veal, fish or vegetable
   Brown Stock: chicken, beef, lamb, game or veal

Apart from the difference in the ingredients, the only aspect that sets white and brown stock apart is that the bones and vegetables are colored by frying or roasting, which gives the brown stock its colour and a variation of flavors from that of white.

Bones provide the main flavor in a stock, but a small amount of meat is necessary if a good meaty flavor is to be achieved. Tougher joints of meat provide more intense flavours than tenderer cuts, and are less costly; a good example is shin beef. Because of its well worked muscles and high connective tissue content it is an ideal choice for use in making beef stock.

TIPS for making stocks
Do:
1. Use good quality ingredients: excess fat should be removed from bones. In the case of beef and lamb stock, it is probably prudent to ask your butcher to chop the bones up for you; the smaller the bones size the less simmering time is required, in order to extract their flavours.
2. When making white stock, the bones can be blanched prior to use, this removes some of the materials that later forms scum on the surface of stocks. It is not necessary to blanch bones that will be roasted for brown stock.
3. Blanch bones, simply place in a pan, cover with cold water, bring to the boil, remove from heat, and pour off the water. Give the bones a rinse and then they are ready to make the stock.
4. Pork and ham bones make a flavorsome stock, however they should be soaked in cold water to remove salt. I recommend soaking in cold water for two to three days with a change of water every twenty four hours.
5. Always peel and wash vegetables and leave in large pieces or whole, if they are cut too small they will break down into a mush and will cloud the stock. A good thumb rule is to put the vegetable into the stock about one hour before the end of the cooking time, this is long enough to extract all the flavours.
6. Use the correct ratio of bones and vegetables to water. Too few ingredients result in an insipid stock. Other vegetable trimmings may be added to stocks such as mushrooms, tomato skins and seeds but not in excess.

7. Try to use fresh herbs rather than dried, but be aware that they have strong flavours and can be overpowering. Use herb types appropriate to the main flavour of the stock (e.g. thyme and rosemary for lamb and chicken, thyme for beef).
8. Skim frequently; this is particularly important when bringing the stock to the simmer for the first time. Skim off any scum that rises to the surface with a ladle or slotted spoon. This, however, will diminish with continued simmering.
9. SIMMER gently, this will ensure a clear stock; boiling rapidly will lead to a cloudy stock. Replace loss of liquid by topping up with cold water when necessary; ingredients sticking out above the liquid level will not be adding flavor.
10. Observe the correct cooking time; under-cooking will result in an insipid stock, as insufficient time will not allow the full flavours to be extracted from the bones and vegetables (see recommended cooking times below).

Don't:
1. Boil stock; any scum rising will be mixed back into the stock, this will make it cloudy and give it a slightly bitter taste.
2. Cover with a lid: you have more control by being able to see the surface of the stock; it also allows the surface scum to bind together further, making it easier to remove.
3. Add SALT, this is added much later when the stock is used in soups, sauces etc.
   This is very important especially if the stock is to be boiled down in order to reduce volume.
4. Use highly flavoured or starchy vegetables such as turnip, swede, parsnip, and fennel (can be used in fish stock) or potatoes should not be used as these overpower the intended flavour of the stock and, in the case of starchy vegetables, make stock cloudy.

Stock cooking times:

Beef, veal, venison: 6 to 8 hours depending on size of bones.
Lamb and mutton, small furred game: 2 to 4 hours depending on size of bones.
Poultry and feathered game: about 2 hours.
Vegetable: about 45mins.
Fish stock: 20minutes.

Scum

Small particles of protein from the bones, skin and connective tissue, blood protein, bone dust if large bones have been sawed, cell particles of vegetables and fat globules. These particles all add to make the stock cloudy initially (Tindal effect); the more particles, the cloudier the stock. As the meat stock reaches about 50°C, the proteins begin to denature and coagulate. In fish stock, the proteins begin to coagulate at an even lower temperature of about 40C. As these proteins coagulate, they bind with the other food particles into a solid mass and rise to the surface. The resulting surface scum must now be removed to prevent the stock from becoming cloudy. The majority of scum appears during the first few minutes, when the stock reaches boiling point, and diminishes as simmering continues.

If at the end of the cooking process, the stock is still a little cloudy, it is possible to make it clearer. Here is one method: freeze the stock in containers (anything from ice cube to 2 liter amounts). Line a container which has some holes in the bottom (plastic containers are ideal) with two or three layers of muslin or a clean tea towel). Place the frozen stock into the container, cover and allow to melt in a cool room or refrigerator. When done, reboil the stock and chill. The cloth will have removed most of the particles that have made the stock cloudy.

One obvious sign that a stock has been made well is that it will become jellied when cold. The prolonged cooking not only extracts the gelatine from the bones but also converts the collagen in the connective tissue into gelatine. Further concentration of a stock will result in a very firm almost rubbery set.

Stocks can also be reduced in volume by gentle boiling. Reducing the volume/amount of stock intensifies the flavours, in fact reducing right down to thick syrup or glaze is often a technique carried out by professional chefs, where a small amount of glaze or glace is added to a soup or sauce to intensify the flavor.

Unfortunately, boiling for long periods alters some of the stocks flavour as the volatile molecules (the cooking smells of food in a kitchen) are driven off from the surface of the stock with the water vapour. This is unavoidable, as covering with a lid to prevent this loss would not allow evaporation. Distillation is one way of concentrating stocks whilst keeping their original flavours, but this requires expensive technical equipment and expertise.

Because of the nature of stocks, they must be treated as high risk foods and be kept refrigerated (or frozen) at all times (see Chapter 11 on Food Safety).

I have also thought it useful to give some tips and advice on how to make stocks using a pressure cooker:

TIPS on making stocks in a pressure cooker
1. If possible, chop bones into small pieces, especially large dense bones such as lamb, mutton, beef, veal or venison, and trim off any excess fat.
2. For brown stocks: sprinkle with a minimum amount of oil, roast in a hot oven until golden brown, turning them over occasionally. Keep the fat from the bones for roasting the vegetables.
3. Place only the bones only in pressure cooker to start with and cover with cold water. DO NOT fill above the maximum mark on the cooker.
4. Without the lid on, gradually bring to the boil, skimming frequently to remove the scum, place the lid on securely, ensuring the seal is engaged. Simmer gently for about 1 hour.
5. Meanwhile, fry or roast the vegetables in the bone fat until golden brown. It is important to keep the vegetables in large pieces or whole; too small and will break down, become mushy and can cloud the stock further.
6. Remove the cooker from heat source and allow the pressure to drop, remove the lid and add the browned vegetables and herbs/spices.
7. Bring back to boil, removing any scum, replace lid and simmer for about 30mins.
8. When the stock is ready, strain through a fine sieve, reboil, and then chill.
9. Keep refrigerated and use within three days or alternately, freeze.

Please note that I have provided a basic stock recipe in the recipe section at the back of the book

SOUPS

Soups are made from all manner of ingredients and into a never ending range of different flavours, textures and consistencies. They are perfect for using up scraps of leftover food, trimmings and ingredients which perhaps, may be on the cusp of or past their use by date, or can be made simply from one or two prime ingredients. They can be substantial and hearty, warming concoctions served in winter months, or a light and delicate consommé served on a dinner menu. They can also be produced with little effort, requiring very little expertise in the kitchen and in many cases, for the cost of a few pennies.

Soups in general should not cause too many problems even for the most uninitiated cook, but as always, there are pitfalls that can be avoided with a little know how.

Clear soups *(consommé)*

Not really an inclusion in today's repertoire of popular soups but more however a decoction originating from classic French haute cuisine, certainly during Escoffier's time.

Simply put, a consommé is a very clear, richly flavoured soup made from meat stock and other ingredients; technically it is a little more than this and can pose one or two challenges in order to make well.

General principle

Consommés are made of chicken, beef, game or occasionally veal. Though usually served hot, there are one or two classical consommés which are served chilled or jellied. In order to make a consommé, similar principles to stock making need be observed. Added to the stock, are amounts of ground meat (beef, chicken of game, depending on the required flavour), vegetables and flavourings (i.e. herbs). By way of ensuring the clarification process is successful, raw egg white is also added. All the ingredients are mixed together and, it is essential that the stock is added cold. Gentle heat is then applied with occasional stirring as the liquid increases in temperature.

At about 60°C, the proteins in the egg white and ground meat begin to coagulate and most of the tiny particles which give the stock a cloudy appearance become bound up. The crust or clarification, as it is sometimes referred to, solidifies on the surface of the liquid. At this stage, the stock is already beginning to clear, and to stir any further would damage the clarification causing the liquid to become cloudy again.

The drawback of using egg whites is that they unavoidably remove some of the water and fat soluble flavour molecules, contributing to a very slight loss of flavour.

There are other methods of clarification; finings such as methylcellulose or gelatine can be used to clarify consommés. Vacuum filtration and centrifugation are also more scientific methods requiring highly specialised and expensive equipment, but these are more likely to be seen in Michelin star restaurant kitchens.

After the appropriate length of cooking time is reached; usually about one hour, the consommé is carefully decanted off into a clean container through a strainer lined with muslin.

If a stronger flavour of consommé is required (consommé double), then reduction can be done by slowly boiling down the liquid, during which, it may be necessary to remove small amounts of scum that may appear on the surface.

Consommés are also good for preparing savoury jellies or aspic; these are simply prepared by adding a measured amount of gelatine to the consommé whilst hot, although this may not always be necessary as there may be sufficient gelatine in the original stock to give a set.

I have included a basic consommé recipe at the back of this book.

Purée soups
Without doubt the easiest of soups to make. They can be made from almost any vegetable or pulse, fresh or dried (lentils, beans, peas, split and chick peas). The body of the soup is created by the main ingredients, and therefore should not require further thickening additives. The soup should be cooked long enough to break down and soften the cellulose fibres of the vegetable or pulse so that they can be more readily liquidised to a smooth purée. This process can be speeded up by cutting the vegetables into small pieces, especially the root varieties and by pre-soaking of pulses such as split peas and beans for a few hours or overnight in stock or water. If the vegetables/pulses are still a little firm, they will not break down sufficiently and this will produce a soup that is lumpy and a texture that is coarse and grainy. Passing the soup through a fine sieve/strainer after liquidising is also important, as this will remove any remaining lumps and give the soup a smooth textured finish.

Care needs to be taken when making this type of soup. Because of their viscosity (thickness), they have a tendency to catch and burn on the bottom of the pan, so gentle heat and fairly regular stirring should be applied.

Green vegetable soups are a particular challenge in that they so easily lose their vibrant natural green colour (chlorophyll) due to the heat. Watercress, broccoli, spinach and asparagus are prone to undesirable colour change and when cooked, even for a short period of time, turn from a natural green to an unappetising drab green-brown. In order to retain as much of the green colour as possible, the base of the soup should be prepared and cooked first. The green vegetable element can then be added and cooked for the minimum amount of time necessary. An example of this method can be seen in the recipe for potato and watercress soup in the recipe section at the back of the book.

Starch thickened soups (velouté)
These soups rely upon a roux (equal amounts of fat and flour) to give them viscosity and a smooth, creamy texture.

Key points about using roux:
This type of thickening is ideal for soups where the main ingredients contribute only a little to the viscosity of the soup. Mushroom, chicken, tomato, and asparagus are all suitable for making into velouté soups.
a. Fat content: butter or margarine is normally used, although butter gives a better flavour. Oil can be used in some recipes.

b. Flour content: plain soft flour is the usual choice as this has lower gluten content than hard/strong flour, which can give a slightly stringy texture to the finished soup. Self raising flour (contains baking powder) should not be used and, whilst the use of wholemeal flour provides additional fibre, the appearance of a white soup (e.g. chicken) made with wholemeal flour, does not look appealing.
c. The fat is melted and the flour incorporated until a smooth paste is formed. Traditionally the roux is coloured slightly, and is cooked until a light golden or fawn colour is achieved.
d. The main problems arise during the addition of the stock to the roux. The purpose of making a roux in the first place, is to allow the liquid to be incorporated easily and evenly into the mixture. Without the fat content, the end result will be a conglomeration of lumps and, once this occurs, there is no likelihood of achieving a smooth textured soup.
e. The stock can be added hot or cold but the disadvantage of adding cold liquid is it takes longer to thicken as it comes to the boil and therefore requires prolonged stirring to avoid lumps. The trick is to add the liquid a little at a time, stirring in well until a smooth consistency develops, then add a little more liquid and so on until all the liquid has been added, stirring to the boil. Occasionally it is a good idea to remove from the heat, particularly when there are many lumps, as to continue would consolidate these lumps of roux and prevent them from breaking down.
f. A whisk can be used to incorporate the liquid into a roux, but the traditional way is to use a wooden or nylon spatula. That way the area between the edges of the base and the wall of the pan can be reached where the roux accumulates.
g. It is essential to simmer the soup for some time in order to 'cook out' the starch thickener, failure to do so will leave the soup with a grainy texture and floury mouth feel.
h. Depending on the main ingredient, the soup can be liquidised or simply strained to remove any lumps.

Alternative thickeners

As gluten intolerance is a concern for many people, it has become a necessity to find alternatives to wheat flour which can be safely used in processed foods and cooking. Manufacturers and food processors now produce ingredients and readymade foods that are suitable for those who suffer from the adverse reactions of gluten.

Where such an alternative or replacement is necessary, various plant starch extracts are now used in gluten free products and are available in supermarkets and health food shops.

Potato flour and potato starch
Both of these are available ready to use, but there is a subtle difference between the two.

Potato flour is obtained from whole potato and potato starch is just that, pure starch. Potato starch can be used as an alternative thickener to wheat flour and is ideal for use in thickening soups and sauces. Potato flour is processed, dried and ground, and not only includes starch but other constituents and this gives it a noticeable potato flavour. Potato flour is highly absorbent so is best suited to baking where the end-product needs to retain moisture.

Corn flour or corn starch, millet, rice (white and brown) and tapioca flours also make suitable thickening substitutes.

Broths
A broth can be a simple concoction made from a small number of ingredients and produced in a short period of time. Ingredients usually consist of meat, vegetables and stock, occasionally a cereal grain or pasta is added. The one difference that sets a broth apart from other soups is that it is not thickened.

Beef, Manx broth; chicken, mutton, Scotch broth or vegetable are probably the most well known, and, there are of course, many ethnic soups which can be classified as a broth. Bouillabaisse; a traditional French fish soup is made by cooking cuts of raw fish in a fish stock. The Japanese make dashi, a basic stock made from kelp (type of seaweed) with the addition of ingredients such as miso and noodles.

My own view is that a broth can only be made by using a good quality fresh stock, although, I appreciate this is not always possible.

TIPS on making broths
1. Always use good quality ingredients and fresh stock where possible.
2. Cut vegetables into even sizes, giving them a regular shape will add to their presentation
3. When adding starchy ingredients such as rice or barley, either cook them separately in a little water or stock first, otherwise there is a chance of ending up with overcooked vegetables and meat.
4. Ingredients such as potatoes and pasta will cloud the broth, so consider cooking them separately, if a clear broth is desired.
5. Add green vegetables towards the end of the cooking period, so they keep their natural green colour.
6. Add cooked meats and fish towards the end also, this will prevent them from becoming tough and stringy.

SAUCES

Sauces play an important role in both British and foreign cuisines, whether homemade or shop bought. Many sauces have changed little since their creation; the ubiquitous tomato ketchup and brown have been shaken and squirted onto all manner of foods since time immemorial. But the diversity in readymade sauces and dressings available today has continued to develop in tandem with the influx of new ingredients, particular dietary requirements such as low fat and the expansion of ethnic and fusion cuisines. Today, a plethora of global ingredients allows the cook to create new flavour and texture combinations for dips, dressings and sauces suitable to accompany a whole range of savoury and sweet dishes; snacks, fish and meat dishes, salads and puddings.

One of the earliest recorded uses of sauce, Garum (also known as liquamen), was a strong pungent condiment used in ancient Greek and Roman times. It was made from mainly oily fish, such as sardines, anchovies, or mackerel, which were fermented together with the intestines of larger fish, such as tuna, and was used extensively in recipes during that era.

Escoffier, in the 20th century, created his "mother sauces" (béchamel, espagnole, hollandaise, tomato and velouté), which were based on the grand sauces of French cuisine set forth by Carême a century earlier.

In modern cookery, the only two mother sauces that have stood the test of time and survived are béchamel and hollandaise; tomato sauce is now rarely made using a roux.

Sauces can therefore be categorised as follows:

A. Starch thickened: roux (wheat flour); béchamel (white sauce); velouté (made from chicken, fish or veal stock); brown (espagnole, made from brown beef stock); corn flour and arrowroot (custard and fruit sauces); and potato
B. Egg: hollandaise, mayonnaise,
C. Butter: nut brown butter, beurre blanc and fondue
D. Vegetable: (tomato sauce); fruit (raspberry or apricot sauce); nuts (pesto, romesco sauce)
E. Bread: bread sauce-roast chicken/turkey
F. Convenience/readymade.

A sauce that is poorly made can spoil an otherwise good piece of meat or fish, and can lead to disappointment of the whole dish. A sauce that is well made can enhance a dish, and in many cases improve the overall taste, in particular, when the primary ingredient is lacking in flavour.

The two main attributes of a well made sauce are: flavour and consistency (viscosity). Sauces are carriers of flavours so should have concentrated flavours, especially as they are usually served in smaller amounts than the foods that they accompany. Equally as important is their consistency; too thin and they collect in a watery pool on the serving dish and are difficult to eat; too thick and they look stodgy and unappealing. Further to this, the ability to taste a sauce with a thin consistency is diminished. This is because its lack of viscosity prevents it from being in contact with the surface of the tongue sufficiently long enough to be perceived by the taste buds.

I think it is helpful therefore to remind ourselves about the importance of sauces, and how their attributes contribute to the enhancement of a dish or meal.

Sauces:
1. Add or enhance flavours; the use of similar flavours can amplify flavours already present in a dish, especially if the ingredients are intrinsically insipid. For example, poached chicken in a chicken sauce. Sauces applied to a dish can also provide contrast in flavour, colour and texture to the primary ingredient, a good example of this is chicken provençal (chicken served in a tomato sauce).
2. Adds moisture; this is especially important where a primary ingredient is dry. Many dishes are prepared and cooked in a sauce, in other words, the sauce is an integral part of the recipe: braised meat dishes, pie fillings, etc, while in other situations, the sauce is an accompaniment.
3. Add visual interest; if the primary ingredients look bland in colour, a colourful sauce can improve the eye appeal of the dish, (i.e. a green pesto poured over a bowl of plain pasta).
4. Contrast textures; Sauces can add a smooth mouth feel to primary ingredients that are firm in texture. A good example of this is serving tartare sauce with deep fried fish in crispy batter or breadcrumbs

There are numerous recipes available to today's cook and the potential combinations of ingredients and methods provide an endless repertoire of sauces and dressing for every occasion. Many sauce recipes are straightforward and require a small handful of ingredients, little preparation time or skill. There are those, nonetheless, that can be troubling if not challenging to make correctly. It is these sauces that I have focused on and hopefully provided some insight into how to overcome the problems faced when making them.

Starch thickened sauces
Root starches, such as potato, arrowroot and tapioca and cereal flours such as corn, rice and wheat, are all used as thickeners in cookery.

Starches vary in their ability to thicken. Starches differ in terms of how quickly they thicken, how much they thicken and furthermore, the quality and flavour of a sauce after thickening. Therefore some understanding of the characteristics of starches will help the cook decide on which best suits the purpose. The most commonly used starch thickeners are wheat and corn flour; corn flour is almost pure starch and therefore is a more efficient thickener than wheat flour. Wheat flour not only contains starch but also amounts of fats and proteins, and these give the finished sauce opaqueness and a distinctive cereal taste once cooked.

Some starches begin the thickening process (gelation) at about 55°C whereas others require a higher temperature. Potato starch, for example begins to gelatinise at lower temperatures than finer grained starches such as corn flour and arrowroot. But in order to maximize thickening ability, all starches must be brought to the boil and held around simmering temperature in order to 'cook out' the starch. When making a flour thickened sauce, a roux is made so that the liquid can be gradually incorporated and blended in. This allows a more even thickening process and prevents the formation of dry flour lumps. The sauce is then allowed to simmer in order to 'cook out' the starch.

The cooking out period allows time for all the starch granules to swell and absorb the liquid. Prolonged cooking and stirring of starch thickened sauces will eventually cause a starch to break down, that is lose its ability to thicken, resulting in a soup or sauce that has become runny. Acids also impact on the starch's power (with the exception of arrowroot), breaking down the starch granules and reducing their ability to thicken or gelatinize.

The technique of thickening a sauce with corn flour, arrowroot or tapioca differs, and requires the thickener to be mixed with a small amount of cold liquid (slurry) and then quickly stirred into the hot sauce or gravy, an example of this is in making custard, where the custard powder is mixed with a little milk or water before stirring into the hot milk.

Roux thickened sauces
Béchamel (white sauce), veloute (velvet sauce), espagnole (basic brown sauce).
Béchamel or white sauce: forms the basis of less than a handful of hot sauces used in modern day cookery;

Parsley sauce for fish or boiled ham: with freshly chopped parsley; added to the sauce at the end of the cooking to retain the chlorophyll. Mustard and onion sauces can also be made using béchamel as the base.

The most commonly used extension of béchamel is cheese sauce (Mornay) which is used in egg, fish meat and vegetables dishes.

Because velouté and espagnole are rarely featured in recipe books, I have not discussed their preparation or uses here.

TIPS on making béchamel and cheese sauce
1. Butter or margarine can be used, but butter gives a better flavour. Always use plain flour, never self-raising because it contains baking powder, which would give a soapy texture.
2. Place milk into a saucepan. Add a studded onion (studded with cloves) and a bay leaf. Cloves have a very strong flavour so only 2 or 3 are sufficient for a small amount of sauce.
3. Bring the milk to the simmer and remove from the heat, allowing the onion to infuse for about 15mins.
4. Melt the fat in a saucepan over a low heat and mix in the flour. The ratio of fat to flour is always 1:1
5. Away from the heat, pour a small amount of hot milk onto the roux and mix in using a wooden spoon or spatula. Mix well until smooth, then add a little more milk, and mix again until smooth.
6. Return the pan to the heat and bring to the simmer, stirring continually until smooth; the sauce will still be very thick.
7. Continue to add more milk, stirring all the time. Remove from the heat occasionally until all the lumps have gone.
8. When all the milk has been added, the studded onion may be added back to the sauce to give further flavour. Allow to simmer very gently for about 20mins, stirring occasionally.
9. The addition of a little English mustard improves flavour and raw egg yolk also adds richness to the sauce and improves glazing (browning) of the surface (i.e. as in cauliflower cheese au gratin). Cream may also be added to improve mouth feel and richness.

Corn flour and arrowroot thickened sauces

These are not too challenging to make, but basic steps need to be followed if smooth, lump-free sauces are to be achieved.

Both these starch flours must be mixed with a cold liquid before adding to a sauce for thickening purposes. The flour is usually mixed with water to form a smooth runny consistency or slurry and is then stirred into the liquid which should be boiling. Thickening happens almost instantaneously, so there is no necessity to cook the sauce for more than one or two minutes.

Because corn flour and arrowroot are almost pure starch, in comparison to wheat, which contains proteins, fibre and sugars, smaller amounts can be used. Secondly, because of their nature, they do not impart any undesirable flavours to sauces.

In all cases, unfortunately, starch thickened sauces do have a tendency to go lumpy easily and form a thick surface skin if left for any length of time. Stirring the sauce after it has formed a skin, will only make matters worse, because the broken skin will simply form lumps. To avoid this, cover the surface of the sauce with a piece of greaseproof paper (cartouche) which has been lightly oiled or buttered.

Ultimately, once a sauce has become lumpy, it can only be rectified by straining through a fine sieve.

Sweet sauces, whether jam or fruit juice based, require a slightly longer cooking out time than savoury thickened sauces. The high sugar content of sweet sauces inhibits the thickening process by binding up the water molecules. This in turn, inhibits the rate of gelatinisation of the starch, necessitating further cooking time. In some instances where the sugar content is so high the sauce will not thicken at all.

Emulsion sauces and dressings

Hollandaise, béarnaise and other derivatives are classed as warm egg sauces. These classical sauces are created by the formation of an emulsion of vinegar, egg yolk and melted butter, with the addition of flavourings such as herbs.

Many a good cook or chef has succumbed to throwing the odd tantrum when trying to make hollandaise or béarnaise sauce, even when it may not have been their first time. Whilst they can appear formidable to prepare, there is some gratification in being able to overcome failure by finally producing a sauce to be proud of, regardless of the number attempts.

How emulsions work - Oil and water!

Water is immiscible in oil and vice versa, in other words neither will mix with the other and this is where the challenge lies when faced with making an emulsion sauce. If you have ever made a basic vinaigrette or French dressing you will have noticed that after a period of time the vinegar and oil separate out; the oil on top, vinegar below, agitation does little to remedy this, though a temporary emulsion is created if only for a few minutes, eventually they will 'separate out'.

Whilst this temporary preparation may be used in making an acceptable dressing for immediate use, a more permanent emulsion must be produced if the sauce is to maintain its integrity over a period of time.

Emulsification is the process of combining two or more liquids together that will not normally mix into a permanent state (immiscible). In the context of sauce making, we only need be concerned with fats (butter and oil) and water based (vinegar, lemon juice, wine) ingredients.

In simple terms, an emulsion can be either a fat dispersed into water or water dispersed into fat. Hollandaise and mayonnaise are fat in water emulsions, whereas vinaigrette and whole butter are classed as water in fat emulsions.

In every emulsion such as mayonnaise, there is also a continuous phase and a dispersal phase. In oil- in water emulsion (O/W), the continuous phase is the vinegar and the dispersed phase is the oil, while in a water in oil emulsion such as vinaigrette, the roles are reversed.

Vinaigrette is regarded as water in oil emulsion (W/O), because the vinegar is being dispersed in the oil or continuous phase. However, by adding an emulsifier, such as lecithin (in egg yolk) the mixture becomes oil in water emulsion.

Egg yolks contain lecithin (a type of lipoprotein) which is a good emulsifier, hence the reason for using it in sauces such as mayonnaise and hollandaise. Emulsifiers are both water loving and hating, or hydrophilic and hydrophobic respectively. The hydrophilic end forms chemical bonds with water but not with oils, and the hydrophobic end forms chemical bonds with oils but not with water. It is this reaction that binds both solutions together and makes them unable to separate out.

Mustard also acts as an emulsifier. Soy lecithin and gums, such as zanthan, are used extensively in processed foods where strong long lasting emulsification of ingredients is required (e.g. bottled sauces and ketchups).

A further important requirement for creating an emulsion is mechanical force. This is necessary to break down the dispersed phase (butter or oil) into small droplets so that they can become suspended in the continuous phase (vinegar). In the kitchen, this can be accomplished by hand with the use of a whisk or by using a blender. With the introduction of food blender/processor- cookers which heat and blend at the same time, this process is made much easier and makes light work of emulsion sauces. Regardless of how the mechanical action is applied, it is essential to break up the liquid butter or oil into tiny droplets, this, along with the emulsifier (lecithin), helps prevent coalescing (clumping together of the small drops) of the fat.

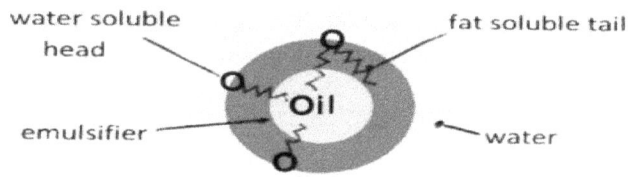

Image showing how an emulsifier holds water based liquids and oil together to form an emulsion

Emulsified vinaigrette/French dressing

Vinaigrettes can be made into an emulsion quite easily, which means the dressing will not separate out on standing once made. In the method below, mustard acts as the emulsifying agent, although the emulsion will only be stable for a short period, it is not permanent. In many brands of shop bought vinegar and oil dressings, the liquids are emulsified and stabilised by use of zantham with ensures a permanent emulsion.

Method:
1. Place the mustard and vinegar into a bowl and mix well.
2. Very slowly drizzle in the oil, whisking vigorously all the time. It is possible to do this in a food processor as long as there is a sufficient amount of ingredients.
3. Once all the oil is added, the dressing is ready. If it is a little too thick, then a little vinegar or lemon juice may be added.
4. If the mixture is 'split', i.e. an emulsion hasn't formed. In this instance, start again, and then add the split dressing very slowly to the new one.
5. Additional ingredients, such as seasoning, herbs or spices may now be added.

Mayonnaise

Mayonnaise and its sauce extensions, such as tartare and Marie rose are classified as savoury cold egg sauces and, like their warm counterparts, are also made by emulsification of primary ingredients, but in this case with vinegar (water), egg yolk and oil.

If you have never made mayonnaise before or perhaps your first attempt was a disaster, you may find it useful to refer to the key points (below) regarding the process involved in its preparation.

It is interesting to note that the basic principle of preparing emulsified savoury sauces is applicable to all types regardless of whether cold or warm.

Don't expect homemade mayonnaise to taste like shop bought, you may be disappointed and reach straight for the Hellman's. However you may be surprised and wish you had learned how to make before, it is all down to personal taste and what you are accustomed or conditioned to.

The process
Mayonnaise
1. Ensure all ingredients are room temperature; the oil will be less viscous and will help with the emulsification. The type of oil, mustard or vinegar makes no difference to the process, only the flavour and colour.
2. Use a stainless steel, plastic or glass bowl for mixing the

mayonnaise in.
3. Mix the egg yolk, vinegar and mustard together, until they are combined.
4. Drizzle the oil slowly onto the yolk mixture with continuous whisking, either by hand or machine, until all the oil is incorporated.

NOTE: if the oil is added too quickly or whisking is not sufficiently vigorous, the emulsion will not form. The fat globules will coalesce, that is they will clump together to from large drops of oil, eventually forming one large globule and the water based ingredients will react similarly. Any amount of whisking however will not reverse this situation.

Faults and tips:
a) If the mayonnaise is too thick, then add a little water or lemon juice.
b) If during its preparation, the mayonnaise becomes very thick and there is still oil to add, add a little water of lemon juice before adding more oil.
c) If the mayonnaise has curdled or split then start again using another egg yolk. You will have to add extra oil to compensate for the extra yolk.
d) If fresh egg yolks (i.e. non-pasteurised) have been used to make the mayonnaise then the sauce must be kept refrigerated between use.

Savoury warm egg sauces: Hollandaise, béarnaise

You will find it beneficial if you carry out a little groundwork before making these sauces. Both salted and unsalted butter can be used, as the finished sauce will be tested for seasoning before use. To save time, the butter can be melted and the butter fat decanted off the butter milk. The reason for this is that only the butter fat is used, while the butter milk is not; although the amount of butter milk present represents a very small amount.

The butter must be melted gently; if it is boiled, the butter will not separate out, but mix together. When it has melted, refrigerate, allowing it to solidify. Once done, the butter milk can be poured off, leaving a block of pure butter fat; incidentally this is how ghee is made (used in Indian cookery). This operation can be done a few hours or a day or two before. Fresh eggs should be used when making either cold or warm emulsion sauces because during prolonged storage, the lecithin emulsifier present in egg yolk breaks down and forms cholesterol, and this also affects its abilities to emulsify.

The process
1. For the reduction: In a small pan, add the vinegar, herbs and/or spices.

2. Gently heat until the liquid has reduced by about 1/3, add to this the same amount of water, and then strain through a sieve.
2. In a bowl place the reduction and egg yolks. Ideally the bowl should be stainless steel as this will conduct the heat quicker than a glass bowl; don't use a plastic bowl.
3. Place the bowl over a container of simmering water. Begin to whisk immediately; be aware that, if making small amounts, the margin of error is higher as this procedure does not take very long and can quickly spoil. The objective is to whisk the mixture over gentle heat until it forms a soft foam (similar to that on a cappuccino coffee). Remove the bowl from the hot water at <u>any time</u> if it feels too hot. Once the foam has been created, remove from the heat, do not return to the heat again, and continue to whisk for a minute or two afterwards to reduce some of the residual heat in the mixing bowl. If, during the process, the mixture becomes too hot, it will over cook (coagulate) the proteins in the egg yolk, resulting in something similar to scrambled egg; in this scenario the only option is to discard it and start again.

Once the foam mixture or sabayon is made, then the prepared melted butter can now be added. It is important that the butter is warm-hot (between 65°C and 75°C), as it will cool down during the whisking and, if allowed to become too cool, will begin to solidify.
4. The incorporation of the butter is akin to that of adding the oil in mayonnaise: little amounts added slowly with continuous whisking. Continue to whisk the butterfat into the egg yolk mixture, unless the buttermilk was already been removed, make sure not to include any in the fat. If the sauce is becoming very thick and there is still butter to add, pour in about 5mls of hot water, this will make the sauce a little thinner, allowing the remainder of the fat to be incorporated and reduce the possibility of it splitting or curdling.
5. Check the sauce for seasoning, a little lemon juice can be added to offset the richness.
6. If the sauce is to be kept warm, cover it with a cartouche to prevent a skin forming and keep it at 63 to 65°C. Warm egg sauces, because of their nature of their ingredients, are considered high risk and should therefore be kept at this temperature for no more than two hours. If the sauce becomes too cold, it will solidify and the emulsion will be broken, in this scenario it should not be reused but discarded.

NOTE: If the butter is added too quickly or whisking is not sufficiently vigorous enough, the emulsion will not form; the butterfat globules will coalesce, that is, they will clump together to from large drops of fat, eventually forming one large globule and the water based ingredients will react similarly, the final result being a layer of melted butter floating on top of the water based ingredients. Any amount of whisking however will not reverse this situation. Vigorous whisking while adding the butter is necessary to break the fat down into tiny globules making them more readily bond with the emulsifier in the egg yolk.

Rectifying a split sauce:
This type of emulsion sauce can separate out easy during preparation or storage, however, it is possible to amend it. The first method is to start again with a new egg yolk and reduction and slowly whisk in, little by little, the split sauce: further melted butter will need to be added to compensate for the extra egg mixture. The second method is to start with a small amount of hot water (5-10mls) in a clean bowl and very slowly whisk in the split sauce a little at a time. The addition of water will inevitably produce a less viscous sauce; to improve viscosity further melted butter must be added.

Key point: by adding more fat, the thicker the sauce will become; by adding more liquid (e.g. vinegar, water, and lemon juice), the thinner, less viscous the sauce will be. It is also important to note that one egg yolk will only emulsify a certain amount of fat, usually about 100g

Most recipe ratios will be similar to these:
200g butter : 2 egg yolks : 10mls reduction liquid + flavourings
Variations on hollandaise are: Maltaise-addition of blood orange juice, Choron – addition of tomato pulp, Mousseline-addition of whipped cream, horseradish-addition of grated horseradish.

Butter sauces –Beurre blanc
Beurre blanc (white butter) and Beurre fondue (melted butter) can be exacting to make, but the process for their preparation is the same. The principle is to form an O/W emulsion; in this instance, it is the case in proteins in the butter milk that act as the emulsifier. Unlike hollandaise and béarnaise sauces, where the butter is added in a melted state, the butter is incorporated in to the water or wine (continuous phase) in small chilled lumps.

There are some interesting variations on Beurre blanc which can be achieved by using different wines, vinegars and herbs and spices e.g. red wine, balsamic vinegar, basil, saffron, and vanilla.

The process
1. Pour the liquid (e.g. vinegar or wine) and flavourings (such as chopped shallots, herbs etc) into a shallow saucepan and bring to the boil. Reduce in volume to about 25%.

2. Cut a block of chilled butter into about 15-20g lumps. Any type of butter can be used, but for a low salt sauce, use unsalted.
3. Remove the pan to the side of the heat source and begin to whisk in lumps of butter, one or two at a time, adding more simultaneously as some melt and begin to form the emulsion.
4. Return the pan to the heat occasionally; the sauce can be allowed to boil a little but not for long periods.
5. It is important to keep whisking throughout the process, shaking the pan simultaneously, also helps.
6. If the sauce starts to thicken slightly at about the halfway stage, then the initial emulsion has been formed. Continue adding the remainder of the butter and whisking continually. Check for seasoning, strain through a sieve and finish with a little lemon juice.
    The sauce must be kept warm and if allowed to go cold will solidify and the emulsion will break.
7. This sauce is easily prone to splitting/separating. In this case, chill the split sauce and drain off the liquid. Pour the liquid back into a clean pan. Cut the solid butter fat into chunks and repeat the procedure from step 2.

Most recipe ratios will be similar to these 200g butter : 20mls reduction liquid + flavourings
  Some variants to the traditional beurre blanc are:
  Red or rosé wine beurre blanc, saffron beurre blanc, herb beurre blanc.

Beurre fondue (melted butter or butter sauce)
This sauce can be served as an alternative to simple melted butter. The advantage of this sauce over melted butter is that it is slightly viscous. Its viscosity allows the sauce to from a thin coating when poured over food, giving it a glossy shine, unlike melted butter, which quickly runs off. Beurre fondue is ideal for serving with fresh vegetables, such asparagus or new potatoes.
  To make Beurre fondue, follow the method for making beurre blanc, using water instead of vinegar or wine.

Nut brown butter or hazelnut butter (beurre noisette)
A classic finish to fish cooked meunière style (shallow fried), it can also be used as an alternative to melted butter on vegetables and pasta. It is used in bakery, in the preparation of Madeleine and financier cakes. The technique involves heating the butter in a frying or omelette pan; as the heat intensifies, the butter begins to foam, which is then followed quickly by a colouring of the butter milk solids; these should be a medium brown nut colour. At this critical stage, a little lemon juice is added, then

the sauce must be immediately poured over the food item. Insufficient browning will not produce the typical nutty flavour; conversely, too prolonged heating causes the butter solids to blacken and burn.

Egg custard sauce (crème Anglaise)

I am sure we are all familiar with the custard made with milk and 'Birds' custard powder; it has been part of our food culture for many years. Where would an apple pie, sticky toffee pudding or a good old trifle be without it? The main ingredient, custard powder, is actually a mixture of three ingredients: corn flour, vanilla flavouring and yellow food colour. If all three ingredients are available you can always make your own. Fresh egg custard, however, in my opinion, is by far superior to the traditionally made custard, in terms of texture, flavour and mouth feel. But if time is not permitting, then there are some good quality brands of readymade, fresh egg custard available to the consumer, in particular those which advertise 'made with real Madagascar vanilla'. An additional ingredient of readymade fresh egg custard is modified starch, and this allows the product to be heated without fear of curdling. The principle in making fresh egg custard is based on the ability of the proteins in the egg yolk to thicken the milk or cream. As the egg proteins are heated, they begin to denature; as the proteins coagulate, they unwind and form new bonds with the water molecules in the liquid, thus creating a thickening mechanism.

The process for making fresh egg custard
1. Separate the egg yolks from the whites, place the yolks into a bowl with the sugar.
2. Beat the yolks and sugar well until pale in colour: this gives the finished custard a creamy off white colour.
3. Split vanilla pods lengthways and scrape out seeds, place both pods and seeds into the milk and cream. In a saucepan, bring the milk and cream to the simmer, remove from the heat and allow to infuse for about 15mins.
4. Whisk the hot milk or cream onto egg mixture and return to the saucepan, heat gently while stirring with a wooden spoon or spatula. As the custard thickens, it should coat the back of the spoon with a thin layer of the sauce; remove from the heat and continue to stir for about 1min, in order to allow the residual heat in the pan to cool. Strain through a sieve. The consistency of the custard should be similar to that of single cream.

Key points:
a. It is imperative that the mixture does not boil. In the event of this happening the custard will curdle.

b. Most recipe ratios will be similar to these: 250ml milk: 2 egg yolks: 25g sugar: ½ vanilla pod
c. To enrich the custard, substitute some of the milk for cream or add an extra yolk: this will slightly increase the viscosity of the custard. The addition of egg yolks is necessary if the custard is to be used on a trifle where a set is required. The type of milk used will also impact richness and viscosity (i.e. skimmed versus whole milk)
d. Curdling, more than anything affects the appearance of the custard. Tiny white lumps can be seen floating in the sauce and these are the egg proteins that have denatured too far or overcooked. A further sign is that here is also some loss in viscosity.
e. Curdled custard can be partially rectified by adding a little corn flour, reheating the sauce too cook out the starch and then straining through a very fine sieve.

If the sauce is intended to be used as a cold set custard (e.g. for trifle) then the ratio of egg yolk to liquid must be increased.

Gravy

"There is no recipe for gravy, nor should there be", states Hugh Fearnley-Whittingstall in the River Cottage Meat Book

What he actually means by this statement is that every time gravy is made, it will always be slightly different; it never starts and ends the same. The final gravy will depend upon various factors; the type of meat, the size of the joint, whether the meat is on or off the bone, the roasting process (time and temperature), and what additional ingredients are used to make the roast gravy.

In French cookery, jus rôti or roast gravy is commonly described as the natural roasted meat juices, with the fat removed, simmered with meat stock and strained. No thickening is added and therefore the gravy is quite watery. In Britain this is not so, and traditionally, gravy has always been thickened with some form of starch, giving it more viscosity than the typical French gravy.

Jus and reduction sauces

Both of these share a common feature in that they are prepared by gently simmering stock, in order to reduce their volume. During the reduction process, steam vapour is driven off by continual simmering and this generates a gradual concentration of the various solids contained within the stock. These solid are what eventually give the reduced stock its consistency, aroma and flavours.

There is however inevitable loss during evaporation, as small molecules dissipate with the steam, this in turn gives rise to some loss of flavour and aroma, and ultimately contributes to a subtle change in the final taste of the jus.

Neither jus nor reduction sauces are starch thickened, but rely up on an amorphous mixture of proteins, cellulose, gelatine, fat and other food molecules to provide the viscosity.

Jus, (literally means juice) is usually understood to be either of the juices that occur during the cooking process (when roasting meat) or the juices from raw vegetables or fruit.

As the demise of Escoffier's classical French cuisine continued during the 70's and 80's, the popularity of the 'meat jus' since then has risen and has now almost supplanted the 'small brown sauces' of the old cuisine. In today's culinary repertoire, the word 'jus' is taken to mean a fresh stock that has been reduced down (by simmering/boiling) to the consistency of syrup. This also enables development of concentration flavours. Such jus are now common place on good restaurant and hotel menus and form an integral part of many meat dishes.

The secret of a great jus lies in the quality of the stock; a jus can only be as good as the stock from which it is made, so it is of great importance that it has been made with care and attention.

The primary ingredients used for the stock, should be the predominant flavours (i.e. beef, chicken, game or lamb). Subtle background flavours are provided by the addition of certain vegetables and herbs. The intended stock does not have to be clear, but a good golden brown colour is important if the final jus is to have a deep mahogany finish.

If you have wondered how restaurants make those wonderful rich, shiny, mahogany coloured jus here is how it is done:

Method for a basic jus

Firstly, the quantity of jus needs to be determined. On average to produce 250mls of jus about 5 litres of stock is required, however this is slightly dependent upon the quality of the stock to be used.

1. Place the stock in a large, wide, shallow pan. The wide shallow the pan the better; this gives a greater surface area than a tall narrow one and will allow the stock to evaporate more quickly. I f the pan is not sufficiently large enough; add more stock once some has boiled away.
2. Bring to the boil and allow to simmer gently at the side of the heat source so that the surface of the stock rolls to one side; this makes removing of the scum easier.
3. Skim frequently whenever scum accumulates on the surface. When reducing large quantities it is a good idea to down size pans

occasionally.
4. When about 2/3 of the liquid has evaporated off, a reduction can now be added.
5. Gently fry the vegetables and herbs in butter for about 10mins, giving them a little colour.
6. Add the alcohol and boil down/reduce until only a small amount is left, once done add the reduce stock.
7. Continue to reduce the jus until it has a consistency of thin syrup, ensuring any scum is removed. There should be no necessity to add anything further, apart from adjusting the seasoning. Pass through a fine sieve or, for an even smoother finish, pass through a piece of muslin; it is now ready for use. The jus can be stored in the refrigerator or can be frozen. When cold, the jus should be quite solid. This is due amongst other food materials, to the concentration of gelatine from the bones and meat.

Reductions
A basic reduction can consist of finely chopped onions (celery, carrot and leek are optional), a little garlic and herbs. The choice of herbs depends to some extent on what meat the jus is to accompany (e.g. tarragon for chicken or beef, rosemary for lamb or chicken, thyme is good for most meats). Secondly the addition of a liquid which is usually a wine; the choice is again dependent upon the flavour of the jus, examples are: red wine for beef and game dishes, white wine for chicken, sherry or Madeira for beef or pork, port for duck. The addition of redcurrant jelly will provide the jus with a slightly sweet finish, which is ideal for game, duck or lamb.

Reduction sauces
In comparative terms, reduction sauces are the 'small brown sauces' that were popular during the classical French cuisine era. These, of which, were many, were all derivatives of demi glace or half-glaze. Demi glace was the foundation of a multitude of brown sauces which were served with various meat, poultry and game dishes and some fish.
   Reduction sauces are made in a similar fashion to the French jus rôti or roast gravy; that is they are not thickened with starch but rely upon the particles of food matter in the meats juices or stock to give the finished sauce its consistency or viscosity.
   When protein foods such as a steak, chicken breast or small lamb cuts, are pan fried they produce juices. The amount of juices produced, is reflective of the type and cut of meat and its moisture content in its raw state. For example a thirty day dry aged sirloin steak will contain less moisture content than a fresh chicken breast of similar weight.

During the cooking process, juices seep or ooze out of meats and these collect in the pan where they remain as liquid or become encrusted as solids or sediment on the bottom of the pan. These meat residues form the basis of a reduction sauce and are collected by swilling of the pan with a chosen liquid appropriate to the finished sauce (i.e. stock, vinegar, water or alcohol liquor). This procedure is more commonly referred to as deglazing or déglacer. The sauce may then be finished with additional ingredients such as butter or cream and may be strained to produce a smoother texture.

Reduction sauce process

What follows is a general method; it is not possible to give a recipe for ingredient amounts, as the final volume of sauce produced is derived from the pan residues, so it is very much down to experience or guesswork.

1. After removal of the food item from the pan, the amount of juices and sediment will vary. The first stage is to determine the quality of the sediment. The pan may have undergone excessive heating during the cooking process causing the sediment to burn, in this situation it is not worth proceeding as to use it will render the final sauce bitter. If the juices and sediment are not overly coloured, then these can be used.
2. Any water content must now be carefully evaporated off by boiling.
3. The next step is to remove excess fat. In fact, all the fat, unless the intention is to add further ingredients (such as finely chopped root vegetables, shallots, onions or herbs). In which case, they should be gently sweated for two to three minutes then the remainder of fat can be drained off. Any alcoholic liquor (wine, sherry, port, brandy) must be added next and allowed to reduce down by boiling/simmering. The reducing down process also facilitates the burning off of some of the liquor alcohol content which otherwise would result in a sauce overpowered by raw winey flavours. There is a misconception that by adding more alcohol than necessary to a sauce it will improve its flavour, not true.
4. Once the reduction has been achieved, then further ingredients can now be added.
5. Stock can be added to extend the amount of sauce, this may also be reduced down in order to concentrate further flavour and to acquire the right consistency.
6. Cream is added if it is intended as a cream sauce, e.g. pepper sauce (au poivre), whipping or double cream is added to the reduction, then it is again boiled down to achieve the correct consistency. Single cream is not suitable for use in these types of sauces because its fat content is too low, making it unstable at high temperatures, unless there is a starch present.

7. Once the sauce consistency has been realised, all that is required is a final check for seasoning and if a smooth textured sauce is desired then a pass through a fine sieve will be necessary. The shine of a reduction sauce can also be improved by the addition of raw butter mixed in to the finished sauce, this procedure is known as monter au Beurre (with butter).
8. Sauce consistencies can be readjusted by either 'boiling down' to thicken or 'let down' with liquid to make thinner.
9. Adding cream to hot, cooked sauces can be problematic if certain rules are not followed.
   Always use whipping or preferably double cream in a sauce that requires boiling or reducing down. Single cream can curdle or split a sauce if boiled for any length of time.
10. Where a dish contains a considerable amount of cooking liquid, this should be boiled down to a minimum before adding cream, otherwise, to add the cream and attempt to boil the sauce down to achieve the correct consistency can lead to curdling.
11. When adding an acid (i.e. lemon juice) to a cream sauce, add it at the end of the cooking process, to prevent curdling. When finishing a sauce with just a touch of cream, then almost any type of cream is suitable; even vegetable oil based creams.

Dressings
This is where the cook can have hours of fun experimenting with different ingredients and learning about those flavours that complement each other and those that don't. Today, there are so many choices of vinegars, flavoured oils, mustards and seasonings available to the cook. There is also the option of saving a little money by flavouring your own oils and vinegars as retail costs for some 'artisan' products are somewhat pricey. For more information on how to make flavoured oils and vinegars please look in Chapter 9 on Food Preservation.

There are no hard and fast rules with regards to making dressings but a few suggestions may be of help:
   a) When experimenting with a new dressing, especially if using unfamiliar ingredients make small amounts, this way if it doesn't work out then it's not a huge waste. If you are totally unsure where to start, try experimenting by adding new ingredients to a simple traditional sauce or dressing: a shop bought one may give you some inspiration.
   b) Blanch fresh herbs before using, this will help keep their colour.
   c) Mix water based ingredients together before adding the oil; mustard doesn't disperse well in oil.

d) When using an oil and vinegar based dressing, don't dress salads with it until serving, otherwise the salad leaves will wilt and discolour quickly. This is largely due to the oil and not the acid in vinegars (or fruit juices). Herbs and salad leaves have a natural fine cuticle which protects them from the weather; a sort of 'waterproofing' and when the oil is poured over the leaves it blocks the pores causing discolouration to the leaves, more so than the vinegar.

e) Dressings should be stored under refrigeration, and in particular those which contain fresh ingredients such as fruit or herbs. In most cases homemade dressings should only be kept for a short period between one and two weeks, although this depends on the ingredients used.

Chapter 4

FRUIT AND VEGETABLES

Vegetables
Vegetables can make up an important part of any meal, adding contrast in colour, flavour, texture, fibre and nutrients. Vegetables can also make an interesting and substantial meal on their own, especially when an alternative to meat or fish is desired. Fresh vegetables are still an underrated aspect of our cuisine, having a stigma of being, taking too long to prepare and cook and are uninteresting to eat. They also tend to be neglected in favour of the main item (i.e. as in a roast, a steak or fish dish), in the belief that they are not as important as the 'star' protein.

Whether through habit or ignorance, there are many who still boil the living daylights out of vegetables, resulting in an unappetising lump of fibre; void of all colour and texture, little flavour or nutritional value. But with some understanding and direction, vegetables can be prepared and cooked in a way that they can be a tasty and tantalising accompaniment to a main course, or as a dish in their own right.

Vegetable classification
The subject of vegetable classification can be a little confusing as it really depends on which context they are being referred to.

From a botanical standpoint, fruits and vegetables are classified based on physiological characteristics of plant structure, development and organisation. Consequently, vegetables identified in the genus for example, Brassica i.e. broccoli, swede, turnip, cabbage, all share the same characteristics and so on.

From a culinary viewpoint, the shared characteristics of vegetables are those based upon which part or parts of the plant are prepared, cooked and eaten (e.g. root, leaf, stem, flower or bulb). Consequently, while carrots, swede, parsnips and turnips are all recognised as root vegetables, they are not all classified as members of the same taxonomic genus. Botanically speaking, turnips are classed as Brassica, carrots as Daucas and parsnips, Pastinaca.

Many vegetables may be considered as fruits in the true botanical sense, as the seeds are contained within part of the plant. Therefore tomatoes, cucumbers, eggplant, peppers, peas, etc. are classified as fruits, or more specifically, vegetable fruits, based on this premise.

Below is just one example of taxonomic or botanical classification of the vegetable broccoli.
- ORDER: Brassicals
  FAMILY: Brassicaceae (mustard)
  GENUS: Brassica
  SPECIES: Brassica oleracea -Broccoli

The following are all members of the brassicaceae family: cabbage, kale, sprouts, broccoli, cauliflower, swede, turnip and kohlrabi. But in culinary terms they are known as: leaves, flowers, roots respectively.

Culinary classification of vegetables
These are generally categorised as:
Bulbs: onion, spring onion, shallots, leeks, garlic
Leaves: cabbage, lettuce, mustard and cress, spinach, chard, watercress
Roots: carrot, parsnip, beetroot, swede, turnip, salsify
Tubers: potato, sweet potato, yam, Jerusalem artichoke
Flowers: cauliflower, broccoli, calabrese
Stems: celery, asparagus, beans, globe artichoke, kohlrabi.
Fungi: mushrooms; cepes, chanterelle, oyster, brown cap, truffles.
Pods and seeds: broad and butter bean, peas, okra, sweet corn.
Vegetable fruits: tomato, peppers, cucumber, chilli, aubergine

Structure of vegetables and fruits
Perhaps a basic understanding of the structure of different vegetables and fruit will help you to understand why different types of vegetables are more suited to certain methods of preparation and cooking.
- The cell wall is constructed of cellulose, hemicelluloses, and pectin along with smaller amounts of lignin. Lignin develops as a secondary wall in plants as they become older and this accounts for the reason that old vegetables are generally tougher. Pectin acts like a glue and its main role is the adhesion of cell to cell. It is these structures that give the cell and subsequently the plant its shape and strength. With the exception of lignin, all the cell components are polysaccharides (many linked glucose units) and, while cellulose is insoluble in water, hemicelluloses and pectin are and contribute to the softening of vegetables and fruit during cooking.

The amounts and ratios of these components depend upon the type of the fruit or vegetable. Hard vegetables such as swede and turnips contain more concentrated cellulose, whereas soft textured vegetables contain less.

Additionally, fruits and vegetables contain large amounts of water; sugar (in the form of fructose and sucrose), various vitamins and minerals, protein and phytochemicals and all of these are stored in organelles within the cytoplasm. The cell membrane provides protection and, like the cell wall, is permeable to allow for the movement of substances in and out of the cell.

- Cytoplasm: contains fluid and various parts for growth and function.
- Vacuole: contains enzymes, sugars, acids, protein, pigments, flavours, waste and defence mechanisms. In particular the vacuoles hold a large percentage of the cells water contributing to the crispness of a fresh vegetable.
- Chloroplast: this is where the chlorophyll is stored and is involved in the process of plant photosynthesis.
- Chromoplast: the yellow, orange and red pigments such as carotenoids are stored here.

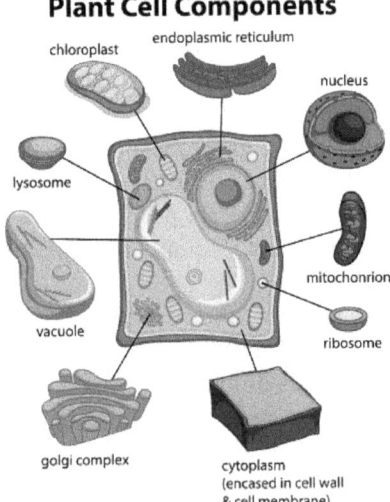

Image 1 showing the basic structure of a plant cell (courtesy of 'colematt' istock)

The colour of fruits and vegetables
The wonderful array of diverse colours that we see in plants, shrubs and trees is due to phyotchemicals or plant chemicals (phyto meaning Greek for plant). Out of over 200,000 different chemical plant compounds occurring naturally, 4,000 of these have been identified as responsible for the distinctive colours of fruit and vegetables

Beta-carotene belongs to a group of phyotchemicals, related to vitamin A, called carotenoids. Their reddish-orange pigment imparts colour to plants, and this can be seen in some vegetables and fruit such as carrots, sweet potatoes, water melons and apricots.

Carotenoids are also found in green vegetables. However, they are hidden by the green chlorophyll pigment during the plants active life, but can become visible in old green vegetables as the chlorophyll degrades.

Carotenoids are generally heat and pH stable, in particular, beta carotenes (orange colour of carrots) are also fat soluble, in other words, they do not dissolve in water. This characteristic, therefore, means that vegetables such as carrots, sweet potatoes, sweet corn, can be cooked in water for long periods without much loss of colour. These natural pigments also contribute to the colour of peaches, apricots and mangos.

Anthoxanthins are a type of water soluble flavonoid (phytochemical) pigment in plants, providing a range of colour from white to cream. Cauliflower, onions, white potatoes, mushrooms, parsnips, bananas and turnips owe their colour to anthoxanthins. Like anthocyanins (below) they are susceptible to colour change under adverse conditions. When certain vegetables containing anthoxanthins are subjected to an acidic environment, such as the addition of vinegar or cream of tartar (acid) to the cooking water, they are bleached, retaining their bright white colour. Conversely, when cooked in water that is slightly alkaline, they turn an undesirable yellow colour. When cooking cauliflower, therefore, it is good practice to add some lemon juice to the water to maintain whiteness. Red onions, radish, red cabbage, red lettuce, egg-plant, red-skinned potatoes and berries contain water soluble flavonoid pigments known as anthocyanins. These phytochemicals give plants a variety of colour ranging from blue to red and purple depending on the pH. Like anthoxanthins, vegetables and fruit which contain these natural colours are sensitive to changes in pH and prefer a slightly acidic environment. In cookery terms, adding an acid such as vinegar, red wine or apples helps to keep the natural deep red/purple colour of red cabbage, while alkaline conditions turn red cabbage purple – blue.

The red colour of tomatoes, watermelon and pink grapefruit is due to lycopene. Lycopene is not soluble in water and is very stable, so it maintains its colour well during cooking, even for prolonged periods at high temperatures.

Similar to anthocyanins are the betalains, these are also water soluble and are colour stable in a slightly acidic environment. Examples of vegetables are containing betalains are beetroot and chard.

Zeaxanthin is responsible for the yellow/orange colour found in corn, saffron and paprika. It is a carotenoid and is present in large amounts in certain green vegetables.

Purchasing, storage, preparation and cooking vegetables

During post harvest and storage, all synthesis of organic compounds stops, though numerous physiological changes continue during storage. Bulbs, roots, tubers & seeds become relatively dormant during storage whereas fleshy tissues undergo ripening after maturation and then continue to senescence (deterioration through aging). Mature vegetables have a tendency to deteriorate less in storage than more immature vegetables. Nonetheless, most fresh vegetables are at their best for only for a few days following harvest.

The action of enzymes rapidly impact on vegetable flavour by converting the plants natural sugars to starch, this is why during food processing, green vegetables such as peas and beans, in particular, are frozen within a few hours of harvesting.

Vegetables contain large amounts of water, prolonged storage, especially under the wrong conditions (i.e. warm and dry), will cause them to become flaccid (limp) and tough. This is the consequence of water loss from the plants cells and the extent of this loss is relative to its environment. Storage in a controlled atmosphere of high humidity between 85 and 95% and low temperature is ideal for almost all vegetables and fruit, as this reduces moisture loss. Some domestic refrigerators now have a built in humidity control for this purpose. Where there is obvious loss of moisture in herbs and vegetables, it is possible to rehydrate (add water) them by soaking in cold water for a few minutes then removing.

A mist spray of water is also useful in keeping fresh herbs, salad leaves and vegetables at their peak condition.

Also noticeable in green vegetables during storage, is the unavoidable loss of colour and this due to the breakdown of the natural pigment chlorophyll (actually chlorophyll A turns a grey-green and chlorophyll B a yellowish colour).

Homegrown vegetables, especially green, intended for freezing, must be blanched in order to inactivate the enzymes which will otherwise continue to cause deterioration in color, flavor and texture. Freezing, alone only slows down the action of enzymes it does not stop the process.

Specific storage temperatures for a wide range of fruit and vegetables can be found at http://www.engineeringtoolbox.com/fruits-vegetables-storage-conditions

Purchasing fruit and vegetables

It may seem obvious to say that we wouldn't buy vegetables or fruit that look old or even worse, beginning to rot. On first inspection we best discern the quality of fruit and vegetables by their appearance; colour and texture are the two most important indicators of freshness. But there are further ways which we can use to tell use more about the quality of the produce:
- ✓ *Colour*: one would expect this to be obvious (i.e. bananas display signs of browning due to over ripening), one or two fruits do however change colour as they ripen; pineapples change from green to a golden/brown colour.

- ✓ Physical damage and bruising: This can be caused by improper handling and, if the produce skin is damaged, can expose the interior to contamination. Bruised fruit can also be a sign of aging.
- ✓ Greens leafy vegetables and salad:, spinach, kale, chard, lettuce should be crisp and firm with no signs of wilt or discolouration.
- ✓ Smell: clearly many vegetables have little or no smell in their natural state, however some fruits such as melons and pineapples do. The smell should be fresh yet not too strong, a musty aroma is generally an indication that the fruit is over ripe and a second inspection by touch can confirm this.
- ✓ Soft fruits (such as berries, grapes, and drupe fruits) are particularly susceptible to rapid deterioration, especially if bought at their ripest. Fruits such as melons and avocados are normally sold under ripe (unless stated) so will need to be purchased in advance. In some cases melons can take up to two weeks to ripen and avocados a week under certain conditions.
- ✓ Root vegetables are more robust and will tolerate storage longer than green. Potatoes with large green patches (Solanin) should be discarded; smaller marks can be cut out. Solanin is toxic, and can be fatal, but only when large amounts are consumed.
- ✓ Fungi or mushrooms age quickly with a noticeable drying out and a woody texture when cooked.
- ✓ For all other vegetables, look for signs of growth of sprouting shoots, shrivelled skin, change in colour, weeping or unpleasant odours.
- ✓ Certain fruits require specific methods for determining ripeness. Avocados need a gentle squeeze when testing. Pineapples should have a feint sweet odour, and their green leaves should pull out easily. Melons vary a little from type to type, but in general, should smell sweet and, the flat end should be quite soft or spongy when pressed with a finger.

Cooking vegetables

Cooking (in water) vegetables softens their tissues by releasing water pressure in the plants cells and dismantling their walls, making the vegetables softer in texture, in older vegetables the cooking time is lengthened due to tougher cellulose structure. The structural characteristics of the vegetable also determines the length of cooking time required; root vegetables such as swede and carrots need longer cooking times than green vegetable.

When vegetable tissue reaches 60∘C, cell membranes are damaged, cells lose water and deflate, tissue goes from firm and crisp to limp and flabby. However, most cell walls remain strong and intact.

Nearer boiling point (100°C), the cell walls begin to weaken though the cellulose framework still remains unchanged. Pectin (cement) and hemicellulose) softens, eventually breaking down and dissolving into the cooking liquid.

Prolonged cooking causes tissue to disintegrate, eventually forming a pulp or purée.

Cooking vegetables in hard or soft water

Household water supplies in the UK tend to be either hard or soft. Southern, North and North Eastern areas generally have hard water, the remainder either moderate or soft.

Hard water contains minerals; in particular calcium and magnesium and this makes the water slightly alkaline (about 8 pH), whereas soft water contains very little or none of these minerals and is slightly acidic (about 6.5 pH).

The calcium, and to a lesser extent, magnesium content of hard water strengthens plant hemicellulose and pectin structures, and this contributes to a vegetable that remains firm in texture.

However, cooking green vegetables for prolonged periods to soften their texture, results in loss of colour. To compensate for the mineral content and preserve colour, a small amount of bicarbonate of soda can be added to the cooking water.

Soft water is slightly acidic and does not contain calcium or magnesium, therefore vegetables cook quicker. Green vegetables however require a slightly alkaline cooking environment in order to retain their colour (chlorophyll), and this can be achieved again by the addition of soda to the cooking water.

Green vegetables

Broccoli, beans, spinach, sprouts, asparagus, and peas all contain significant amounts of chlorophyll. This green pigment has, at the centre of its molecular structure, a single magnesium atom. During adverse conditions, such as prolonged cooking or a change in the pH towards a more acid environment, the magnesium atom is displaced and replaced by a hydrogen atom and this manifests in the vegetables loss of colour.

BLANCHING (colour fixing or shocking green vegetables)

The cells of green vegetables not only comprise of chlorophyll but an enzyme known as chlorophyllase and it is this enzyme which is responsible for the destruction of the green pigment. Blanching in boiling water or steaming easily deactivates the enzyme and thus allows the vegetable to maintain its green colour.

Microscopic air pockets among the plant cells cloud the green colour but, when the vegetable is blanched, the green gases expand and escape from the cells, and the green colour immediately brightens.

Blanching technique
Prepared vegetables are plunged into boiling salt water for between one and five minutes, after which they must be plunged into cold preferably, iced water to remove the heat and halt further cooking. The length of time is dependent upon the type of vegetable: vegetables such as asparagus, peas and beans, will only require about 2-3 minutes, sprouts and broccoli about three minutes. Even these times will vary, depending on the size or thickness of the vegetable. Steaming can also be used to blanch vegetables; times tend to be slightly longer than for boiling, because heat is not transferred through steam (water vapour) as effectively as water.

CULINARY APPLICATIONS
A good example of discolouration is in the use of fresh herbs. Basil especially turns dark brown (and eventually blackens) when cut. Blanching basil leaves for a few seconds before chopping or liquidising them with oil makes for a bright green dressing. Un-blanched herbs will result in a drab finish to a dressing or sauce.

TIPS *for cooking green vegetables*
1. Add plenty of salt to the cooking water. Salt speeds up vegetable softening. It assists in the breaking down of the cellulose cross links and dissolves the hemicellulose
2. The pH of water should be neutral or slightly alkaline - acidity dulls chlorophyll, a small pinch of bi-carbonate of soda can be added to the water to check acidity and retain colour, however if too much soda is used, the increased alkalinity quickly breaks down the vegetable fibres, leading to an overcooked and mushy texture.
3. Green vegetables must always be plunged into boiling water, never start them in cold water.
4. Use a big pan of boiling water, do not overload; the larger the amount placed into the pan, the further the temperature is lowered and therefore it takes longer to return back to the boil - cook in batches if necessary. Plenty of water helps dilute natural plant acids which can cause some colour loss.
5. Test for doneness and cook for the minimum amount of time. Cooked green vegetables should be crisp to the bite.
6. Immediately the vegetables are cooked, plunge into cold, preferably iced water to reduce the temperature and halt the cooking process. Ensure they are thoroughly cold before removing from the water.

7. Steaming, Frying or Baking vegetables: when cooking by these methods, the cell walls are exposed only to the natural acids and moisture in the plant cells (steam is slightly acid) and therefore produces a firmer result than boiling.

Notes on vegetable cookery in general
This is by no means an exhaustive list, but I hope I have covered those vegetables that can be tricky to cook or how to avoid the usual mistakes made when cooking them.

Artichokes: globe (flower head of the thistle family) and Jerusalem (tuber of the Sunflower family) Jerusalem artichoke discolours very quickly when peeled (as dos salsify), so should be left in a solution of salt water or lemon juice for any length of time. The best way to cook these to retain their whiteness is in a 'blanc'; a cooking liquid of water, salt, lemon juice and plain flour. Globe artichokes can be cooked in boiling salted water, baked or barbecued.

Asparagus: if leaving whole as spears, peel about ¼ of the length of skin from the root end. Treat as for green vegetables if boiling or steaming. Grilled or roast from raw. Cooking times vary: between 3 and 10mins, asparagus is easily overcooked. The English asparagus season is very brief: about 8 weeks, starting on St.Georges day and ending on the summer solstice.

Bean sprouts: raw or stir fried, don't be tempted to wash first, unless using in a salad. Keep refrigerated, they have a very short shelf life.

Beetroot: always cook whole with the skin on, don't pierce or will bleed. Beetroot can also be roasted whole or cut into pieces.

Broccoli: will cook quicker and more evenly if cut into florets. Cook broccoli as for green vegetables.

If using in stir fries, keep the broccoli raw

Brussels sprouts: remove discoloured outer leaves, put a cross in the stalk end; this helps the heat transfer deeper into the centre. Separate large and small sprouts, cook the large sprouts first for a few minutes then add the small ones. By the end of the boiling time both will be cooked to the same degree. Sprouts can also be shallow fried or puréed when cooked.

Cabbage, red: shred finely and braise with red wine, vinegar or tart apples to retain colour. Don't boil red cabbage; it loses its colour easily.

Cabbage, green: shred and cook in boiling salted water. If stuffing; remove whole outer leaves, cut out the tough midrib and blanch, this will soften the leaf, making them more pliable.

Carrots: contain natural sugars which dissolve in water, so consider an alternative cooking method such as steaming or cooking in a minimum amount of water e.g. glacé

Cauliflower: Cut cauliflowers into florets, this speeds up the cooking time and cooks the vegetable more evenly; it also helps with portion control. Add a good squeeze of lemon juice to cooking water to retain its whiteness.

Celery and fennel (bulb): both share the same family and can be prepared and cooked in very much the same way. While they are good for use in salads, they require prolonged moist cooking such as braising to tenderize them. Some recommend peeling the outer skin or string from celery stalks before eating or cooking. Fennel discolours easily, so blanch the bulb whole in boiling water for a few minutes prior to braising or roasting. Grated fennel with remoulade sauce is a popular salad accompaniment to cold meats and smoked fish.

Chilies (aka chili pepper): this ubiquitous ingredient is actually classified as a fruit and is more commonly used in savoury foods but has found its way into some desserts and confectionery.

The chilies heat comes from the natural alkaloid capsaicin present in the fruit and this is mostly concentrated in the fleshy part (placenta) which holds the seeds in place. Preparation and cooking has no effect on the intensity of chilies. Chilies can burn the skin, so always wash hands thoroughly after handling and preparing them. Good advice is to wear a pair of vinyl gloves, particularly when handling a large amount.

Eggplant (aubergine): have a very absorbent flesh and easily soak up fat. To avoid a greasy dish, dry fry in slices, especially when making moussaka.

Garlic: grows into a bulb, each segment is called a clove. Garlic can be roasted or cold smoked while still whole. To peel and crush garlic, place cloves on a cutting board and hit or squash hard with the side of a knife, this makes removal of the outer skin easier to peel off. Sprinkle the cloves with a little salt, and again, using the side of a knife and the palm of a hand and mash with a downward and sideways movement. The salt acts as an abrasive and helps to break down the fibers.

Mange tout and sugar snap: sometimes require de-stringing from end to end. Stir fry or sauté in oil or butter to keep crisp, they do not need pre-boiling.

Mushrooms: there is no necessity to peel or wash cultivated mushrooms, remove any compost with a firm brush.

Onions, shallots: contain sulphur compounds and it is these that cause the age old problem of tears during their preparation (caused by a weak form of sulphuric acid). Despite many suggestions and remedies to overcome this, no ideal solutions have been forthcoming. The reason why some onions have high levels of sulphur is dependent upon, amongst other things, the sulphur content of the soil in which they are grown.

Where a recipe calls for sweated onions or shallots, the technique involves partly or totally cooking the chopped vegetable without colour; this should be done using low heat. Caramelized onions are cooked at higher temperatures allowing the natural sugars to brown. In both cases the addition of oil or butter helps the processes. Acid such as vinegar may be added towards the end of the caramelisation to give a slightly sweet/sour flavour.

Parsnips: discolour quickly when peeled. Peel and cook straight away or keep in salted water.

As a root vegetable, parsnips are one of the quickest to cook. For a more even texture, remove the internal woody core. Roasting: blanch quickly; drain and roast in a little fat, the addition of honey will bring out their sweetness.

Potatoes: use the right type of potato for the recipe 9see below). Peeled potatoes should be submersed in cold water if not being used immediately; this will stop the potato from turning black. Potatoes for roasting, should be blanched in boiling water for about 2-3 minutes before, this gelatinises some of the surface starch and stops them sticking to the roasting dish.

Potatoes for mashing should be cooked in minimum amount of water, do not overcook them as they will continue to absorb water. When soft, drain potatoes and return to gentle heat to dry. Every home has a masher, in some cases it is probably one or two generations old; it does the job but, unfortunately, it always leaves the odd lump behind. By using a fine sieve, a much smoother mashed/puréed potato can be achieved. Finally don't feel tempted to use the liquidiser or electric mixer to mash up the potato; the result will resemble something like wall paper paste.

General points
Choosing the right variety of potato is important if you hope to produce a really good quality dish. As different varieties of potatoes contain different levels of starch, the choice of potato is therefore determined by its starch content.

Potato starch varies similarly to rice in that the ratios of the two components vary depending on the variety of potato. Waxy potatoes contain lower amounts of amylose (13-15%) and a higher amount of amylopectin than floury or mealy potatoes; this makes them ideal for layered potato dishes and salads as they hold their structure better when cooked. Floury potatoes are higher in amylose (20-24%) but lower in amylopectin than waxy varieties; in this instance, the cells separate when cooked making them better suited to baking, mashing and chipping. This also makes them able to take up cream and butter without becoming sloppy. The disadvantage of high starch potatoes is that they absorb water and therefore are prone to falling apart and becoming mushy easily.

When potatoes are referred to as 'high starch' and 'low starch' what is really meant is: 'low starch' potatoes contain lower amounts of amylose and have a higher content of amylopectin than 'high starch' potatoes and vice versa.

Medium starch, or all purpose potatoes, contain a little more moisture than high starch potatoes so hold their shape better. This type of potato is good for roasting and baked potato dishes.

Low-starch or waxy potatoes hold their shape better when cooked and are suitable for chipping and salads.

Potato varieties:

High starch: uses – mashing, baking: varieties - Idaho, Russet, King Edward, Maris piper

Medium starch (all purpose): uses - boiling, frying, roasting or mashing (to a degree) varieties Ailsa, Desiree, Wilja, Estima, Maris piper, Golden Wonder.

Low starch: uses - salads, daupinoise, baking: varieties - Cara, Charlotte, new; Jersey royal, Nicola.

To clarify a point here, when the term starchy potato is used, it means the potato has a much higher content of amylose than those considered as low starch or waxy. Waxy potatoes consist of higher amylopectin content than starchy potatoes.

It is also important to note that potato variants differ in characteristics; such as moisture and starch content. Seasonal climate change and storage conditions also impact on the texture and consistency of the cooked potato dish, and the same type of potato may produce a dish of varying quality at different times of the year.

Black or brownish spots on cooked potatoes appear for a number of reasons; improper storage (i.e. too cold or badly handled) causing bruising. When storing potatoes, make sure it is at a temperature above 4°C.

Cooking potatoes in aluminium or iron cook ware can also produce reactions leading to the formation of black spots, so stainless steel or non stick pans should be used.

Black spots can also be formed by chemical reactions between constituents found in potatoes; iron, a phyto chemical known as chlorogenic acid and oxygen. The chemical reaction is more common when potatoes are boiled in water which is slightly alkaline, so a good tip is to add a little acid such as lemon juice or cream of tartare to the cooking water, particularly in areas of the country where the water is hard.

Spinach: is easily overcooked. Remove tough stalks and midribs from leaves, wash well.
Boiling; plunge into boiling salted water for about 3-4mins, refresh and drain, form into a ball and squeeze well to remove excess water. Reheat quickly in a little butter.
Wilted: prepare as above. Heat a little butter in a frying pan, add the spinach, season and cook quickly until the leaves become wilted. A little ground nutmeg or garlic works well with spinach.

Vegetable purées
Some vegetables, including old and sweet potatoes purée (mash) well; spinach, cauliflower, carrot and swede, parsnip, fennel, celeriac and peas. When preparing vegetable purées, it is important to ensure, firstly that they are cooked (not overcooked) until soft. Secondly, any cooking water must be removed; this is best done by drying in the pan over gentle heat. This is crucial with certain vegetables and in particular potatoes if a watery consistency is to be avoided. Whilst most vegetables can be puréed using a food processor, potatoes cannot, they become over-soft and gluey in texture.

SALADS
Salads are usually consumed mainly in the warmer months of the year, when ingredients are readily available and at their prime. Salad ingredients purchased out of the British growing season are more than likely imported and quite often lack in flavour and tend to be more costly.
   Salad leaves deteriorate quickly, so they need to be stored and prepared with care. Keep all salad leaf ingredients chilled by storing in the refrigerator and hydrated (moist). If the leaves are limp, they can be placed into cold water for a few minutes, and then removed, this will help give a crisper texture. Where a dressing is used, apply this just before serving.

FRUIT
In botanical terms, a fruit is the seed -bearing structure in flowering plants formed from the ovary after it has flowered. Fruits are the means by which flowering plants disseminate seeds and it is these seeds which, given the right conditions, become the adult plants of tomorrow
   In culinary terms, fruits do not correspond to botanical classifications, as is much the case with vegetables. Fruits are therefore classed as any edible, sweet-tasting part of a plant. Secondly, fruits are higher in organic

acids and sugar, higher than vegetables and are usually eaten raw, where vegetables in general tend to be cooked.

Further classification of fruits can be based on whether the fruit ripens before or after harvesting; they are either climacteric or non-climacteric. Climacteric fruits are those which, after picking, show a marked increase in ethylene gas, and this acts to engender the ripening process; examples of these are apples, avocados, bananas, peaches and pears. Non-climacteric fruits produce little or no ethylene and show little change after harvesting, in other words they do not ripen further; grapes, raspberries and strawberries are examples of these. However this method is now considered redundant by many, because of the development of new cultivars and genotypes. For example pineapples and melons once classified as non- climacteric, are now known to ripen after harvesting.

FRUIT CLASSIFICATIONS
Berries: strawberry, raspberry, blue and black berry, red and white currants, gooseberry
Drupes: peach, nectarine, plum, apricot, cherry
Citrus: orange, lemon, lime, grapefruit, tangerine, Clementine
Melons: water, honey dew, cantaloupe, ogen, galia
Pome: apple, pear, medlar, quince
Tropical: mango, kiwi, banana, avocado, coconut, pineapple, passion fruit

Fruit storage, preparation and browning
Fresh fruits need low temperatures and high relative humidity (90-95%) to reduce respiration and slow down their metabolic processes. The slowing down of these natural processes prevents fruit from becoming ripe too quickly, or at worst, overripe and rotten.

As a rule, soft fruits such as berries, in particular, require refrigerated storage to reduce spoilage. Hard fruits (such as melons, pineapples) are happy in a warmer environment of 5-13°C, although apples and pears do benefit from cooler storage temperatures.

Consequently, fruits vary in the length of time that they can be stored before becoming past their best. Recent research has found that between fruits cell are cavities which are filled with carbon dioxide and oxygen gas, thus acting like lungs, allowing the fruit to breath. Apparently apples have about five times greater volume of space than pears and it could be for this reason that apples are able to be stored for a longer period than pears.

As mentioned earlier, a characteristic of climacteric fruit is the production of the odourless and colourless gas, ethylene. Ethylene is a naturally occurring hydrocarbon hormone produced by most vegetables and fruits, especially apples, bananas, citrus fruit, melons and tomatoes. This gas generates a softening of the plant cell wall and speeds up the ripening process; a well known practice of this is enclosing bananas with unripe avocados to help speed up ripening.

Oxidative enzymatic browning

We have all experienced the changes in an apple when cut or bitten into and if left even after a short time, begins to go brown.

The agent responsible for this common appearance is enzymatic browning. It is a chemical process, involving oxidases, and other enzymes that create colour pigments from natural polyphenols, resulting in the familiar brown colour. In general, enzymatic browning also requires exposure to oxygen.

Polyphenols are present in fruit cells but are stored separately to the enzyme polyphenol oxidase, but when the fruit is cut or damaged and is exposed to the air both these substances react to form quinones, which then combine to make melanins; the undesirable dark brown colour in fruit.

There are methods that can be employed to prevent or slow down fruit browning. Enzymes can be easily denatured by heat treatment (usually above 45°C), both blanching and poaching creates an unfavourable condition for enzymatic browning.

The addition of salt can inhibit the enzyme system and reduce the browning reaction; this may be acceptable for vegetables but not for fruit as this can generate a salty taste.

Soaking fruits and vegetables in organic acids can also inhibit enzymatic reaction: citric (limes and lemon), ascorbic (grapefruit, oranges), malic (strawberry, mango, oranges, and peaches) or tartaric (wine, grapes, cranberries, bananas) are all effective as the activity of polyphenol oxidase decreases at a pH of 5 and below. Cut fresh fruit, such as apples, pineapple and pears, can be kept in fruit juices or syrups to prevent browning; this has the dual action of excluding oxygen and providing an acid environment.

Elimination of the air either by vacuum packing or by keeping cut fruit in sugar syrup are two further methods of preventing browning. The antioxidant sulphur dioxide is used in processed foods to prevent browning and loss of flavour; dried apricots, apples and raisins in particular

Peeling, deseeding and stoning fruit

One of the most fiddly and sometimes monotonous tasks in the kitchen is peeling and removing seeds or stones from fruit. As in all aspects of cookery, there is a right way, and wrong way of doing things, but occasionally, there is 'no-way'.

I have endeavoured to discuss the 'inns and outs' of preparing fruit with some handy tips and advice along the way.

Peeling:
Most pome fruits such as apples, medlar, pears and quince pose no problems, though by using a knife, rather than a peeler, it is likely that more flesh will be removed, unless of course, you are extremely dexterous.

Apricots, peaches and nectarines seem to cause the most frustrations. Sometimes, these fruit can be peeled easily with a knife and without any prior preparation, however at other times this is almost impossible. When such fruits do not succumb to peeling, some suggest blanching in boiling water for a few seconds to enable peeling, although my experience is that this does not always work; so you're stuck with the skin.

Commercially canned peaches and some brands of tinned apricots are first treated with lye (a solution of potassium hydroxide) to remove the skins prior to processing.

Deseeding/stoning:
Peaches and nectarines fall into two types; freestone and clingstone, and as their names suggest, the stone or pit in the former is not attached to the flesh and therefore releases easily, whereas the pit is firmly embedded in the flesh in the latter.

To the layman, it is practically impossible to discern which is which by looking at them, so apparently the thumb rule is that early season varieties of peaches and nectarines tend to be cling stone, and later season varieties freestone.

Cherry stones are usually easily removed by cutting the fruit in half, but if the fruit is to be left whole, then a pitter should be used. Hand pitters are available in most good cooks' shops and are often sold as olive pitters.

Some grape varieties tend to be seedless, but where pips need to be removed, especially if the grape is to be kept whole, then pips can be removed using the loop end of a hair grip.

Pineapples should be 'top and tailed' and then the skin removed using a large sharp knife, ideally a serrated one. Follow the contour of the fruit and remove about 5-8mm thickness of skin. Don't slice straight down as too much fruit will be left on the skin. Use the tip of a small pointed knife to remove the eyes. Gadgets are available which cut out the central core, while leaving the pineapple whole.

Strawberries require little preparation apart from the removal (hulling) of the green leaves and stalk (calyx) and this should be done with the point of a small knife to minimise loss of the fruit. All soft fruits and berries in particular should be rinsed just before being consumed as they deteriorate quickly once prepared.

Segmenting citrus fruits with a knife requires some skill, but practice makes perfect!

Top and tail the fruit using a small sharp knife. Stand the fruit on one of the cut surfaces, and follow around the contour of the fruit with the knife, removing the zest and white pith. The thickness of the peel depends upon the fruit; grapefruit generally have a much thicker pith layer than lemons or oranges.

Work around the fruit, and trim off any remaining pith. To segment, hold the fruit in one hand and cut to the centre and to the side of the thin vein which separates each segment, cut again to the centre following the opposite vein of the segment. When two or three segments have been removed the remaining segments can be removed by following the vein to the centre of the fruit, then turning the blade outwards and following the opposite vein back out of the fruit.

To avoid mushy fruit, it is important to ensure that the fruit is firm and not over ripe and minimise the amount of handling during preparation. A good thumb rule for removing the skin from fruit is to ensure the knife is sharp, this avoids bruising; use a large bladed knife for large fruit such as melons and pineapples. Follow the contours of the fruit; at the same time be aware of the thickness of the skin.

COOKING FRUITS

The challenges of cooking fruits are due mainly to their softness and high water content, although some are less susceptible to breaking up during cooking than others. Undue prolonged heat dismantles the fruits structure, causing it to break up and this in turn produces fruits with a pulpous texture. Some fruits, like eating apples, pears and apricots, however are less prone to breaking up during cooking.

Fruits are at their best when ripe, they are at their peak in terms of sweetness, texture and flavours, but it is also at this stage that they are the most challenging to cook. In apples, the amount of acid and sugar determines the balance between tartness and sweetness. Bramley apples are a good example of this, though they maintain their flavour during cooking, are easily turned to a pulp. Conversely, eating apples are good at holding their shape during cooking.

Of course, there are times when the fruit needs to be cooked to a stage so that it can be puréed easily, as in apple sauce or for fruit fools, so cooking times will not only be dependent upon the type of fruit but also its ripeness. Slightly under ripe 'soft' fruits, climacteric in particular, are less sweet but firmer, mature/ripe fruit will have maximum sweetness but will more than likely have a softer texture. The general thumb rule is the softer the fruit the shorter the cooking time.

Pectin content

Pectin is a polysaccharide that is found in cell walls of plants, it also acts as glue where it binds cells together. Pectin is present in varying amounts in fruits and vegetables. Citrus fruits high in pectin content contain between 0.5 to 1.5% of weight. Vegetables, carrots especially, contain the highest amount of pectin about 1.5 %. Because pectin helps keep cell walls intact, fruits that are highest in pectin maintain their structure; apples, pears, quince, blackcurrants and plums contain large amounts while soft fruits such as strawberries, grapes and cherries, contain smaller amounts. Pectin levels also vary with degree of ripening. Pectin peaks just before fruit reaches full ripeness.

For further information regarding pectin and its role in jam and marmalade making please see Chapter 9 on Food Preservation.

Poaching fruit tips:
1. Prepare the cooking liquid first. This is usually a mixture of sugar and water or wine with the addition of herbs and or spices. Pre - cooking of the cooking liquor is good practice as it will allow time for the herbs and spices to add their flavours, important where the cooking time for the fruit is short. Use whole spices rather than ground if clear poaching liquor is required, ground spices give a slightly cloudy appearance. In the case of apples and pears, a further reason for preparing the syrup first is that the fruit can be placed straight into it, therefore reducing the likelihood of discolouration due to enzyme browning.
2. Cooking in highly sugared syrup helps ripe, juicy fruits hold their shape. This is due to osmotic effect of sugar. If the sugar concentration in the cooking liquid is lower than that of the fruit, then the fruit will draw more water into the cells. This causes the fruit to swell and become overly soft. In order to prevent this ensure that there is sufficient sugar in the cooking syrup. The addition of calcium, which is present in molasses and brown sugar, will bind with pectin to strengthen the cell walls, thus preventing them from becoming mushy.
3. Finally, cooking at low heat for a longer period of time (see slow cooking below) is gentler and does less damage to the fruits structure, allowing it to maintain its original shape. Agitation, due to simmering or boiling of fruit speeds up the breakdown of the cell walls leading to overcooked and mushy fruit.

Poached fruits are also good for preserving, either in bottles or jars. In the summer when there can be an abundance of some fruits, it can be a great opportunity to preserve them so they can be enjoyed 'out of season.'

Slow cooking

Cooking fruit at low temperatures is beneficial as it prevents the cells from completely breaking down, as is likely in traditional methods such as stewing or poaching. This means that the fruit is cooked but still hold its shape.

All fruits can be cooked slowly but the cooking time and temperature need to be adjusted depending on the type, firmness of the fruit. For example, pineapple will take much longer to cook than peach. Ripeness of the fruit also impacts the cooking times.

Sous vide (under vacuum) is a process that cooks many different types of food, at low temperatures, usually under vacuum and is therefore an ideal method for cooking many different types of fruit.

For more information on sous vide please see Chapter 2. There is also a recipe for poaching rhubarb at low temperature in the recipe section at the back of the book.

Guideline fruit cooking times and temperatures
Apples and Pears: 85°C for 40–60 minutes
Plums, peaches, nectarines and rhubarb: 75°C for 30–60 minutes
Pineapple: 80°C for 90 minutes
Note: these times will vary depending upon the ripeness of the fruit

Fruit purées and coulis

To prepare fruit pulps or purées, it is necessary to cook the fruit at a temperature higher than that for poaching. Gently boiling the fruit will breakdown the fruit fibres, stirring will help to hasten the process. Because of the high moisture content of some fruit types, only a small amount of liquid is necessary in the process; too much and the purée will be watery. However, each fruit should be treated differently, in some cases sufficient moisture will come from the fruit itself and therefore require no further addition.

Preparation of a fruit purée can be speeded up by doing away with the peeling and coring stage; in the case of apple purée (using baking apples), the apples can be simply cut into quarters and cooked gently in a little butter and sugar in a covered pan. When the apple is completely soft, it can be pressed through a sieve. The end result is a smooth apple purée, the skin core and pips are left behind in the sieve. Purées can also be made by liquidising the fruit, but it is necessary to remove the peel and core first before cooking.

Couli.

Coulis were very popular in the 1970 and 80s and despite a drop in popularity since then, still have a place in any sweet sauce repertoire. They have the advantage of being inexpensive and very easy to prepare and can provide contrast in colour, texture and flavour to hot and cold desserts. (i.e. the creaminess of a rich vanilla cheesecake or ice-cream can be compensated for by the fresh tartness of a raspberry coulis). Fruit coulis are made from fresh or frozen fruit, either cooked or uncooked, with the addition of sugar, where necessary, to add sweetness. Coulis rely upon the fruit pulp to give the sauce its viscosity so no starch thickening should be necessary.

The following is a simple method for making fruit coulis:

Prepare fruit by removing stalks, core, skin, hulls etc where applicable. Wash the fruit under cold running water; this important as it removes any pesticides and wild yeasts which can ferment the coulis over a period of time.

Liquidise in a food processor. Taste the coulis before adding sweetener (sugar or sugar substitute) there may be sufficient sweetness especially if the fruit is very ripe.

Strain through a fine sieve to remove any seeds or pips, in particular raspberries.

If the coulis is too thick, add a little water or fruit juice

Note: Frozen fruits are usually ready prepared and can be used straight from the freezer.

Fresh fruit syrups

The juices of fresh fruits have natural flavour and colour; however their lack of viscosity makes them unsuitable for use as syrups for puddings and desserts. Reducing a fruit juice by boiling to achieve a thicker consistency may work, however the fresh flavours and colour can be compromised by the heat process. The addition of a thickener which does not require heat to thicken is a far better alternative.

Modified starches have been used by food manufacturers and processors for many years. They are used to great effect where traditional starch thickeners are unsuitable. There are many applications of these starches, some of which include freeze-thaw stability and retrogradation, preservation of flavours and enhanced viscosity and mouth feel. But for the purpose of thickening fruit syrups, pre-gelatinised or cold-water swelling starch is ideal. Such starches are now available from specialist ingredient suppliers and are sold under a number of different brand names, 'Ultratex' being one.

Chapter 5

DESSERTS and PUDDINGS

Once again, I have concentrated on the preparation of sweet items which can either be tricky to get right and those which pose considerable challenges in their making.

It cannot be stressed too much the importance of following recipes correctly and without the temptation to cut corners, unless you are totally confident that any changes made, will not impact on the quality of the end product. This is especially so in the weighing and measuring of ingredients and the steps involved in the method. Secondly, substituting an ingredient when the right one is not at hand may seem unimportant, but this could prove to be a regrettable mistake.

DAIRY BASED

Brûlées and baked egg custard

There are subtle differences between these two baked egg dishes. Brûlées are usually made with only the egg yolk, whereas egg custards utilise the whole egg. Secondly, brûlées recipes use cream, which makes them richer, whereas in baked egg custard recipes milk is normally used. The use of whole eggs in baked custards produces a firm set when cold. This is important if the custard is to be cut into portions e.g. custard tart or it is to be unmolded as in caramel creams. Brûlées, however, are usually made and served in the dish they are cooked in and have a softer, creamier, spoonable, consistency.

A variation in ratio of eggs to liquid also alters the firmness or softness of set. With brûlées, increasing the ratio of egg yolks to cream produces a firm set as does using a high fat content cream.

What remains constant in the preparation of these puddings is the cooking temperature. This must be at a temperature high enough to coagulate the proteins in the egg but not too high as to overcook or curdle the egg mixture. There are recipes which use oven temperatures ranging from 140°C to 180°C, but I have found that a minimum 150°C and a maximum of 160°C is an ideal range. Baked custard desserts (not custard tarts) should be cooked in a bain-marie to avoid overheating. A bain-marie is a shallow oven proof container filled with hot water in which the baked egg custard dish is to be cooked. Ideally the water level should be about 2/3 up the side of the dish, the hot water acts as a heat buffer so that the temperature of the contents of the dish do not rise sufficient enough to cause curdling.

For best results these puddings are best prepared about a day in advance and kept chilled until ready for use. This is especially important for crème brûlées which will be finished later with caramelised sugar. If not sufficiently cold, the intense heat during caramelising can cause the custard to curdle.

For baked egg custard tarts, the baking dish is lined with pastry (short or sweet) and baked blind. The custard is then baked in the pastry case using a similar oven temperature.

Meringues

Share one thing in common with whipped cream; they are both classed as foams.

Egg white contains about 90% water, 10% protein and almost no fat unlike egg yolk which contains 50% water, 16% protein and 28% fat

When egg whites undergo physical stress by whisking the proteins unfold (denature). A matrix or structure is formed through the bonding of the air bubbles with the water and proteins as they unravel. A temporary foam structure is thus formed. Egg white proteins have both water loving and water hating (hydrophilic and hydrophobic) areas, in the case of meringue the exposed water loving part of the protein bonds with the water in the egg and the water-hating element bonds with the air bubbles.

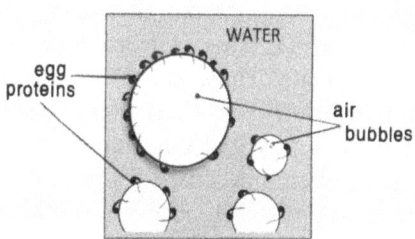

Image showing unravelled egg white proteins bonded with air bubbles and water

When meringues go wrong

Advice for both manual or machine preparation
1. Eggs should be brought up to room temperature before using, this helps improve the volume of the beaten egg white. Eggs should be fresh as possible; the end result is a more stable foam.
2. EGG WHITE DOES NOT LIKE FAT OR OIL, make sure the mixing bowl and whisk are free from any form of grease. If there is even a trace of grease on the equipment the whites will NOT foam well, in some cases the egg white will not foam at all.
3. Use a stainless steel or glass bowls or ideally copper if available, but

not plastic as these scratch easily and can harbour traces of fat.
4. A small amount of acid helps to strengthen the egg white foam: a little lemon juice or cream of tartare, but vinegar should not be used as this imparts an unpleasant flavour.
5. STAGES of foam: are A) Soft peak, this is when the egg white has volume but is still soft, forming shallow peaks when the whisk is removed. B) Full peak, this is where the foam is at maximum volume and forms stiff peaks which do not collapse when the whisk is removed.
6. Where recipes such as soufflés and mousses require whisked egg white, it is better to keep the foam slightly soft, this way they it will fold in and amalgamate with the mixture more quickly. If too stiff, it requires more effort to fold in the whites and there is a likelihood of loss of some aeration.
7. It is crucial not to whisk egg whites until they are ready to be added to a recipe. Whites whisked too far in advance will collapse and when re-whisked small form specks of white denatured protein, this will also cause loss of aeration.
8. If the egg white is over whisked especially if it has sugar added (as in English meringue) the meringue will lose much of its aeration and become runny, in this advent there is little that can be done but to start afresh.
9. Cooking meringues (e.g. lemon meringue pie). Occasionally meringue can seep liquid. This is a mixture of sugar dissolved in water from the egg white. There are few reasons for this. Either the meringue has not had sufficient time in the oven, this can also occur with over baking. It is possible that not all the sugar has dissolved during whisking. To overcome this, corn flour can be added to the egg whites during whisking this will absorb some of the moisture content. Italian meringue is also an option as it is far more stable.
10. Drying meringue should be done in an oven no higher than 110°C, higher than this and it will begin to colour.

Cream
During the 'standardisation' stage of processing milk, all the butterfat is skimmed off milk. Some of this fat is put back to make whole, semi or skimmed milk, and the remainder is sold as cream of differing fat content.

Cream is very similar in characteristics to milk in that it is a colloid; in this instance, the fat and water content of the cream forms the emulsion. The milk fat globules are encapsulated in a globule membrane (FGM) and amongst other substances such as vitamins and minerals; the membrane contains lipoproteins (natural emulsifiers). When the FGM is damaged or broken as in the practice of churning cream to make butter, the fat globules join together (coalesce) into a solid mass during which the water (whey) is purged (squeezed out).

Cream is normally produced as single, whipping, double, extra thick double, clotted each one containing a different percentage of fat content and this contributes to their varying thickness (viscosity)

- ❖ Single: 18% minimum fat. Uses - pouring cream, finishing soups and sauces.
- ❖ Whipping: 35% minimum fat. Uses - pouring, whipping, cooking
- ❖ Double (heavy cream in the US): 48% minimum fat. Uses - pouring, whipping, making butter, cooking
- ❖ Clotted: 55% minimum fat. Uses - spreading i.e. scones

Cream is used in many aspects of cookery; it adds richness and a smooth, silky mouth feel to soups and sauces, it can also improve viscosity by slight thickening.

Cream adds moisture and a contrast in texture to pastries such as cream horns, éclairs, pies and tarts. It can carry different flavours as in Chantilly cream (vanilla and sugar). Cream is used as an integral part of so many cold dessert recipes such as cheese cakes, mousses and soufflés

Whipped cream; is a foam, a suspension of air bubbles in liquid cream. It is formed by mechanical aeration i.e. whisking or by the injection of gas (carbon dioxide or nitrous oxide) under pressure such as in aerosols and siphons.

The action of whipping forces air into the cream, although initially these bubbles burst, because the surface tension of the cream isn't strong enough to hold on to them. After continued whipping, fat globules begin to break down as the phospholipids membrane break apart by the force of whisking. The fat surfaces are now exposed and start to bond with each other. Those that can't, bond with air bubbles rather than water molecules (remember fat and water don't mix). This fat structure forms a kind of network around the air bubbles making it a stable mixture.

The low fat content of single cream does not allow it to be whipped, it cannot form a foam. On the other hand, whipping and double cream can, because they both have a higher fat content of 30% and more.

To what extent cream is whipped, is usually determined by its use. Cream that is whipped to soft or half peak whipped cream has increased in volume but not achieved its maximum. At this stage it is quite soft and is easier to fold into mixtures when making mousses and soufflés. Full -peak whipped cream has reached its maximum volume and is quite firm in texture; more so with double cream. This makes it ideal for the purposes of piping and layering in gateaux and cakes, but because of its consistency, takes longer to incorporate into a mix, the result of which is a loss of some volume due to the physical activity of folding or mixing in.

Care must be taken when whipping cream especially when using an electric mixer as it can be easily 'over whipped', in such an eventuality the cream is no longer usable.

However, over whipped cream does have a second chance; continue to whip or beat the cream until the butter fat content clumps together and water is squeezed out and what is produced? butter, just add a little salt, wrap and refrigerate, hey presto

Cream should always be kept refrigerated, if left in a warm environment even for a short period of time will turn, whipped cream will also separate out, leaving a pool of milk in the bottom of the mixing bowl and a frothy top.

Naturally sour cream or cream that is just 'turning' can be used in the preparation of cheesecakes and is a traditional ingredient for goulash and stroganoff.

Processed sour cream has a fat content of about 20% and may include ingredients such as gelatine and thickeners to improve viscosity and stability. It is made by introducing lactic acid producing bacteria to cream; this gives the cream a slightly thicker consistency and a slightly sour or tart taste.

Crème fraiche has a higher fat content of about 30%, it is thicker than sour cream but does not contain stabilisers or thickeners. It is also made by adding bacterial cultures to cream.

Acidulated cream is cream usually mixed with lemon juice, giving it a tangy taste, it also thickens it slightly. It was once very popular, served as an accompaniment to roasted game and poultry salads.

Chocolate

Evidence showing the use of chocolate as a food dates back to about 3,000 years ago. Its origins can be clearly traced to countries of Central and Southern America, with Mexico and Guatemala in particular producing the earliest evidence.

Today, chocolate is one of the world's most popular food type. According to Statista (www.statista.com) "from 2015 to 2016 approximately 7.3 million tons of retail chocolate confectionery were consumed worldwide" with the British public consuming about 13lbs per head during the same period.

Block chocolate is produced as dark or plain, milk and white, although it is argued that white chocolate is not actually chocolate because it does not contain any cocoa powder or solids, only cocoa fat/butter, milk and sugar.

Milk chocolate, as the word suggest contains milk with sugar, cocoa solids, cocoa butter and other ingredients such as flavouring and emulsifiers.

What sets milk and dark or plain chocolate apart is that dark does not contain any milk solids. Dark chocolate also has a higher percentage of cocoa solids which can range from between 30% and 80%

Plain or dark chocolate is probably the most popular type of chocolate used in the preparation of puddings and desserts because its flavours are more pronounced than those of milk. Chocolate is also found in savoury food cookery and is used to make mole, a traditional sauce originating in Mexican cuisine.

Cacao or cocoa? Many people falsely believe that one is an alternative spelling of the other. But while they are both derivatives of the cacao bean, there is a marked difference between the two. Cacao is the natural raw product of the bean and remains practically unprocessed. Cocoa is subjected to more processing than cacao, and this includes roasting at high temperature; it can also contain additional ingredients such as sugar and flavourings. Both these chocolate ingredients are produced in powder form, i.e. raw cacao powder and cocoa powder (being the more common). Both powders can be used interchangeably as they contribute similar characteristics when used in cooking. Drinking chocolate should not be confused with either cacao or cocoa, as well as cocoa powder, drinking chocolate also contains sugar, powdered milk and flavourings. Baking chocolate is unsweetened which makes it very bitter, also it does not contain any additional flavourings. Bitter sweet and semi-sweet are also baking chocolates, but contain varying amounts of sugar.

Chocolate has a reasonable shelf life if stored properly. It should be stored in a cool dry place and out of direct sunlight, unsatisfactory conditions can cause bloom. This is a distinctly recognisable off-white coating or spots which appear on the surface of the chocolate. Fat bloom is brought about by a change in the fat structure, however this does not make the chocolate inedible and such blooms can be easily removed by re-melting the chocolate. Sugar bloom is caused by exposure to moisture which precipitates the formation of sugar crystals in the chocolate. Moisture bloom is irreversible and the chocolate should not be used for baking.

CULINARY APPLICATIONS

Cold mousses, soufflés, cheesecakes and ganache, sauces, cakes, gateaux and sponges, biscuits and cookies, icings and butter creams

Chocolate also makes a very good medium for moulding, shaping and carving, so much so that every year national and international competitions are held to give the opportunity to pastry chefs and chocolatiers to

showcase their skills in chocolate work. The pinnacle of which is the World Chocolate Masters and each year the competition attracts entrants from all over the world to compete in the final, which every year is hosted by a different country. It is worthwhile taking a look at some of their incredible chocolate creations:
www.worldchocolatemasters.com

TIPS for using chocolate
1. Breaking large blocks of chocolate into smaller pieces is not easy, so great care needs to be taken especially if using a knife. Some commercial manufactures produce chocolate in callets or chips, and these are much easier to use because no chopping is required.
2. Melting chocolate can be done by using a microwave ,but this can be tricky as hot spots can very quickly form within the chocolate very quickly, causing the chocolate to burn. This is particularly likely to happen if the microwave is switched on for too long, even ½ minute can make the difference between melted and burnt chocolate.
3. A more controllable method is to place the broken chocolate into a clean glass, plastic or stainless steel bowl; chocolate will melt quicker in a metal bowl as it is a better conductor of heat.
4. Place the bowl over a pan of very hot to simmering water and stir continually, removing the pan from the heat source if it becomes too hot/boils. If the chocolate is allowed to get too hot it will start to break down. This is noticeable as the chocolate clumps together and becomes grainy in texture. It also results in the chocolate losing its glossy appearance.
5. As soon as the chocolate has melted, remove the bowl from the pan; it is important not to allow any water to get into the chocolate. It is now ready for use.

Tempering chocolate
This is a process of heating and cooling chocolate to different temperatures. Tempering chocolate improves its handling characteristics, increasing brittleness and prevents it from melting when handled. Chocolate must be treated this way if it is to be used in moulding and shaping. It is a process used by pastry chefs, confectioners and chocolatiers in the making of chocolates, Easter eggs and chocolate show pieces. Because of the specialised nature of the process, I have elected not to go into further detail here.

Carob

There was a surge in popularity in this alternative to chocolate during the 70s and 80s and this was due, in part, to the increasing interest in vegetarian and veganism at that time. Carob or locust bean tree is native to the Mediterranean region. The dried pods are ground to make carob powder which is used as an alternative to cooking with chocolate. Unlike chocolate carob does not contain caffeine, theobromine or saturated fat.

Soufflés (hot)

Soufflés essentially consist of two parts: a base and whisked egg whites. In traditional recipes, the base is a thick béchamel with the addition of egg yolk and sweet or savoury ingredients, but some modern versions do not use a starch base. Regardless of whether the soufflé is sweet or savoury, all additions are added to the base before the egg whites are incorporated.

When preparing the whisked egg whites, great care must be taken not to allow any egg yolk into the white, the fat content of the yolk will inhibit foam development. Utensils used in the process must also be free of grease; stainless steel or glass is best for this purpose as plastic bowls are easily scratched and can harbor traces of fat.

The key to whisking is to incorporate as much air as possible into the white, so vigorous whisking is necessary; using an electric mixer will obviously do this more quickly. A 'soft-peak' consistency is ideal for soufflés as too stiff a foam requires more blending in, resulting in a loss of some aeration. The foam can now be gently folded in, usually about a third is mixed into the base first and then the remainder gently folded in until the mixture shows no streaks of egg white. It is important to fold and not mix the whites in to maintain as much volume as possible.

Baking dishes should be greased well with either melted butter or margarine; this will allow the soufflé to rise evenly and not stick to the sides of the dish.

Soufflés should be placed into a bain-marie of hot water; using hot water speeds up the cooking and therefore the rise. Soufflés are cooked in a hot oven at about 220°C or gas mark 7; baking times vary from 15 to 25mins.

When a soufflé cooks, the air in the bubbles expands, causing the soufflé to rise. The proteins in the egg coagulate and the starch in the flour gelatinizes, giving the soufflé its structure.

Faults and tips:
Soufflé
1. Didn't rise: insufficient beating or over beating of egg white or over mixing in.
2. Collapsed after taking out of oven: insufficient cooking or not enough

base mix or too wet/runny.
3. Rose and then collapsed in oven: whites not beaten enough or the base mix is too runny or a drop in oven temperature.
4. The top is brown but centre is undercooked: oven is too hot or the dish too large; consider using individual portion or smaller dishes.
5. Chewy texture: ovens is too cool or the dish too large.
6. Top splits, sticks to sides: inadequate greasing of inside of the dish.
7. Uneven rise: inadequate greasing of dish or egg whites not folded in sufficiently.

Gelatine/agar set desserts

Gelatine is available in sheet or leaf, flakes or powdered form. Agar is usually produced and sold as flakes or powder.

Gelatine is made from animals, usually pigs, by boiling the skin and bones etc, agar is obtained from the cell walls of certain red algae (type of seaweed). Both are used to set liquids (i.e. jellies; sweet and savoury, mousses, bavarois, cheesecakes brawn and meat pies). Although gelatine has been used traditionally for many years, agar has seen a rise in its popularity due mainly to its suitability for vegan and vegetarian consumers.

Gelatine is produced in four different strengths or blooms (bronze, silver, gold and platinum) but, for consistency sake, the differing strengths are compensated for by the size of the sheet/leaf.

A large percentage of recipes simply stipulate leaf and nothing more, so the question of knowing which type of gelatine to use becomes irrelevant.

The advantages of using gelatine leaf/sheet, is that it does tend to produce a clearer set, have a cleaner taste and is easier to bloom (hydrate) and incorporate into a recipe.

The disadvantages of using gelatine is that it has a lower melting point (35°C) than agar, which has a higher melting point, so a dessert set with gelatine on a hot summer's day will not hold up as well as one set with agar, Secondly gelatine does not set liquids with high acid, salts or alcohol content. Setting temperatures for agar vary depending upon the type of seaweed used, but normally setting starts at about 45°C. Once set agar jells will not melt until heated to about 80-90°C

Powdered agar and flakes also differ in strength; powdered agar is stronger than flakes; one tablespoon of agar flakes is equivalent to one teaspoon of agar powder. Agar is a more powerful setting agent than gelatine; the general guideline for substituting gelatine is 3:1 gelatine and agar respectively. However to ensure consistency in a recipe it is highly recommend that teaspoon and table spoon amounts be converted into grams, this then makes for far more accurate measuring and consistent end product.

Protein digesting (proteolytic) enzymes in pineapple, mango, fig and kiwi also inhibit gelatine and agar setting unless first deactivated by heating. Chocolate also interferes with the gelling properties of agar.

Agar
TIPS on using agar
1. Agar cannot be added directly into a recipe without it first being hydrated.
2. Agar has to be heated to almost boiling point or above 90°C and simmered for a few minutes.
3. Where a recipe does not require the liquid to be heated, then a small amount of the liquid. can be heated in order to hydrate the agar, this can then be incorporated back into the mix.
4. Agar, like gelatine, does not set well in high acid liquids; therefore hydration must be carried out in a neutral liquid, before being re-introduced to the rest of the ingredients. Agar jellies will collapse if stirred or shaken before they have set completely.
5. Agar will not set if in contact with grease, so make sure moulds are free of this.

TIPS on using gelatine
1. To bloom (hydrate or soak) leaf gelatine, place in cold water and leave until it becomes very soft, remove and squeeze out all the water. It is important to use cold water; if the water is warm the gelatine will begin to melt before soaking is complete. To bloom powdered or granule gelatine, sprinkle into a measured amount of cold water and leave for about 10mins. It is advisable to then heat the soaked gelatine to ensure complete hydration and enable smoother and consistent incorporation into the dish.
2. Add to the hot liquid and stir, it should melt and mix in immediately.
3. In warm weather, it is advisable to increase gelatine amounts a little.
4. Gelatine is relatively slow at setting and needs to be kept at refrigeration temperature for at least a couple of hours to allow it to solidify and it will continue to set firmer over a longer period.
5. If the dessert is to be set in a mould and then turned out when set, no preparation of the mould, such as greasing or lining should be necessary.
6. To turn out, dip the mould up to the rim in hot water for a few seconds. This varies and is dependent upon the material of the mould. If a metal mould is used then dipping times will be less than those for plastic or porcelain.
7. Remove and dry the mould then quickly up turn onto the serving

dish, sometimes a shake is necessary.
8. Do not leave too long in the water as this will melt the sides and base too much, resulting in a pool of liquid on the serving plate. In this situation return the mould to the fridge and allow the contents to reset.

Panna cotta (cooked cream)

Perhaps one of the simplest desserts to make yet can impress even the most discerning of diners. The fat content and ratio of cream to milk determines the richness and consistency of the panna cotta; the higher the cream or fat content, the richer and creamier the texture and the firmer the consistency.

Tips:
1. Leave the panna cotta to cool down before straining into the mould or serving dish, this will prevent a thick skin forming on the setting mixture.
2. The texture of a panna cotta should be smooth and just set; too much gelatine or agar will make it rubbery. If the panna cotta is intended to be turned out of the mould or if the weather is particularly warm, there is a risk of the dessert collapsing or even melting. In which case, it is advisable to add a little more gelatine or agar to prevent this.
3. The volume of additional flavouring liquids such as alcohols or fruit purées should be taken into account when measuring the total volume of liquid to gelatine or agar amounts.

Bavarois, mousses and cold soufflés

There is very little difference between these cold desserts, they are all set with a gelling agent and are aerated by whipped cream and or whipped egg white to give a light airy texture.

TIPS:
Bavarois:
1. Do not whip the cream or egg whites too stiff. They should be whisked to soft peak, by doing this they are both be easier and quicker to incorporate into the custard base.
2. If the egg whites are whisked too far in advanced they will fall and begin to separate out and, when re-whisked, will form white speck; these spoil the appearance of the finished bavarois.
3. The temperature of the custard, cream and whites will impact the speed of setting. There must be sufficient time to fold in both cream and whites completely and be able to pour the mixture into moulds before setting begins. Therefore make sure the whipped cream and

egg whites are not chilled and the custard is very slightly tepid.
4. Using a large spoon or spatula, start by folding all the cream in, when almost mixed in, fold in the whites and continue to gently fold in until smooth.
5. When the whipped cream is folded into the custard it should begin to form a smooth consistency. The whisked egg whites can now be folded in.
6. As soon as the mixture becomes smooth and even, it must be poured into the mould immediately before it has time to set. If during the stage of adding the cream, it appears to float on top, then the custard may still be too warm. In this event, dip the custard in a bowl of iced water for a few minutes; this will help with the incorporation of the cream. If however it becomes too cold or starts to set during the first stages, it must be gently warmed until melted again.
7. Refrigerate well be before serving or turning out of the mould.

Mousses and soufflés:
The same tips for bavarois are applicable to these. Where the mousse or soufflé base is chocolate or egg yolk mixture, it must remain liquid until the cream and egg white has been incorporated. In other words it must not set until it is in the moulds.

Ice – cream
Shop bought ice creams are produced and sold in a wide range of flavours, from the traditional single flavours of vanilla or chocolate to the more exotic multi-flavour and texture ices. Ice-cream quality also varies considerably and this is due to the ingredients used rather than the process. Soft scoop and economy consist of a high volume of air bubbles. Premium ices are made using dairy ingredients that have higher fat levels and because of this, such ice-creams contain smaller amounts of air.

The process of making ice cream is almost the same for both mass and home produced; however the use of vegetable oils, flavourings, emulsifiers, stabilisers etc used extensively in many brands, makes one question the wholesomeness of such products. At least the home cook has control over what goes into their ices.

Most homemade ice cream recipes consist of about a handful of ingredients, but their final composition is quite complex, how they are made therefore requires a little understanding of the ingredients used and the process involved.

Without the use of an ice-cream machine or sorbetière as it is otherwise known, it is difficult to achieve the smooth texture that can be found with readymade ices. There are, however, recipes which use non-churn methods, and these seem to produce a reasonable quality ice-creams.

The key objective in making ice cream is the emulsification of the main ingredients; the fat and water content of the dairy ingredients, with the addition of air cells, must all homogenise to form a smooth, lump free mixture. The emulsification process begins during the preparation of the egg custard base, where the heated egg proteins denature and create a network (lecithin in the yolk also assists in emulsification), thereby thickening the mix.

Secondly and equally as important in preparing ice cream, is minimising the size of the ice crystals i.e. the smaller the crystal formation, the smoother the mouth feel.

The water content in cream and milk is responsible for the formation of these ice crystals and these are controlled by the effective process of freezing whilst continually stirring or churning the mix.

Churning continues to maintain the emulsification of the mixture as it freezes, at the same time breaking up any large ice crystals which may form.

Factors including the fat and protein content of the milk, cream and egg yolk, sugar and alcohol also impact on the texture as well as adding flavour. The fat or butter milk adds richness, increases flavour and adds stability. A smooth texture is also developed by fat content which prevents the formation of large ice crystals thus enhancing mouth feel. There is no minimum fat content requirement for home-made ice-cream, suffice to say the lower the fat content the less creamy and buttery the texture or mouth feel; some mass produced low-fat ice-creams have a fat content of only 2-4%. The ideal maximum fat content is about 25%, above this the ice-cream tastes greasy and there is the likelihood that the mixture will separate during churning, ending up as butter.

Sugars and sweeteners (honey and corn syrup) improve texture and give body and also lower the freezing point so as to prevent the ice cream from becoming too hard.

Air, in the form of tiny bubbles is incorporated into the ice cream during churning and this in turn impacts the consistency, texture and in particular the volume. Some mass produced brands of ice cream contain large quantities of air, allowing the product to be produced cheaply. This is known as 'over run', where the volume of ice cream produced can be 100% more than the volume of the initial base. In order to achieve high overruns, ice cream bases have a low percentage of fat content. When ice cream is prepared using ingredients with high fat concentrations such as double cream (48%) then a very small increase (low over run) in the final volume of the ice cream can be seen.

Solids such as proteins (in milk, cream and eggs), minerals and flavourings such as syrups, alcohol, nuts, chocolate and fruits give body, texture and smoothness; they also prevent the formation of large ice crystals. Food gums (Xanthan, guar), gelatine and agar can also be used in ice creams to stabilise and prevent large ice crystal formation.

Most domestic freezers operate at temperatures below the ideal temperature for serving ice cream, this can be both an advantage and a disadvantage. On the one hand, storing ice cream at temperatures below -18°C (more commonly -20 to -25°C) slows down the growth of large ice crystals and thereby prolongs the texture quality of the ice cream, but at these temperatures the ice cream is extremely hard and difficult to scoop or portion. Tempering or removing the ice cream from the freezer to soften up before consuming makes handling and serving easier but this can enable the development of large ice crystals. In such a case, when making ice cream, it may be better to produce small batches which can be consumed entirely, without the need to refreeze.

Commercial ice cream freezers and dispensers operate at temperatures between about -12° and -16°C and this facilitates easy portioning and serving while maintaining a frozen product.

I have been making ice creams for some years now and enjoy experimenting with new flavours and combinations. I have even won several awards for them at various competitions.

I do recommend the use of an ice-cream maker, especially if you intend making ice-cream on a regular basis; it is well worth the investment.

I have included one or two basic ice-cream recipes at the back of this book; you can always experiment and create your own flavour combinations.

For further information on making ice-cream go to:
www.icecreamnation.org/science-of-ice-cream/

Parfaits, biscuit and bombe glaceés.

As with ice cream these frozen dairy based desserts are made with egg yolk, sugar and cream, but unlike their counterpart, are not churned during freezing. Both of these preparations have their origins in classical French cuisine and like many other aspects of this era have now all but disappeared from modern day cook books, although parfaits seems to have experienced a revival in recent years.

Biscuit glaceés like parfaits are very rich and this is because they consist mainly of egg yolks and whipped cream and unlike bombes, they also contain Italian meringue. Bombes are in fact dome shaped moulds which are filled with different flavoured ice-cream like mixtures, frozen hard and then removed and decorated. Parfaits, in particular, are a good alternative to traditional ices especially where an ice-cream machine is not available.

I have included a recipe for strawberry parfait in the recipe section. Furthermore you can find some interesting recipes at:
www.greatbritishchefs.com/collections/parfait-recipes,

Cheesecakes

Cheesecakes exist in two forms; the baked and the un-baked or cold set, both of which comprise of a biscuit type base and a cream cheese filling or topping. The combination of types of biscuits, cheese filling and additional flavours and ingredients such as nuts, fruit, and chocolate is endless.

Baked cheesecakes are little more than baked egg custard, where the milk is replaced by the cheese, however some recipes incorporate starch. The addition of flour or corn flour ensures a more stable mixture during baking, that is, it is less likely to curdle if the heat is too intense, though some creaminess of texture is forfeited with this addition. As with baked egg dishes such as crème brûlée and crème caramel, the correct baking temperature is therefore crucial. It may be prudent to use a bain-marie to bake a starch free cheesecake in order to maintain further control over the oven heat. Towards the end of the baking period, the cheesecake may still appear slightly unset or very soft in the centre, this is normal and to continue the baking process until the whole area is firm will inevitably lead to an over baked cheesecake. One of the tell tale signs of over baking is when a crack develops on the surface.

Cold set (aka no-bake) cheesecakes:

Most recipes rely totally upon the main cheese ingredient to give the final consistency and texture and therefore do not need the addition of a setting agent, such as gelatine or agar. Where warm conditions prevail, however, it may be necessary to add an amount of gelatine or agar to the cheesecake mix to add stability.

Cream cheeses such Philadelphia for example, ricotta or mascarpone are all popular because of their mild flavour and ease of incorporation with other ingredients. The perfect texture of cheesecake is achieved by the correct balance of ingredients. A lighter texture of cheesecake can be achieved with the addition of pouring or whipped cream; this can also lessen the sharpness of the cheese.

TIPS for cold set cheesecakes
1. Always use good quality ingredients and ensure they are measured out correctly
2. Always line the cake tin/mould with greaseproof paper
3. Make the biscuit base well in advance, allowing it to set firm
4. For the biscuit base: For a coarse base, break up the biscuit in a clean cloth with a rolling pin, use a food processor to break down the biscuit to a fine crumb
5. Bring cream cheese and cream to room temperature
6. Place gelatine in cold water to bloom or if using agar follow instruction on packet: usually add to water and boil for a few minutes
7. Beat the cream cheese in a bowl until soft and smooth.
8. For a lighter cheesecake filling, whip the cream to half peak
9. Squeeze gelatine and melt in a little (about 25mls to 25g gelatine) hot water or lemon juice.
10. If adding sugar, dissolve this in the hot gelatine mixture.
11. Mix the cream into the cream cheese using a whisk, when smooth, add the melted gelatine.
12. Quickly pour into cake tin, level off the top and refrigerate.
13. The cheesecake will continue to set and firm up over a 24 hour period.
14. When ready, take out of the refrigerator and immediately remove the cake tin and greaseproof paper.
15. Cut into portions while still chilled using a sharp knife dipped in hot water.
16. Always remove cheesecakes from the fridge about 30mins before consuming, this allows the texture to soften slightly and flavours can become more prominent.

I have included a basic recipe for both types of cheese cake in the recipe section at the back of the book.

Sugar boiling
Working with boiled sugar does set its own demands and challenges and requires considerable expertise in some areas such as pulled and blown.

More often, sugar is boiled to specific temperatures in the process of making various types of confectionary. The characteristics of boiled sugar change as temperatures are increased. Within a very narrow margin the syrup can change from one stage to the next. Therefore, ensuring sugar is cooked to the correct degree is crucial.

Below is a list of the different temperatures used for boiling sugar and at each stage, examples of its use.

The expert confectioner can recognise the varying degree of boiled sugar without the necessity of a thermometer, however for the layman, the use of a one is essential if the right degree of boiled sugar is to be achieved.

If a sugar thermometer is not available, there is a simple test which can be done to establish the stage or degree of the sugar syrup:

Use a teaspoon, take out a small quantity of sugar syrup, pour it into a cupful of cold water and allow to cool. Use fingers to determine the consistency or stage of the sugar.

Apart from achieving the right stage of boiled sugar, crystallisation is also a problem to be aware of. As sugar syrup is boiled, water is driven off and the sugar concentrates. The more water driven off, the higher the concentration of sugar. There then comes a stage where insufficient water is present to keep all the sugar in solution (syrup), so sugar crystals can begin to form. Crystals can form on the sides of the cooking utensil or spoons used to stir the sugar solution. Given the right temperature these few crystals can cause the formation of many more, culminating in the crystallisation of the whole batch.

Wet or dry?

A wet caramel is made by heating sugar and water together in the pan. A dry caramel is simply sugar heated without any liquid.

TIPS on sugar boiling
1. To avoid re-crystallisation make sure that the sugar is free of impurities and that the pan used is clean.
2. If using the wet method, try to resist stirring as this encourages crystals to clump together. Ensure all the sugar has dissolved before increasing the heat.
3. To prevent crystals forming, use a pastry brush or similar to wash down the sides of the saucepan with cold water. Keep stirring utensils etc. in a separate container of water.
4. A pinch of cream of tartar, lemon juice or glucose will reduce the risk of crystallisation.
5. When using the dry method, use a heavy bottomed saucepan and sprinkle the sugar evenly onto the bottom. As the sugar is heated, the edges and bottom will melt first and start browning. A gentle stir will help to combine the liquefied and sugar granules together.
6. It is important to watch the sugar as it changes very quickly from pale to dark amber and if ignored will turn black and burn. To stop

the caramel from colouring further, the pan can be dipped into cold water for a few seconds to remove some of the residual heat.
7. Any further ingredients added, such as butter or cream will halt the caramelisation process.

Thread stage: 110-112°C
Sugar concentration: 80% - characteristic: thin syrup and when dripped into cold water forms thin threads

Soft Ball stage: 112-118°C
Sugar concentration: 85% - characteristic: forms a soft ball when dropped into cold water
Uses; confectionery - fudge, pralines, and fondant

Firm Ball stage: 118-121° C
Sugar concentration: 87% - characteristic: a firm stable ball is formed though very sticky to the touch.
Uses; caramels

Hard Ball stage: 121-130° C
Sugar concentration: 92% - characteristic: very firm stable ball though a little sticky.
Uses; confectionery –nougat, marshmallows, rock candy

Soft Crack stage: 132-143° C
Sugar concentration: 95% - characteristic: forms firm, pliable threads
Uses; confectionery - toffees, brittles, and butterscotch

Hard Crack stage: 146-154° C
Sugar concentration: 99% - characteristic: forms brittle threads, and will crack
Uses: confectionery - toffee, nut brittles, and lollipops

Caramel stages: 165-170° C
Sugar concentration: 100% - syrup begins to turn golden brown, but turns darker very quickly

Brown-Liquid stage 170° C
Sugar concentration: 100% - characteristic: turning darker brown colour, beginning to break down and form many complex molecules that contribute to aroma and flavour.
Uses: desserts, decorations and nut coatings.

Burnt sugar stage 177° C
Sugar concentration: 100% characteristic: almost black in colour, very pungent odour and bitter taste

These temperatures and characteristics are based on the use of granulated table sugar

Chapter 6

PASTRY AND BAKED GOODS

Pastry work has probably caused more tantrums and bouts of high blood pressure in the world of bakery and cookery than any other aspect. Whist cookery books, food writers, food experts, et al attempt to explain why pastry faults happen, it still doesn't appear to appease or help those who continue to falter on the pastry treadmill.

If it is of any consolation I still make blunders when preparing short pastry, I suppose it is because I no longer make it on a regular basis, perhaps there lies the answer, as William Hickson once penned 'if at first you don't succeed, try, try again'.

Anyway here are some tips which hopefully may help answer some questions.

Pastry common faults:
Choux:
Problem: mixture too runny
Reason: too much water/insufficient flour. Flour, fat and water mix was not cooked out enough. Too much egg, check size of eggs used.
Problem: didn't rise or collapsed after rising.
Reason: flour not cooked out. Oven too cool or a drop in oven temperature during baking. Taken out of the oven too soon.
Problem: greasy and heavy
Reason: flour, water and fat mixture are overcooked

TIPS:
1. It is important to measure ingredients out precisely. Margarine or butter can be used and the difference in taste is unappreciable. It is important to consider egg sizes as there is a difference in volume between a small and a large/jumbo.
2. Ensure the fat has totally melted in the water before adding the flour. All the flour must be added at once and not a little at a time. Most recipes use plain flour; however I use strong flour, as this tends to give the choux pastry a slightly firmer structure.
3. Remove from the heat at this stage and beat well until there are no lumps of flour and mixture is smooth. Return to the heat and continue stirring well until the mixture forms a stiff ball and leaves the sides and bottom of the pan.
4. Remove from the heat and leave to cool, it doesn't have to be cold.
5. Beat the eggs and stir in a little at a time until all the egg has been

incorporated; this can be done a little quicker in an electric mixer.
6. Bake at 220°C gas 7 for the first 10mins, reducing the oven temperature to about 170°C to dry and crisp up.

Short crust:
Problem: hard/tough, warped, and shrunk.
Reasons: too much water, the gluten has started to develop, this also happens in tandem with over mixing/handling. Insufficient fat coverage of flour grains due to insufficient rubbing in or not enough fat to flour, wrong type of flour used, oven too cool.
Problem: too short/crumbly
Reasons: insufficient fat to flour, not enough liquid.
Problem: soggy pastry.
Reason: pie/tart filling too wet or the oven was too cool.
Problem: blistering of the surface.
Reason: fat not rubbed in evenly, water added unevenly.

Sweet or sugar:
This pastry is very rich and extremely short and while it is perfect for making sweet pastry desserts such as flans, tarts and pies, handling and rolling out can be challenging. This pastry must be chilled for several hours before using and then brought up to cool-ambient before use.

TIPS:
1. Make and chill well in advance of use.
2. Only roll out enough pastry for the purpose, try not to over handle; warm hands will quickly make this pastry very soft and difficult to roll, in this event re-chill.
3. Use sufficient flour to keep the pastry from sticking to the work surface.

Problem: speckled pastry
Reason: undissolved sugar grains, use caster sugar instead of granulated.
Problem: very soft and difficult to handle.
Reason: insufficient chilling
Problem: difficult to roll out after chilling; pastry breaks up.
Reason: pastry too cold, allow to warm up slightly.
Problem: pastry is not short or tough.
Reason: over mixing or handling.

TIPS for short crust and sweet pastry
1. Soft pastry flour (all purpose) should only be used; it contains less gluten than strong flour. Sifting the flour before rubbing in the fat

improves aeration.
2. Cut the fat into small pieces and rub into the flour using finger tips. Occasionally rub a handful between the palms of the hands, this will show up any lumps of fat. It is important that the flour grains are covered in a layer of fat. This provides a waterproof coating and prevents the water from mixing with the flour's gluten forming proteins.
3. Ensue the water is cold and sprinkle onto the fat flour mix rather than pour in. Mix with a knife using a cutting movement.
4. Replacing the water with alcohol such as vodka has become popular (see below).
5. Do not over mix or handle; wrap in food film and leave to relax in a cool place for about 30mins.
6. Roll out just enough pastry for the purpose; this reduces the amount of trimmings. Re-rolling and over-handling the trimmings can make the pastry dry and difficult to roll. It will also work the gluten, causing the pastry to become tough.
7. Use only a very light dusting of flour for rolling out; too much and the pastry will become dry and crumbly.
8. Move the pastry around during rolling to ensure that it is not sticking to the work surface.
9. Use two thin pieces of wood appropriate in length to the size of pastry to be rolled out. The thickness of wood corresponding to the thickness of pastry. Place either side of the pastry and using them to guide the rolling pin over, this will ensure a more even thickness of the pastry.
10. For lining and topping large pies and tarts, use the rolling pin to lift the pastry from the work surface, gently unrolling it across the baking dish from one side to the other.
11. When lining baking tins and dishes let the pastry lie over the container, ease it gently into the corners then up the sides, pulling or stretching can tear the pastry.
12. Where a flan ring is to be lined and baked blind: some prefer to leave the excess pastry draped over the rim of the ring then bake it, trimming off the excess cooked pastry with a sharp knife afterwards. This method ensures that the pastry sides/walls do not fall in when baking, however this does not always leave a neat edge. The alternative method is to trim off the raw excess pastry before baking and although this leaves a neat edge after baking, there is always the tendency for the pastry sides to collapse unless supported with greaseproof paper and baking beans.
13. For fruit pies and tarts, cooking the filling first allows better control of the water content. Excess water from fruit can either be driven off

by rapidly cooking, or by thickening the fruit juices with corn flour. This reduces the amount of moisture that would normally soak into the pastry as it cooks. Cooking pastry blind does NOT reduce the possibility of soggy pastry; it actually makes it worse, as more liquid is absorbed by the dry pastry. Brushing the inside surface of the pastry with egg wash or egg white can act as a barrier between the pastry and the moist filling.

14. All pastry items should be allowed to relax again in a cool place, after rolling and before baking.
15. Ensure the oven is pre-heated to the right temperature.
16. If bakery goods are at the stage where they have sufficient colour but are not thoroughly cooked, either reduce the oven temperature, prop the oven door open slightly or cover with a piece of foil or greaseproof paper.
17. For a deeper brown and higher gloss finish to pastry goods, brush with raw egg yolk only.

Please see the section at the back for a sweet and short crust pastry recipes.

Suet:
Problem: heavy
Reason: insufficient or old baking powder, not enough baking powder will cause the pastry to be heavy. Baking powder stored for a long time does lose its aerating ability; check by sprinkling a little into warm water, it should fizz/effervesce when in contact with the water. Not enough suet to flour
Problem: tough.
Reason: over handling and re-rolling develops gluten, this gives the pastry a tough chewy texture.
Problem: soggy.
Reason: dish not properly covered or protected from the steams moisture or Insufficient steaming or boiling.

TIPS:
1. Vegetable suet is available as an alternative to the traditional shredded beef suet, which makes it suitable for vegans and vegetarians.
2. Use self raising flour or plain soft flour with the addition of baking powder.
3. The most important part of making this pastry is not to rub the suet into the flour. It should be just folded in and, when the water is added, a gentle mixing to form a soft dough but with the suet lumps still present.

Rough puff:
Problem: not risen sufficiently/too few layers.
Reason: oven was too cool, insufficient rolling, turning, or folding. Fat breaking through dough layers or fat was too soft.
Problem: excess loss of fat.
Reason: oven was too cool.
Problem: heavy, tough pastry.
Reason: over handling, insufficient fat, or incorrect oven temperature.
Problem: excessive shrinkage.
Reason: over stretching during rolling, insufficient resting.

TIPS:
Rough puff
1. Always use ice-cold water.
2. Don't knead the pastry dough.
3. Cut the fat into even sized 2cm cubes, these should be firm but not hard.
4. Only partially rub in the fat, leaving small lumps distributed throughout the flour.
5. Give four double turns. Making sure the pastry is relaxed for about 30mins. between each turn.

Puff :
Problem: not flaky.
Reason: fat was too warm, poor lamination (layering) achieved or over rolling.
Problem: fat oozes out.
Reason: fat or dough was too soft. Edges not sealed or oven was too cool.
Problem: hard
Reason: too much water. Too much flour during rolling or over handling.
Problem: shrinkage.
Reason: insufficient resting between turns or over stretching.
Problem: under baked.
Reason: oven was too hot; has browned before being cooked.
Problem: uneven rise.
Reason: uneven distribution of fat. Edges not straight or uneven folding and rolling

1. There are three methods for making puff pastry: English, Scottish and French, any of these methods can be used, but it is a good idea to use the one you feel most confident with.
2. Use a little lemon juice or cream of tartare with the water. This helps develop the gluten making the dough more elastic.

3. It is important that the dough is of the same texture as the fat. If the fat is too hard it will break through the dough during the first roll. If the fat is too soft it can ooze out of the sides during rolling.
4. Make sure, when rolling out, that the sides and ends are square.
5. Press one, two or three indentations into the pastry to denote number of turns, otherwise it is easy to forget how many have been done.
6. Relaxing in a cool place is most important between folds and turns, but don't refrigerate, this makes the fat too hard and difficult to roll.
7. Puff pastry freezes well, so it can be made well in advance.
8. When using puff pastry, any trimmings left over after rolling, that are to be reused, should be collected together in layers, and not squeezed together into a ball, which will spoil the layering.

Tarte tatin

A traditional French pastry and dessert consisting of a baked puff pastry base with a topping of apple halves in caramel syrup. The dish can be served hot or cold; but many believe it is better served straight from the oven accompanied with cream, fresh egg custard or ice-cream.

The first stage is to make the caramel, so the baking container needs to be robust. A round cast iron skillet or frying pan is ideal, but a heavy based frying pan will do just as well, (non-stick tarte tatin baking tins are available to buy).

Apple varieties such as Braeburn, Cox's, Granny Smith are recommended, these have a slight sharpness to them which counteracts the richness of the caramel syrup. Variations on the original apple tatin, include the use of apricots, nectarines or pears, in fact most fruits that will hold up to the high temperature during baking can be used.

TIPS:
1. Cut the butter into about 1cm cubes.
2. Prepare the apples. Peel first. If the apples are to be arranged in layers of overlapping slices, then cut in half, remove the core and slice thickly; this method can be time consuming. If the apples are small, then cut in half, remove the core and place neatly into the caramel, core side up. Alternatively the apples may be cut in half and arranged end up in the caramel.
3. Heat the sugar in the pan. It will start to melt then quickly colour, stir it so that it colours evenly.
4. When a medium amber colour caramel is reached, carefully add the butter .Stir until the butter mixes with the caramel. If there is still some undissolved sugar then add a little water or fruit juice.
5. Whatever method, arrange the apples neatly; this will enhance the presentation of the dish.

6. Make sure the apples are covered with the puff pastry and there is extra tucked down between the inside of the dish and the apples.
7. Pierce one or two holes in the pastry to allow excess steam to escape; there is no point in egg washing the pastry as this forms the base.
8. Bake at between 180 to 200°C for anything between 25 and 40mins.
9. Allow to cool slightly before turning out of the dish.

Hot water:
Fault: cracked pastry.
Reason: insufficient kneading, pastry cooled down too much before rolling, water not boiling prior to adding to the flour.
Fault: dry, difficult to handle.
Reason: as above.
Fault: too soft, difficult to mould.
Reason: incorrect ratio of flour to water, dough too hot
Fault: pastry hard when cooked.
Reason: insufficient water or fat, over handling/rolling.

Tuiles
Tuiles are very light crispy wafer like biscuits and are usually made to accompany a range of sweet dishes.

Originally they were moulded into an arched or curved shape whilst still hot, but they can be made into any shape or size with a variety of flavours.

TIPS:
Tuiles should be very light delicate wafer thin biscuits. They are easy to make but do not remain crisp for long especially in humid conditions, so should be stored in an airtight container.
1. The mixture should be smooth and firm, it may be necessary to refrigerate it which will give more control for spreading.
2. Use good quality non-stick bake ware for preparing tuiles, they must not be allowed to stick otherwise they will break when removed. Silicone baking mats are ideal for this and require no pre-preparation.
3. Shapes can be made from templates cut out of large thin plastic lids or similar material, about 2mm thick.
4. Tuiles that has become soft, can be placed back in a hot oven for a few seconds, this will crisp them up.

Shortbread

TIPS:
1. Pre-heat oven to 150°C. This low temperature will ensure that the shortbread does not become too coloured. It is generally accepted that shortbread should be very pale in colour.
2. Salted or unsalted butter can be used, but if using the later, add a good pinch of salt.
3. Use butter at room temperature, add the sugar and beat well.
4. Use a mix of plain flour in a ratio of between 2 and 3:1 plain flour to rice, corn flour or coconut. E.g. 100g plain flour and 30 or 50g rice, corn or coconut flour.
5. Use caster sugar, not granulated.
6. Form into a dough ball and keep rolling to a minimum, or pat into shape with the fingers.
7. Chill for about 15mins. before baking.

Fats, oils and flour in pastry making

Butter, margarine, vegetable shortening, lard and oils can all be used for making short crust. It is important to be aware of the characteristics of the various fats and oils as each one performs differently in pastry making.

Butter gives a superior flavour over all other fats and has good shortening properties. The use of salted or unsalted makes little difference to the finished product, although unsalted is marginally better for pastry used in items like fruit tarts and pies and salted for savoury such as meat pies and quiches.

Butter has a lower melting point (about 35°C) in comparison to other fats and this makes it prone to becoming too soft if over handled. Butter also has a water content (about 18%) which can lead to some early development of gluten if over mixed, and this can lead to slightly tougher pastry when cooked. Better results have been observed using butter with the water content (whey) removed

Using half butter and half shortener/lard produces a good balance between flavour and texture.

Lard is a very effective pastry shortener and contains no water; however it does impart a flavour which may be off putting. The advantage of using lard is that it has a higher working temperature threshold (about 44°C, leaf fat) so is less prone to becoming too soft even with over handling.

Margarine Soft margarine can be used straight from the fridge as opposed to butter which needs to be taken out before use. Margarines, in some cases, contain a significant amount of water. Fat spreads however should not be used because they contain higher quantities of water (up to 50%)

Margarine is more suitable where there are concerns of using animal fats which can result in increased cholesterol intake levels or those with special dietary requirements.

Shortening is a general term for a fat which is solid at room temperature and is used to rub into flour to minimise gluten development and therefore achieving a pastry which is short i.e. has a crumbly and or flaky texture. More specifically, it is a fat that is produced from hydrogenated vegetable oils and is used in place of animal fats such as butter and lard. The advantage of shortening is that it, like lard, has a greater working temperature range (melting point around 47°C) than butter and therefore less likely to become too soft or melt.

Oils, such as corn, cottonseed, coconut, olive and vegetable can all be used successfully in the making of short pastry and in general results in crumbly, tender pastry. Oils are usually added to the dry ingredients (flour) first with the water added later, or a mixture of oil and water can be added then mixed into the flour.

Flour

White wheat flours differ mainly in their protein content. High protein (i.e. strong or hard) flour produces a greater amount of gluten than one with less protein. Using the correct type of flour for a particular pastry or bread dough is important because the potential gluten content determines the structure and texture of baked goods.

All-purpose flour

Usually sold in the UK as 'plain flour' and like self-raising flour has a protein content of about 10%

It is ideal for making pastry and baked goods, except where a flour with a higher amount of protein is required such as enriched and bread dough. Plain flour is also used for cooking in general.

Self-raising flour

Readymade all-purpose flour with the addition of baking powder which acts as the raising agent. It is suitable for all bakery items where aeration is required; examples are scones, cakes and some biscuits. It can also be used as a substitute in recipes which utilises yeast for aeration.

Cake or sponge flour
This flour has very low protein content (between 7 and 9%) and therefore a low gluten potential, so it is ideally suited to making cakes and sponges.

Strong or bread flour
Of all the refined white flours this contains the highest percentage of protein, between 12 and 16%. This characteristic makes it ideal for making bread products. Once combined with water and mixed, it provides strength and elasticity which is also essential in the preparation of fresh pasta and puff pastry.

Wholemeal flour
Coarse, unrefined flour containing the whole bran, with a protein content ranging from 9 to 12%. It can be used as an alternative to all-purpose flour where higher fibre content is required. There are some brands of strong wholemeal flour specifically for bread dough products.

Gluten free flour
Gluten free flours are now widely available in shops, but it should be noted that they vary somewhat in their nature and, though most are easy to use for general cooking purposes, such as thickening a sauce or for coating food prior to frying, they cannot be used as a direct substitute for wheat flour in most bakery goods.

Gluten free flours, by their very nature, do not contain the proteins glutenin and gliadin (it is actually gliadin that causes sensitivity to gluten)

Alternatives to wheat flour vary from single plant flours to blended gluten free flours. Amaranth, arrowroot, buckwheat, chia, chickpea (gram), corn, potato, quinoa, rice, soya, and tapioca are all gluten free..

Blended flours consist of a mix of anything from two to six different flours, but to be able to use these substitutes in baking and achieve a good end product; many brands add an ingredient that will act in a similar way to gluten. Zantham and gum guar are just two of the most popular ingredients added to gluten free blended flour for baking purposes.

For more information on gluten free flour go to www.coeliac.org.uk

Alcohol in pastry making?
Substituting alcohol for water in short crust pastry recipes has become very popular. How does it work?

Alcohol is about 40% ethanol and 60% water. Alcohol does not participate in gluten development as does water and therefore the substitution of water with alcohol means a reduction in gluten development. Vodka is the most neutral with regards to flavour so the most suitable, although gin, whisky or brandy can also be used.

Cakes and sponges

It could be argued that the main difference between the two is that a cake is made with fat and a sponge is not. Whatever the argument both can and do cause the baker some irritation and distress at one time or another. Cakes and sponges take on many forms so I have tried to keep the faults and tips to a more general basis

Creamed in method

Creaming in is the first stage in cake making by combining fat and sugar until a light, fluffy texture is achieved. This is brought about by vigorous beating of the two ingredients and, during this process, air is incorporated, which adds to the final, light texture of the baked cake. The type of fat used can have an influence on aeration levels; butter and margarine are the most often used fats in baking. Although butter is fairly consistent in its characteristics, margarines vary considerably in their ingredients, especially fat spreads, and these differences can impact the quality of the baked cake. Creaming- in must be maximised to trap as much air as possible, overbeating can make the fat too warm, in which case it becomes so soft that the trapped air becomes lost; under-creaming does not produce maximum entrapment of air.

Victoria sandwich, cup, fairy, Madeira and fruit cakes are all made by the creamed in method.

Whisking: Swiss roll, Genoese/genoise sponge

Genoise and Swiss roll sponges are very light and airy in texture; they make good alternatives to cakes, which have much higher fat contents. Genoise sponges are used predominantly in the making of gateaux and are filled with fresh whipped cream or butter cream, fruits or flavourings. Black forest, chocolate and strawberry are popular gateaux. Swiss rolls are generally jam filled plain or chocolate sponges and logs, formed into a roll. The essence of making perfect genoise sponge is in the aeration of the eggs and sugar; this is what makes it rise and gives the sponge its lightness. The second crucial step is the folding in of the flour.

TIPS for making genoise and Swiss roll sponges

1. Baking tins should be lined with greaseproof or baking parchment to ensure easy removal of the sponge when baked. The shape of a Swiss roll tin is designed to produce a shallow rectangular sponge which can be filled and rolled after baking.
2. The whole eggs and sugar must be whisked vigorously; some advocate doing this over a pan of simmering water, others do not find it necessary. The main objective is to achieve a very light stiff

foam, similar to that of shaving foam; this is called the ribbon stage. If whisking over hot water, the danger is to heat the mixture too far and end up overcooking/coagulating the mix, resulting in sweet scrambled egg.
3. The flour should be sieved first and sieved again and folded into the egg foam in batches of about 1/3. Gentle folding in of the flour is crucial and this should be done using a spatula, large balloon whisk or large spoon, some prefer to use an open hand to incorporate the flour. Fat can be added to a genoise but is not necessary if the sponge is to be used straight away; the addition of fat will improve the shelf life, but will contribute to a slightly heavier sponge texture.
4. For chocolate sponges, the flour and cocoa powder should be mixed together well, and then sieved before incorporation. For a dark chocolate coloured sponge, chocolate colouring can be added to the egg mixture before whisking.
5. For Swiss rolls, the mixture should be levelled off when poured into the tin. If it is left uneven, the resulting sponge will not roll into an even cylinder shape. Too much mixture will also result in a thick sponge and will be difficult to roll.
6. It is important not to over bake Swiss roll sponges as they quickly become dry crisp and this can cause them to crack or break during rolling.
7. While still hot, the baked Swiss roll sponges must be turned upside down onto a sheet of greaseproof paper sprinkled with caster sugar (the baked surface is in contact with the sugared paper) and the baking tin left on top to trap in steam.
8. Some recipe methods suggest rolling up the sponge, allowing to cool and then unrolling for filling. This method is essential if the sponge roll is to be filled with fresh cream. Alternately, the sponge can be spread with filling and rolled whilst still warm.
9. Do not spread with too much jam or filling as this can ooze out of the ends during rolling.
10. The sponge can then be rolled by pulling the greaseproof paper over the bottom half, leaving the seam underneath. Leave the roll wrapped in the greaseproof until firm, to prevent it from unrolling.

Melting: *gingerbread, brownies*
These are fairly easy to make and therefore should not pose too many concerns. As a rule, cakes made by this method are generally heavier and firmer in texture than those made by creaming in or whisking, though baking powder can be used to create a lighter texture. The key point to observe is not to heat the fat content too high a temperature and that

cooling down of the fat and sugar mix before adding the other ingredients is important.

Chocolate brownie
Always use good quality ingredients, in particular chocolate; baking chocolate is unsuitable. Whilst the addition of cocoa powder will give a more intense, slightly bitter, flavour it also tends to produce a drier less gooey texture. Use the right size baking tins, too shallow and the brownie will not have depth.

Ensure all ingredients are at room temperature. Melt the chocolate carefully; if is too hot, let it cool before adding to the eggs to avoid overcooking them. Under- baking results in undercooked brownies, not a more gooey texture. Use a wooden skewer to test doneness, it should been almost clean when pulled out. Brownies are still very soft when removed from the oven, so they must be left to cool down before cutting into.

Rubbing- in
Rubbing-- in is actually the first stage in preparing short crust pastry. The fat is rubbed into the flour to form a water- resistant coating, which denies moisture from reacting with the proteins in the flour and therefore unwanted development of gluten. Rubbing in should be done gently with the fingertips, so starting with a firm fat will help avoid overheating. The liquid (usually milk or water) should be added all at once and handled just enough to form a soft dough.

Much the same problems can arise at the various stages; over handling during rubbing in causes the fat to become too warm and melting.

Once the liquid is added, handling should be kept to a minimum, to avoid a product with a tough and chewy texture due to gluten development.

Plain flour, with the addition of baking powder or self-raising flour, both achieve similar results; too much or too little raising agent can impact on rise and texture of the finished product. Sour milk, yoghurt, and buttermilk can also be used in the preparation of these baked items.

Scones, rock buns and shortbread are examples of rubbing- in baked products.

Cakes-common faults
Fault: fat, sugar and egg mix has curdled
Reason: eggs added too quickly or too cold. Remove eggs from the fridge before using and beat so they can be added slowly.
Fault: flat heavy cake.
Reason: Insufficient creaming in, insufficient raising agent.
Fault: cake sunk in middle.

Reason: too much raising agent, too much fat, too much sugar, drop in oven temperature during baking. The main reason is usually incorrect measurement of ingredients.
Fault: cake collapses at sides.
Reason: too much liquid.
Fault: crack in the top of the cake.
Reason: oven too hot, the crust is forming before the cake has finished rising; check the oven temperature.
Fault: cake peaked in the middle of the top.
Reason: over mixing, tough batter, too much raising agent, oven too hot.
Fault: shiny crust on cake top
Reason: too much sugar, sugar not mixed in adequately.
Fault: fruit sank in cake:
Reason: batter too wet, fruit too wet, too much raising agent.
Fault: cake size is smaller than should be:
Reason: insufficient aeration either by creaming in or raising agent. Batter too dry, more liquid needed. Over mixing and gluten development. Oven too hot.
Fault: soggy or wet area at base of cake.
Reason: batter too wet, too much liquid, under baked.
Fault: gooey centre
Reason: not baked for long enough.
Fault: open or coarse texture:
Reason: too much raising agent, oven too hot, insufficient creaming-in, incorrect measurement of ingredients.
Fault: dry and crumbly texture.
Reason: insufficient fat, too much raising agent, oven too cool, cooked too long.

Fermented, enriched dough pastries: Savarin (ring shape), babas (bouchon/champagne cork shape), marignans (round or barquette/boat shape).

For the uninitiated, these are probably best described (in texture terms), as a cross between a doughnut and a sponge cake, soaked in flavoured syrup. They are all made using the same type of enriched dough; the only differentiation between them is their shape, though babas usually contain currants or raisins.

For those who have had some experience working with yeast (i.e. bread making), you will be happy to know that the same principles apply.

TIPS
1. While savarin and marignans are made with plain dough, babas have the addition of dried fruit.

2. If using dried yeast, hydrate first in a small amount of warm liquid (about 37°C).
3. Prepare moulds by greasing with butter or margarine. It is important to ensure that all the surface of the mould is greased, otherwise the sponge will stick.
4. Once all ingredients are incorporated (except the butter), beat well for a good ten minutes. The dough should be quite soft, sticky and stringy.
5. Proving: finding the right storing temperature is important: too hot, and the mix can over prove or even begin to cook, too cool and proving can take much longer. When proved, the mix should be about double its original size.
6. Only fill the mould about a half to two thirds, the mix needs to rise just above the rim of the mould, any more and it will overflow during the second proving or baking. Using a piping bag will give better control when filling moulds.
7. Turn out of the mould while still warm and allow to cool.
8. Soaking: one method is to return the sponge to the mould and soak it with the syrup, gently turning out when soaked. Warm or hot syrup will be absorbed more easily.
9. If gazing with jam (apricot is traditionally used), make sure the jam glaze has been strained of any lumps.
10. When applying the glaze, always use a soft pastry brush. Ensure that the glaze is hot and of the correct consistency; too thin and it will merely soak in without giving a good glaze, too thick and it is difficult to apply and can damage the surface of the sponge.

Summary of baking advice
1. Use a reliable recipe and read through thoroughly, especially one that has never been used before or is complex in its method.
2. Always follow the method properly; it's there for a reason. If you don't understand a baking term, look up the definition.
3. Make sure you have all the ingredients for the recipe and they are measured /weighed out correctly, double check if need be. Check the age of the dry ingredients; those that have been the cupboard for months, they could be stale. Baking powder loses its ability to work when kept for a long time.
4. Don't substitute or add extra ingredients. While butter, margarine and oil are fats, they do not work in the same way, and can't be swopped gram for gram.
5. Ensure all ingredients are at room temperature. Cold butter does not cream properly and chilled eggs cause the batter to curdle, resulting in a cake with a coarse texture and a greasy mouth feel.

6. Ensure the baking equipment is clean and ready for use; cake tins may need greasing or lining with greaseproof paper.
7. Use the correct size cake tin for the recipe yield. Too big and the cake or sponge will turn out too thin, too small and the mixture may overflow. Baking times are also affected by using different sized cake tins.
8. Arrange shelves to the right position before turning the oven on, hot shelves can be dangerous.
9. Always pre-heat the oven and set to the correct temperature for baking. Delaying baking by waiting for an oven to heat up can mean a cake does not rise well.
10. Don't open the oven door too soon, this drops the oven temperature and can lead to a cake with a sunken middle. Check cakes after about 75% of the baking time has been achieved.
11. Use cooking timers where appropriate and check the oven regularly to make sure the contents are baking correctly. Quite often biscuits, cakes, sponges etc. need moving round to ensure even cooking and colouring.
12. Electric mixers are without doubt labour saving and have been used for many years by both the amateur cook and professional alike in bakery. Because of their speed and efficiency they can easily ruin pastry. At the rubbing in or creaming in stages over mixing can occur and due to the friction of the motor, overheating can cause fats to break down.
13. Sample and above all enjoy the fruits of your labours.

There are a considerable number of websites offering much information and advice about baking in general. There are also hundreds upon hundreds of books covering every aspect of baking and am sure the keen baker will already have their small library of books on this subject.

As bread making is not an expertise of mine, I have provided references to a couple of highly respected websites that offer the definitive information for bread making, faults encountered and tips and advice:

www.bakingmad.com/tips/
www.bakeinfo.co.nz

PART 2

Chapter 7

Heat transfer *(kinetic energy)* and cooking

The origins of when man first learned to control fire and use its heat to cook food is a highly debated subject. In fact, there has been much research done with contrasting results. Suffice to say that it marked the beginning of a new era in the history of mankind. As Richard Wrangham postulates in his book **Catching Fire: How Cooking Made Us Human** *(2009)*,"cooking food was an essential element in the physiological evolution of human beings and it was cooking that caused the transformation of our ancestors from apelike beings to Homo erectus".

So what is cooking? The *Oxford English Dictionary* defines cooking as:
1. The practice or skill of preparing food by combining, mixing, and heating ingredients.
1.1 Food that has been prepared in a particular way: authentic Italian cooking.

Clearly, the above definitions only give an insight into food and cooking and do not really give us the ability to understand cooking in any depth; it is therefore necessary to look further into what exactly happens when food is cooked using the application of heat or *kinetic energy,* more specifically *thermal energy.*

It is important to remember that when two objects with different temperatures are in contact with each other, energy is directly transferred from the hotter material to the colder material; when food is placed into a hot pan during frying, the heat is transferred from the hot pan to the food. A further example, when cream is poured over hot apple pie, the heat is transferred from the pie to the cream, not the reverse of the cream cooling the pie down.

Cooking, then, is primarily the process of producing safe and edible food by preparing and combining ingredients, and (in most cases) with the application of heat . Secondly, cooking with heat is a means of initiating numerous chemical and physical reactions which ultimately improves flavour, texture and in many cases, the visual appearance of the food.

The control of heat (*thermal energy*) and the length of time that heat is applied to foods are the key elements of cooking. Too much heat reduces certain foods to a dehydrated, chewy, flavourless lump, as in the case of over roasted meat, undercooked food, however, can not only be unpalatable and indigestible but dangerous for consumption through bacterial contamination.

In fact, food is heated in order to:

A) Destroy harmful food poisoning and food spoilage micro organisms; usually bacteria that are present on almost all raw foods.
B) Make the food more palatable and easier to eat and digest.
C) Release or make nutrients more easily available for digestion and take up by the body..
D) Make the food more appetising by improving organoleptic/gustatory qualities such as appearance, aroma, texture and flavour.
E) Add further variety to the diet.
F) Allow different flavours to be interchanged with different foods (e.g. as in adding herbs to a braised meat dish).
G) Lengthen the shelf life of food (as in preservation methods such as jamming, pasteurising and sterilising).
H) Boil water for tea and coffee to release the volatile oils and flavours which dissolve better in hot water. These volatile substances are vaporized by the heat then reach our nose and create aroma and flavour.

How is heat transferred to food?

Cast your mind back to school days and you may remember being taught the three ways in which heat is transferred:

Radiated and conducted heat from a ceramic hob heats the pan, which in turn heats the water by conduction and convection currents

Conduction

In simple terms, heat (thermal energy) is passed through solid objects that are in contact with each other: heat from a pan to the water contained in it.

More specifically heat is transferred between adjacent molecules in a solid substance. When heat is applied, the molecules begin to vibrate, the faster they vibrate, and the more energy is generated. Conduction in liquids and gases is the similar, however these are less dense i.e. the molecules are not as tightly packed as in solids such as metals, that is why energy transfer between molecules is less efficient and require longer to heat up..

To sum up, metals, some more than others are good heat conductors that is why they are used in cooking utensils. Poor conductors, such as wood, cloth and plastics are used to provide protection or insulation against heat: oven gloves and plastic pan handles.

As a rule, foods are poor conductors (have low thermal conductivity), though as expected, there is some variation and this is due to differences in temperature and composition of the food. Two good examples of this are a roasted joint of meat, even when removed from the oven, will continue to carry on cooking, similarly a steak will also continue to cook (conduct heat) when removed from the grill or frying pan. This slow conduction of heat through a food is commonly referred to as residual heat.

In terms of the efficiency of liquids as heat conductors; consider a pan of cold water placed on the cooker, it will eventually come to the boil nicely without the necessity to stir it. However place a pan of cold thick soup or sauce onto the cooker, if it isn't stirred there is a strong likelihood that it will stick to the pan base and singe or even burn. The reason is that because water is not viscous, the water molecules are free to move around and so the energy created is moved around the liquid quicker and more evenly. The soup or sauce is very viscous (thick), so the molecules are only able to move about a little, causing a build up of heat in pockets or hot spots, these regions can reach temperatures well above boiling point (superheating) causing the solids in the liquid to scorch and burn. By stirring though, this distributes the heat to other areas and therefore prevents a build up of heat near the bottom of the pan

CULINARY APPLICATION
Many methods of cookery involve the conduction of heat to cook food.

Convection (currents)
The transfer of heat through currents of air (oven) or in a liquid (water or boil).

Molecules that contain high heat energy in a liquid or gas rise to take the place of molecules with less heat energy. The heat is transferred from hot areas to cooler by convection currents and this continues until equilibrium occurs throughout the whole of the liquid or gas.

Natural Convection uses the principle of a heated gas or liquid that rises while cooler gas or liquid falls, thus creating circulation. Boiling water involves movement of hot water by convection currents (as well as conduction).

Mechanical Convection is used in ovens that are fan assisted where the heat generated by the heat source is wafted by the fan around the oven space; this produces a more consistent temperature throughout than that achieved by conventional ovens.

CULINARY APPLICATION
Examples: Baking in an oven where the heat is transferred by convection currents of heated air emanating from the heat source. Roasting of meats, at high enough temperatures promotes the Maillard and caramelisation reactions.

Radiation
Thermal radiation
When an object is heated (above absolute zero), it emits infrared radiation; a type of electromagnetic radiation producing 'heat rays' or waves. The hotter it becomes the more Infrared radiation is emitted. It does not require physical contact between the heat source and the food, unlike in conduction and convection, so radiation can even work through the vacuum of space.

CULINARY APPLICATION
Examples: Infrared red radiation: a glowing heat lamp over food, a toaster or a grill.
   Foods are placed under and close to the heat source. Because of the direct intense heat, the surface moisture of the food is quickly evaporated enabling Maillard and caramelisation reactions to take place. In toasted bread the reaction involved in browning is dextrinisation; breaking down of starch through dry heat into dextrins.

Microwave cooking
Microwaves work on the same principle; however their wave lengths are slightly longer than those of infra red rays. They also have higher frequencies and shorter wave lengths than radio waves. Microwave ovens rely on the ability of microwaves to penetrate about 1 cm into food. They are absorbed by water molecules in the food, which vibrate (they actually spin back and forth) and generate heat and cook food at the same time.
   As we know, food cooked in the microwave cooks much quicker than conventional cooking because heat transfer is more effective and efficient.

CULINARY APPLICATION
Example: cooking, re-heating and de-frosting
   Most methods of cooking involve more than one form of heat transfer. Consider baking a cake: the oven is heated by convection currents rising from the heat source, heat is also radiated from the oven walls. As the cake tin heats up it conducts heat to the surface of the cake and from there the

heat is conducted towards the centre of the cake, cooking it as the heat increases.

Residual or 'carry over' cooking *(passive cooking)*

This is an important aspect of cooking and one which, quite often, is given little thought. Residual heat refers to the amount of stored thermal energy in a substance. In cookery, this can be seen as the heat that is retained in a cooking appliance or a piece of equipment, after the heat source has been turned off; as in an oven or ceramic hob. It also applies to the heat which food retains after it has been removed from a heat source. The effect of this residual heat in food is the continuation of the cooking process, the length of which is dependent upon the type, density and size of food and the heat level.

Although seldom mentioned in recipes this 'carry-over' cooking period should be accounted for in the overall cooking time for a particular food. The impact of residual heat can mean an increase in the internal temperature of a food item by temperatures between 3 and 14°C. The larger and denser the food being cooked, the greater the amount of temperature increase due to this retained heat. Also, foods with higher water content are more subject to residual cooking as water has a higher heat capacity and will therefore have more heat to distribute throughout the food.

The residual heat therefore, can make the difference between perfectly cooked or over-cooked as the temperature continues to increase inside the food.

A good example of this can be seen in the roasting of meat. If the core target temperature of a small roast chicken is 65°C, then to compensate for the residual heat, the chicken needs to be removed from the oven before this temperature is reached; a fair estimate would be a temperature of 60°C

The term 'resting time' (meat) is synonymous with residual cooking in that they both infer cooking is continuing despite being removed from the heat source. Furthermore resting, also allows time for internal juices to redistribute throughout the meat, until the different internal temperatures reach equilibrium. Consequently, the resting period facilitates the retention of the meats juices and flavour and produces a more tender texture.

Chapter 8

COOKING PROCESSES

Cooking can be best defined as the practice, skill or art of preparing food by combining and mixing ingredients and often with the application of heat.

The aim of cooking is to meet a range of criteria, many of which are both essential and desirable, and these include the necessity to make the food safe to eat, appetising and digestible.

Nearly always some chemical reactions take place during the preparation and cooking of food. These reactions bring about changes, many of which are visibly apparent, though more than often the change is subtle, for example, egg white loses its translucency and becomes opaque on heating, milk turns to a solid during the process of cheese making, when cream is whipped it forms a foam. Many reactions however go unnoticed to the human eye, though the foods intrinsic characteristics will have changed.

So what causes these chemical reactions to take place?

Heat, the action of enzymes and a change of pH environment are the three main agents that bring on reactive chemical changes in food. During these reactions, new chemical structures are made, energy changes occur and the food is then transformed from its native state into a new substance with its own distinct characteristics.

HOW DOES HEAT CHANGE FOOD?

The application of heat is the action or process which transforms food from a raw state to a cooked one. As a result of this, chemical reactions create molecular changes. How this transformation is achieved successfully in the kitchen is dependent upon the correct use of heat and time.

Whilst recipes give details of cooking times and temperatures, there are occasions when cooks need to use their own judgement, especially in situations where no recipe is available. The experienced cook will be able to decide when an item or dish requires further or reduced cooking time or higher or lower temperatures than stated in the recipe.

Heating causes complex physical and chemical changes to occur and these changes vary depending on the type of food being cooked and the method of cookery. Therefore these changes are a means at arriving at a desired outcome e.g., by improving or altering the organoleptic qualities such as flavour, texture, consistency, colour and digestibility. The down side of these chemical changes is in many cases, a reduction in the nutritional value of the food, the extent to which is dependent upon the type of food and the cooking process involved. Secondly, the generation of undesirable compounds or the production of potentially toxic substances is an unavoidable occurrence, especially where particular food types are subjected to high temperatures during the cooking process. Heat also has a direct effect on the moisture content of foods. Meats, fish, vegetables and fruit contain large amounts of water, which is lost through evaporation. Shrinkage and changes in structure (see food shrinkage below) are also symptoms of exposure to heat. However, without this loss of water, caramelisation and the Maillard reactions cannot take place. In many methods of cooking food, the initiation of these reactions is encouraged so that new flavours and aromas can be developed and intensified.

Below are the main changes that occur in different food types during cooking:

Caramelisation
More specifically, the thermo chemical decomposition of organic substances by pyrolysis. When we think of caramelisation we automatically assume it is referring to the caramel that is produced for confectionery and desserts. That is one aspect, but all foods containing sugars can be caramelised to some degree; onions, parsnips, carrots, courgettes and peppers are examples of vegetables that we caramelise to add colour and bring out further sweetness and flavours.

The process of caramelising in cooking produces volatile chemicals which give foods, a nutty flavour and brown colour. During the reaction, water is driven off and sugars break down.

Both caramelisation and the Maillard reactions are causes of non-enzymatic browning in foods that have undergone some form of heating. Pyrolysis occurs whenever food is exposed to high temperatures (160°C +) in a dry environment (i.e. in baking or toasting bread). Caramelisation should not be confused *with Maillard reactions*; the former occurs with sugars, the latter in the presence of an amino acid (protein) and a reducing sugar (see Maillard reaction below).

CULINARY APPLICATIONS
Foods with high sugar content are cooked to caramelise the natural sugars they contain (e.g. onions, carrots and parsnips). This imparts new flavours, produces different aromas and adds colour.

During sugar boiling, changes occur that give the syrup different characteristics at differing temperatures and it is these varying characteristics that are used in different ways in confectionery.

Evaporated milk has a slightly brown tinge and caramel flavour and this is due to the high heat process during canning, which causes the milk sugar (lactose) to caramelise.

For further details on sugar boiling see Chapter 6 Pastry and Baked Goods

Maillard reaction

The Maillard reaction is a chemical reaction between an amino acid and a reducing sugar. The reactive sugar; e.g. glucose or fructose, interacts with the amino acid of the protein chain. This process generally begins from about 145°C and continues to about 260°C. At lower temperatures, meat, for example, will have less developed flavours and colour, as temperatures rise these changes become more apparent; meat begins to brown and flavours and aromas intensify and become distinctive and unique to the food. During these reactions, the type of amino acids that make up the protein; whether it is a beef steak, lamb chop or fish fillet, will contribute to the final flavours, texture and structure of the cooked food. Maillard reactions are not a simple process, numerous different compounds are created temporarily, only to be broken down and replaced with yet more new ones. Over a thousand different molecules have been identified during the Maillard process, many of which are responsible for the browning in meat, while others contribute aromas and flavours.

What is especially noticeable of roasted, shallow fried or grilled meats, apart from their particular aroma, is the characteristics of the meats surface; deep brown in colour, dry and crisp texture. The crispness of chicken skin or the brown colour of a pan fried steak would not be possible without Maillard reactions.

CULINARY APPLICATIONS

In the kitchen: roasted, pan fried and grilled meats, chipped potatoes, baked products

In processed foods: coffee, malted barley, condensed milk, peanuts, caramel, maple syrup, chocolate.

Starch gelatinisation and retrogradation

Starch is a *polysaccharide,* or a *carbohydrate polymer* of many units or molecules of *glucose* joined by glycosidic bonds. It forms an energy store for most plants and is found in large amounts in staple ingredients such as flour, potatoes, vegetable and grains.

It consists of two types of molecules: linear chains of amylose and branched amylopectin. The amounts of amylose to amylopectin depends on the type of plant, but are generally found in a ratios of 3:1 amylopectin to amylose.

Starch is insoluble in cold water; this can be seen, for example if corn flour is mixed with cold water and left to stand for a while. The corn flour settles to the bottom (i.e. it does not dissolve in the water but forms a suspension). However, as soon as a certain amount of heat is applied, it will dissolve in the liquid, thickening it during the process.

Gelatinization is the result when starch granules of a plant are mixed with an aqueous liquid and then subjected to heat. The gelatinization temperature of starch is generally between 55 and 85°C but again this is dependent on the type of plant starch. Other factors that impact on starch gelation are the amount of liquid present, the pH of the environment, and the presence of fat, protein, salt or sugars.

Starch granules undergo a transition process, they begin to soften and swell by absorbing water. When the liquid is heated, the hydrogen bonds begin to break down allowing water to penetrate the starch molecules. As the starch swells, the liquid begins to thicken. The result of the thickening process is that the water content becomes 'bound' within the starch framework and forms a gel. Gels are made whenever starch is used as a thickening agent and can be observed in the process of making starch thickened sauces and puddings.

The opacity of a cooked starch is not always noticeable or a consideration in many aspects of cookery, and the degree to which starches become opaque or translucent, is dependent upon the type of starch involved.

Arrowroot, when used in thickening, not only has the advantage of giving sauces a more translucent finish, but because it contains no protein, unlike wheat flour, the resulting sauce has a high gloss finish. These characteristics therefore make it an ideal choice for thickening fruit sauces, particularly where clarity, colour and neutral flavour is important.

Corn flour or corn starch is ideal for thickening dairy based sauces, custard for example, gravies and puddings, but in acid environments the starch breaks down and loses its thickening potential.

Wheat starch is not pure but contains protein (gliadin and glutenin) and other substances, so larger amounts are required to thicken where other forms of starch require smaller amounts. Wheat starch also has a tendency to reduce flavour profiles of sauces, so sauces thickened with this type of starch can taste a little bland and may impart a slightly nutty, cereal taste.

It is important to choose the right type of starch as the thickening agent, as each one is more suited to certain uses than others. Root starches, such as tapioca, arrowroot and potato, though thicken at lower temperatures, break down with continued boiling, so should be added to sauces towards the end of cooking.

Cereal starches thicken at higher temperatures and do not break down as quickly, therefore this makes them more suitable for sauces which will undergo high temperatures for prolonged periods (i.e. baked cauliflower cheese or lasagne).

CULINARY APPLICATIONS
Gelatinisation occurs in the following when cooked:
Blanc mange; a cold set dessert using corn flour as the gelling agent.
Choux paste, bread dough, pasta, sauces, batters and soups.

Two examples of starch gelatinisation occurring in cooking:
a) *Béchamel sauce*; when milk is added to the flour and fat mixture (roux), subsequent heating of the milk liberates the starch granules and in turn causes the sauce to thicken as the liquid is absorbed.
b) *Custard*, when corn flour is mixed and heated with milk, the starch grains swell. The starch continues to swell during cooking and by doing so, thickens the milk.

As a thickener, corn flour is more efficient because it is almost pure starch (amylose), whereas wheat flour also contains proteins, fat and sugars. Once left to cool down both the béchamel and custard will continue to thicken and set firm. The resulting firmness will depend upon the degree to which the starch is 'cooked out', and the ratio of thickener to liquid.

Using béchamel sauce to further explain this phenomenon:
When hot milk is added to the flour and fat mixture (roux), the starch granules begin to swell and absorb the milk. This process continues over a period of time as prolonged heat allows more and more starch granules to swell and absorb further liquid until a status quo has been achieved. That is, all the starch granules have swollen to their maximum volume and absorbed free liquid in doing so. At this stage, the sauce has reached its determined viscosity. To add further liquid would lower the sauces viscosity. Conversely, to withhold some liquid would result in a very viscous sauce. It is important therefore that recipes are accurate in their predetermined ratio amounts of thickener to liquid so that the required viscosity of sauce is achieved consistently. It is also important to remember that, as starch thickened sauces cool, they become thicker/increase in viscosity, which makes them more difficult to use for the purpose of coating food. A good example is in the preparation of cauliflower cheese, where the cauliflower is coated with cheese sauce. Here the right consistency is important in order to achieve an even coating over the vegetable; too thin and it will run off and collect in a pool at the bottom of the dish, too thick and it will not coat evenly, resulting in a lumpy, stodgy appearance. Using the sauce to coat food with the correct

consistency and whilst still hot, will also ensure a more consistent, smooth coverage.

Retrogradation
I have included this purely out of added interest as it is a by-product of the gelatinisation process of starch over which the cook has very little control. Retrogradation is the realigning of the two types of starch molecules (amylose and amylopectin) during cooling of a mixture. One main consequence of this reaction is syneresis, which is the oozing of a liquid from a gelatinised structure when left to stand and cool down. It can be seen in items such as in the filling of home-made lemon meringue pie and starch thickened sauces especially after being frozen and defrosted. Food manufacturers use 'modified starches' to overcome this problem in many readymade meals and desserts.

Staling of bread is due to starch retrogradation and not simply moisture loss through storage as some believe.

Colour change during cooking
It is perhaps best to categorise these as desired and undesirable changes-

Desirable
Foods are deliberately coloured, in most cases by browning; by the Maillard and caramelisation reactions (see above), during roasting, grilling, baking and frying. As well as creating flavours and aromas, these reactions also provide foods with an appetising eye appeal; the crust on bread and baked goods, the crisp brown skin of a roasted chicken. Convenience foods also undergo colour changes as they are treated to similar processes; for example, the roasting of coffee beans not only contributes to the aromas and flavours of coffee but also the colour.

Some shellfish, notably lobsters, change colour when subjected to heat, they turn from a blue to a pink colour. This is due to a natural pigment astaxanthin (pink-red colour) in the shell. Whilst the shellfish is alive, the pigment is also bound to the protein crustacyanin. However crustacyanin is not heat stable so when shellfish are cooked, the protein denatures, allowing the colour of astaxanthin to show through.

Sugar is heated to a caramel stage which adds colour as well as flavour, the caramelised sugar topping on crème brûlée is a good example

Undesirable
Changes occur when vegetables are cooked, especially when overcooked; green vegetable lose their colour as chlorophyll is denatured, other vegetables lose some of their colour, becoming less vibrant. Some vegetables change colour totally and become unappealing and

unappetising. Observing the correct procedures for cooking vegetables is crucial then if their natural attributes are to be retained.

Apart from looking and tasting unappetising and therefore undesirable, food that has been burnt during cooking is avoidable. When food is exposed to too much heat or to heat for too long it becomes dehydrated and blackens or burns. Burnt food takes on an unpalatable flavour and has a greatly reduced nutrient content. Intentional charring foods such as fish, meat and vegetables is very popular, but ultimately the food is still burnt, if only the skin or outer surface. Recent research has given rise to concerns that burnt or charred food contains carcinogens which is thought can lead to the formation certain cancers.

Protein changes through heating

Denaturation is the change in the structure of a protein, either due to heat, acid, alkali, or other agents. Heating proteins, changes their carefully ordered structure, making them lose their original or native state. The consequence of this is that the process is normally irreversible. In other words, because the protein has denatured, it has lost its functional ability, it cannot be used again for the same purpose. The properties of a raw egg for instance differ from those of a cooked one; it is not possible to make meringue with cooked egg white, neither is it possible to prepare Gravlax or ceviche using cooked fish.

Proteins are said to coagulate during denaturation so the terms are really interchangeable. Some of these changes are physical and can be seen taking place when food is cooked. In many cases, though, chemical and biological changes cannot. Different proteins require different considerations, in terms of how they should be prepared and cooked so that their function, flavours, texture, aroma and visual appeal can be maximised.

When egg whites are subjected to heat, they become solid and opaque, with excessive heat they take on a rubbery texture. Egg yolks similarly become firm when cooked, but a crumbly texture can be seen when overcooked.

The characteristic ability for egg proteins to form gels is used to advantage in the preparation of custards and quiches for example.

All foods contain enzymes (proteins) and, when heated during cooking, lose their ability to efficiently catalyze chemical reactions. Enzymes have specific temperature ranges where they are at their most active (usually around 35-42°C), above these they become denatured and are ultimately destroyed, at lower temperatures they are either inactive or work very slowly.

In cooking, deactivation of enzyme activity in food is a necessity if the integrity of the foods natural properties (i.e. colour, flavour and texture) are to be maintained; green vegetables are blanched in boiling water to deactivate natural enzymes that are present, if these are allowed to remain active, they would denature the chlorophyll in the vegetable causing colour loss.

In the manufacture of cheeses such as parmesan and Emmental, cheese curds (casein protein)are heated from between 48°C and 56°C to denature the proteins, thus allowing further whey to be drained off. During the process of making halloumi, the curds are cooked in the whey which is heated to 90°C and it is partly due to this that halloumi has a high melting point and can be fried or grilled without melting.

Tenderising meat

While collagen softens in moist heat, muscle fibres become firmer as their proteins unfold and form new linkages during cooking. Various proteins in meat fibres (*actin and myosin*) denature over a range of temperatures, usually between 40° C and 90°C. The higher the cooking temperature, the tougher the muscle fibres become, and the more they shrink in both length and width. Between about 40 and 50°C meat enzymes begin to denature and become inactive. At about 50°C, meat develops a grey/white colour as the protein myosin denatures and, during this process, there is loss of moisture from the muscle tissue. Connective tissue, collagen, is also beginning to shrink and denature. Reaching about 70°C, collagen begins to dissolve and turn to gelatine and continues during prolonged cooking. The meat fibres are now becoming dryer but, because the connective tissue has denatured, the fibres are able to break apart, making the meat tenderer; pulled meats are a good example of this. As collagen is converted to gelatine and intramuscular fat renders down during cooking, both of these give meat the impression of moistness and succulence.

Food shrinkage

Is brought about by the loss of moisture content of food and on many occasions is, to some extent, unavoidable when heat is used in the cooking process. Protein molecules in meat are packed into coils and when heat is applied the proteins unfold and shrink and simultaneously water is squeezed out. This water loss accounts for the loss of some of the juices in meats. The inevitable impact of this is that the longer the cooking time or higher the temperature, the greater the loss of moisture in the meat and therefore the greater the shrinkage. Of all the food types, meat can suffer the greatest loss of moisture when cooked, it can also succumb to shrinkage as the internal and external fat content renders down and melts away from the meat.

By taking better control of the cooking process, this loss of moisture/water can be minimised by cooking food at optimum temperatures to retain the maximum moisture content. i.e. roasting a joint of meat at the correct temperature and length of time to preserve the meats juices.

Preservation

There are different ways in which heat is applied to foods as a method of preservation. Boiling and steaming are used to denature and deactivate natural enzymes in food and to destroy both food poisoning and spoilage microbes; pasteurisation and sterilisation are good examples of the use of heat to make food safe to consume and extend shelf life. Removing or reducing the moisture content of food by using heat enables it to be kept for longer periods than would normally be possible if left in its natural state. Dried, processed food products such as dried milk, instant potato powder, coffee granules, and packet soups, are all examples of raw materials treated to extend their shelf life and prevent the growth of unwanted microbes.

Fruits, in the preparation of jams and marmalades, are preserved by being boiled with sugar; this in turn, makes an unsuitable environment for the growth of harmful microbes.

CULINARY APPLICATION

Food preservation: curing, drying, smoking, pickling, canning and bottling, chilling and freezing.

Desirable and undesirable compounds

Cooking food allows chemical changes to occur which promote the release of complex flavour compounds and volatile aroma molecules. These can be found in many cooked foods but are most noticeable in proteins and carbohydrates that have been cooked at high temperatures; examples are cooked meats; the smell and flavour of roast meats caused by Maillard reactions and the distinctive flavour and aroma of sugar that has been boiled to a caramel stage.

Fats release flavour when they melt. In animals, fat contributes flavours to its meat and it is not until certain temperatures are reached that these fats begin to break down (render) giving off volatile flavour and aroma molecules.

Vegetables and fruit release flavours when heated; their cells release flavours when the walls breakdown. During the process of jam and marmalade making, pectins in fruit are released from plant cell walls when boiled and form a gel with the liquid and fruit pulp, this in turn produces the characteristic ability to set once cooled.

The sulphur molecules of onions are destroyed and, at the same time, heat also caramelises the sugars present giving the vegetable a less pungent and a sweeter taste.

Undesirable compounds:

There are some concerns, leading to research being carried out into the regular consumption of foods, in particular carbohydrates, which have been cooked using high temperatures. Certain foods subjected to temperature s in access of 120°C, have been found to contain levels of acrylamide, but not in foods treated at temperatures below this. Acrylamide, a chemical found in processed foods such as bread, coffee and breakfast cereals, has been directly linked to the incidence of cancer; fried, grilled and roasted meats are also implicated. However, because of insufficient data, there are no recommendations as to how much can be consumed safely. Some studies estimate that the amount of acrylamide obtained from food cooked in the home is lower than that which is present in processed foods or from meals prepared in a restaurant. As yet, there appears to be no government guidelines with regards to what are considered safe levels, however FSA studies have concluded that regular consumption of certain foods cooked at high temperatures expose consumers to higher levels of acrylamide than is desirable.

Moisture content of food

Water is one of the most abundant chemicals on the planet. Water sustains most forms of life. Water is needed for growing plants and rearing animals for food. Water is used as a solvent: a universal solvent as it is capable of dissolving many substances, washing and removing waste products. It is used in huge volumes in manufacturing and processing of a wide range of materials, commodities and foodstuffs and, of course, it is used extensively in the kitchen; without it cooking would be virtually impossible.

All food contains varying amounts of moisture unless they have been dried; though these still contain a small amount.

Fresh fruits contain high percentages of water, some as much as 90% whereas, fresh meats a little less at around 75% water content. If you have ever wondered why, when a pineapple or a piece of steak is cut into, the water doesn't come flooding out? The reason is the types of water involved.

The moisture present in food is a combination of 'free,' 'bound' and 'trapped' water. Free water is unbound, that is, it can move freely out of foods when cut or squeezed. For example, free water makes up about 10% of the moisture content in meat muscle.

Bound water molecules may be physically or chemically bound to the other constituents of the food, such as carbohydrates or proteins, and the bonding is such that the structure of these molecules differs from that of free water. Bound water is held tightly by proteins and is not affected by heating or freezing. In meat muscle, this water type represents about 1%, a much smaller amount than that of free water.

Trapped or immobilised water contributes the highest percentage of moisture content in foods. It is held within pockets and channels of some foods, and is held in place by physical barriers which prevent the water from escaping. In meat, the water is trapped within muscle fibres and in the cells and contributes up to 80% of the total moisture content in meat muscle.

Flavours and aromas

Flavour is a result of a combination of human gustatory senses: salty, sweet, bitter, sour and umami derived from water soluble compounds. These tastes are perceived during chemical reactions with taste receptor cells in the mouth.

Aromas are evolved from the numerous substances present in food in its natural state or developed through various chemical reactions and it is these volatile compounds which contribute to the distinctive flavour of the food. Flavours and aromas are not easy to separate because many flavour properties are the result of molecular odour sensations.

Heat is both an ally and an enemy to the cook, while it is essential for the development of both flavours and aromas; it also has the unfortunate ability to diminish or destroy many.

Flavour and aroma compounds are generally developed during cooking. Different organic volatile aroma compounds contribute flavours to meat, and this is brought about by the partial breakdown of the protein and fat through heating. In meat, these compounds are bound within the fibres and fat matrices and, it is the structural makeup of these that determines when the flavours and aromas are released. Finally, it is the release of the different aromas from the melting fat which give beef, lamb and pork their distinctive characteristics.

It is a known fact that heat or lack of it has a direct effect on the flavour and aroma profiles of many foods that we eat. For example, food eaten straight from the refrigerator can suffer from a diminished, almost bland taste and smell and it is not until it is brought up to ambient temperatures (20-25°C) that its attributes can be really appreciated. Many food smells or aromas are not perceived by the nose unless they are at a certain temperature.

This is why some food types should be served at room temperature; cheese, red wine and nuts, yet other foods; salads and fruit drinks are served chilled or in the case of ice cream and sorbet, frozen.

CHANGES TO FOOD OTHER THAN BY HEATING

Whilst I have discussed the many changes that take place either when food is cooked or during the processes applied as part of food preservation, there are other agents that are used in cookery to change the characteristics of foods.

One of the main aims when cooking some food types is the attainment of tenderness; roasting or stewing meat to make it tender, boiling vegetables to soften them. There are also other well known methods used to tenderise meat for example. Mincing gives the impression that meat is tenderer by breaking down and reducing the length of muscle and connective tissue fibres, as in burgers.

Batting out meat when preparing escallops; the mechanical activity of hitting the meat with a mallet stretches and tears the meat and connective tissue fibres, making them shorter and therefore more tender.

Commercial tenderiser powders are available which contain natural fruit enzymes; bromelain in pineapple, papain in papaya, ficin in fig and actinidin in kiwi are all proteolytic (protein digesting) enzymes which help to break down connective tissue in the meat.

The addition of acid to some raw foods can work in a useful way. When preparing the South American dish ceviche, citrus fruit juice (usually lemon or lime) is applied to sliced or diced raw fish. The citric acid in the natural fruit juice acts on the fish flesh and in doing so denatures the proteins; that is they are changed from their native form, giving the appearance and texture of traditionally cooked fish.

In Chinese cookery, bi-carbonate of soda is added to small pieces of beef and pork prior to cooking, to make the meat more tender. This process has the advantage of making cheaper, tougher cuts of meat suitable for stir-frying

Brining is a process of soaking meat in a salt solution. During this chemical process, protein structures denature during which they have a greater capacity to absorb water. The uptake of water makes the meat more tender and juicier.

Marinating: A marinade is a mixture of wine, sherry, citrus juice or vinegar with the addition of other ingredients such as herbs, spices and vegetables. The purpose of the marinade is usually two fold; primarily to add further flavours and secondly to tenderise meat prior to cooking.

Much debate, argument, a fair of amount of scientific and other (myself included) research has been carried out over the years and the consensus is no, marinating meat does not tenderise or add flavours, certainly not in the way that is generally thought.

Marinades can only penetrate about 2-3mm into the meat, although this is increased with the addition of salt. Therefore a marinade cannot tenderise the internal muscle of a thick piece or joint of meat.

It is a known fact that acids such as those in lemon juice and vinegar and alcohol such as wine can denature proteins, making meat tenderer. However, excess acid has the reverse effect, making meat tougher and drier and continued marinating will result in the surface of meat becoming mushy once cooked. For marinades to be effective, the pieces or slices of meat need to be no more than about 5mm in thickness for the marinade to diffuse through to the centre. Marinades are therefore adsorbed or accumulate onto the meats surface rather than being absorbed or permeating into the meat.

Thus said, some foods can be marinated effectively, especially where the internal structure of the food is less dense, examples are fish and shellfish and certain vegetables such as aubergines.

For additional information on changes in food see Chapter 9 on Food Preservation

Chapter 9

FOOD PRESERVATION

Differing forms of food preservation has been practiced for centuries in practically every corner of the globe. Many techniques have been passed down through generation to generation, only to be modified periodically with the introduction of new ingredients, materials, techniques or to fulfil aspects food safety.

Food preservation is the process of treating and handling food to halt or slow down food spoilage, in order to alter or retain the texture, taste, smell, appearance or nutritional value of a food whilst prolonging its storage life. The food must also be rendered safe to eat by denying food poisoning microbes the ability to grow and multiply.

Food spoilage can be defined as a change in a food's natural state that makes it become unappetising, inedible or toxic. Biological changes that occur are usually quite obvious: off smells; unpleasant taste; and visible changes in food, such as colour, texture or viscosity. Some foods develop a surface slime, while others promote the growth of yeast or moulds. Various factors are responsible for food spoilage and are usually a combination of two or more factors: air and oxygen, moisture, light, microbial growth, temperature and time. Whilst we find unintended food spoilage disagreeable and, at most, potentially toxic if consumed, in some cases we actually promote and encourage food spoilage in the process of preserving many foods for consumption.

Causes of food spoilage
Food deterioration can occur during various times in the food chain. Crop foods begin to deteriorate post harvest, meat, fish and dairy products also succumb to spoilage until they are processed, cooked or consumed. The spoiling of food can be due to various factors; physical, chemical, microbial and enzymatic. While one or more of these factors may be to blame, the deterioration of food by microbial action (bacteria, yeasts and moulds) is the most important in terms of food preservation.

Bacteria
These are single celled organisms, able to reproduce rapidly under the right conditions. Not all are harmful, like food poisoning bacteria. In fact, there are far more types and strains that are harmless. Many are useful and these are utilised in a positive way in food preservation. The production of cheeses, yoghurts and probiotic drinks are good examples.

Bacteria need certain conditions in which to grow and multiply. Temperature; the optimum (ideal) temperature range for bacterial growth is 30°C – 37°C.

Most bacteria however grow between 10°C and 60°C. A large percentage of bacteria are destroyed at temperatures above 63 °C.

At very cold temperatures, bacteria become dormant - they do not die, but growth and reproduction slows down and in many cases, stops.

Like all living animals, bacteria need food and water to survive, grow and multiply. Foods high in protein and moisture, such as meat, fish and dairy products make ideal habitats to support the growth of many types of bacteria.

Yeasts

Like bacteria, yeasts are found throughout the world in soils and on plant surfaces. They are single celled fungi particularly fond of environments where sugars are present, such as fruit skins and flowers. Yeasts can spoil the taste of food but do not make it harmful, just unpleasant to eat. They will grow well in suitable conditions; sugary food, although do not survive concentrations above 50%

They prefer warmer temperatures; although above 75°C will be destroyed. Yeasts also tolerate neutral to acid conditions.

Moulds

Moulds are classed as fungi. They need moisture and prefer slightly acidic conditions. Moulds grow best at a temperature range of 20°C and 40°C but are killed off above 70°C and below freezing point. The presence of moulds on food indicates staleness or inappropriate storage, as in the case of freshly baked bread which has been packaged whilst still warm and stored in similar conditions. Unlike yeasts, moulds do not grow well without the presence of oxygen.

Some moulds, however are used to our advantage, as in some blue and white mould cheeses, such as camembert and brie.

Enzymes

Autolysis or self destruction is a natural process resulting from enzyme activity within foods.

In many cases it is not possible to prevent, however intervention by the grower, food processor/producer and the cook can help in slowing down food deterioration by applying correct preparation, processing, handling and storage requirements.

Two important aspects of enzyme action in fruit and vegetables is ripening and browning. In both situations, the organoleptic qualities of food over a period of time are progressively impaired.

In meat, enzyme activity or proteolysis continues during storage, causing meat muscle to mature, become tender and develop flavour. This process however, can be slowed down by chilling the meat.

Moisture content of food

Water is one of the most abundant chemicals on the planet. Water sustains many forms of life. Water is needed for growing plants and rearing animals for food. Water is used as a solvent: a universal solvent as it is capable of dissolving many substances, washing and removing waste products. It is used in huge volumes in manufacturing and processing of a wide range of materials, commodities and foodstuffs and of course it is used extensively in the kitchen, without it cooking would be virtually impossible.

But there is another aspect of water, and one which should not be taken for granted when cooking and that is the intrinsic water content of food. It is this moisture that we strive to preserve when food is prepared and cooked; the moisture content of cooked meats and fish for example.

All foods contain varying amounts of moisture or water unless they have been dried; though these can still contain small moisture residues.

Considering that most fruits are made up of nearly 90% water and about 75% for a meat, have you ever wondered why after cutting into a pineapple or a steak, the water doesn't come flooding out? The reason is the type of water involved.

The moisture present in food is a combination of 'free,' 'bound' and 'trapped' water. Free water is unbound, that is, it can move freely out of foods when cut or squeezed. For example, free water makes up about 10% of the moisture content in meat muscle.

In bound water, water molecules may be physically or chemically bound to the other constituents of the food, such as carbohydrates or proteins. The bonding is such that the molecular structure of these water molecules differs from that of free water. Bound water is held tightly by proteins and is not affected by heating or freezing and in meat muscle only represents less than 1%.

Trapped or immobilised water contributes the highest percentage of moisture content in foods. It is held within pockets and channels of some foods by physical barriers which prevent the water from escaping. In meat, the water is trapped within muscle fibres, cell bundles and membrane and contributes up to 80% of the total moisture content in meat muscle.

Water activity (aW): water that is not physically or chemically bound or tied up to food molecules can support the growth of microbes such as bacteria and moulds. Water activity describes the energy status, or the tendency for water to escape from food, or the amount of water available for hydration (drying). In other words, water activity is an indication of the amount of free water in food. During dehydration of foods, the water activity of a food is lowered thus prohibiting the growth of bacteria. Dried foods therefore are able to be stored (under the right conditions) for long periods without deterioration. However, once rehydrated they become susceptible to microbial contamination and so must be treated as foods similar in nature.

Jams and marmalades, whilst considered as gels, are not capable of sustaining bacterial growth because the sugar and water molecules present bond strongly, denying the microbes' access to the moisture.

However, the water activity of a food is not the same as its moisture content. Water activity is a measure or the energy status of the water in a food and does not depend on the amount in food. Moisture content is the amount of water in a food, dry or wet, and does depend upon the amount present.

Determining water activity in foods is of particular importance in the food processing industries, when determining packaging and storage requirements.

Methods of food preservation
Whilst many methods of 'food preservation' are no longer done on the same level as our ancestors during Victorian times, there are, however still many who carry out some of these practices today.

While the traditions of canning and jugging are now almost nonexistent, jamming, smoking, curing and pickling remain in vogue.

The overriding concern associated with all forms of food preservation is food safety. Regardless of whether the food involved in the process is high risk, such as meat and poultry, or low risk, as in fruit and vegetables, ineffective or faulty procedures during preparation and preservation can ultimately lead to contaminated food illness. It is less likely, however, that a pot of homemade jam will cause food poisoning, but an incorrectly cured ham could lead to severe or even fatal consequences.

Curing
This is a preservation and flavouring process, especially of meat or fish, by the addition of salt, (nitrates or nitrite and sugar. Curing works on the principle of food hydration (i.e. the removal of water) and is one of the earliest forms of food curing.

Some curing of foods involves additional forms of preservation; smoking after the food has been cured, for example smoked salmon, and drying, such as salt fish. One of the staple diets of Portugal is Bacalao (salted and dried cod).

With some foods all three methods of preservation are involved; salting, smoking and drying. Westphalia ham and Spanish chorizo sausage are produced using these curing methods.

Concerns of food contamination are with the contamination of foods with food poisoning bacteria. Without thorough knowledge and observance of correct curing procedures in producing food that is safe, bacteria levels will not have been reduced to safe levels and this will culminate in foods that are potentially poisonous to consume.

Pickling

This is the process of steeping fruits and vegetables in an acidic liquid or by fermentation in brine to prolong the shelf life.

Pickling food in vinegar, or quick pickling, is a relatively simple process of steeping prepared raw fruit or vegetables in a liquid consisting of water, vinegar, salt sugar and herbs and spices. In order for the pickling liquor to be effective, a pH level of about 4.5 or lower is necessary. The pickles are then sealed in airtight jars ready for consumption, usually after a week.

Fermented or brined or better known in the United States as crock pickle, they rely on bacteria (lactobacillus) which are present on all fruit and vegetables. The bacteria live on the natural plant sugars, converting these to lactic acid and it is this which acts as the preservative, giving treated foods a distinctive sour taste. Good examples of this process are sauerkraut, kimchi and pickled dill cucumbers.

The process begins with immersing vegetables in a salt solution or brine which can also have the addition of flavourings such as herbs and spices. During the fermentation process it is important to ensure that the vegetables are totally submerged in the brine at all times and must not be allowed to become exposed to the air. Lacto bacillus are anaerobic (don't need oxygen to survive) microbes so will continue to thrive well in the brine and, during the pickling stage, produce lactic acid and carbon dioxide; it is the production of this gas which signifies that fermentation is taking place. Yeast, moulds and some spoilage bacteria are aerobic (need oxygen to survive) so, while they will not survive in the brine, they are happy to live and prosper on any vegetables above the surface of the pickling liquid, thus resulting in spoilage of the vegetables.

TIPS on pickling:
The key objective here is the exclusion of air/oxygen during the process. It is worthwhile doing some research on which containers are best suited to pickling food

1. Use produce that is as fresh as possible. Some fruits sold in supermarkets are coated with wax to protect them during transport

and storage and to reduce moisture loss by evaporation. This treatment can prevent the pickle solution diffusing into the food so these should be avoided if possible.
2. Clean fruit and vegetables well, removing any outer leaves or roots and, if not being left whole, cut into uniform pieces. When pickling cucumber, about 1cm of the flowering end must be cut off. This part contains an enzyme which causes cucumbers to become over-soft.
3. To remove excess water from vegetables, they should be treated with either dry salt or immersed in a salt water solution and left for 12 to 36 hours. This process helps to keep the vegetables crisper. Once the salting is complete the food item should be rinsed in cold water.
4. Use unrefined salt, such as sea salt, not iodised table salt which can also contain an anti-caking agent, and can lead to a cloudy pickle.
5. If the pickling liquid is too weak it will cause the pickles to become soft, but if the liquid is too concentrated the pickles will shrivel and become tough.
6. Alum (potassium alum) was used in earlier recipes to keep vegetables crisp, however because of concerns of using chemical additives, this practice has disappeared.
7. Use good quality vinegar (minimum 5% acidity). To prevent discolouration of cauliflower use white distilled vinegar. Malt and cider vinegars are also good for pickling purposes
8. Sterilise jars and lids in boiling water or a cool oven (130°C) for 15-20mins.
9. Ensure vegetables and fruit are completely submerged below the pickling liquid and make sure lids form an airtight seal. Store in a cool dry place.

Faults:
1. Cloudy brine: this can be due to using table salt instead of unrefined salt. Hard water can also cause clouding.
2. Discoloured: Mixing vegetables which have strong colours such as beetroot. Reaction of the acids in the brine with certain metals during fermentation, avoid using zinc, brass, copper, iron, aluminium or chipped enamelled containers and utensils. Contamination by moulds or yeast.
3. If vegetables that have become soft, slimy and bad smelling before fermentation has begun, they must be discarded.
4. A white film can occur on the surface of the brine, this is not a mould but kahm, a harmless yeast.
5. Dull or faded colours can be because of exposure to direct sunlight or the vegetables were not fresh and at their best condition before pickling.

Relishes and chutneys

These share similar characteristics to pickles, but pickles are usually preserved in a water/salt/ vinegar solution.

In general, relishes and chutneys can be cooked or uncooked, it depends upon the recipe and how long the item is expected to be kept for. Apart from the addition of flavourings, both of these condiments usually contain sugar and vinegar which add to their preservative qualities.

TIPS on making chutneys and relishes:
1. Always use good quality ingredients and for consistency, always follow the same recipe. Experimenting with a chutney or relish recipe can be good fun and some great flavour combinations can be produced; make sure you have made a note, if the same recipe is to be repeated again.
2. Where the recipe is cooked, ensure that it is cooked for the correct length of time. Undercooking will result in too sharp a taste as not all the vinegar acid will have been driven off. A simple test is to press a spoonful of chutney or relish against the side of the saucepan, if the liquid runs off slowly, like syrup, then it is ready.
3. Overcooking results in more of a jam consistency, this is because too much moisture has been driven off.
4. As with all forms of preserves, all aspects of food hygiene must be observed. Sterilising of bottle, jars , lids and seals is crucial if contamination during bottling is to be avoided
5. Chutneys and relishes do improve with age and many do not fully develop flavours until after a few weeks.

Flavoured oils and vinegars

These condiments are easy to prepare and cost a fraction of the price that readymade varieties are sold for in shops and supermarkets.

To make flavoured oils, in most cases, it is simply a matter of marinating the flavouring (herb, spice, fruit, flowers or nuts) in the oil or vinegar for a few days. This is particularly true when using dried herbs and spices.

Oils flavoured with fresh herbs, however, need further consideration, as they can become contaminated with food poisoning bacteria already present on the herb. Because of the high acidity of vinegars, however, this is less of a concern.

Fresh herbs grown in the soil, are contaminated with bacteria; clostridium botulinum in particular. This type of bacteria is classed as an anaerobe which means it prefers to live in an oxygen free atmosphere, the sort of ideal environment bottled oil provides and, like any other food items, fresh herbs contain water, which also supports bacteria growth.

Commercially produced flavoured oils contain additives, such as acids to make oils safe and prolong their shelf life.

There are many books and websites on the internet that provide recipes for making these condiments. Some recipes suggest heating the herb and oil in a saucepan for a few minutes and then bottling. This is by far the safest way to ensure that most bacteria, especially clostridium, are destroyed.

TIPS for bottling fresh herb oils
1. Most dried and fresh herbs and spices can be used to infuse oils and this includes: chillies, garlic, lemon grass and ginger.
2. Always sanitise bottles and containers used for storing oils.
3. Use herbs that are very fresh and remove any discoloured or damaged stalks and leaves.
4. Use oils with neutral flavours: use sunflower, canola or rapeseed if the flavour of the herb is to be predominant, olive oil can also be used but gives a distinct flavour.
5. Wash herbs well, dry and bruise slightly to allow flavours to be released more quickly, nuts can be chopped or coarsely ground.
6. HOT-infused oils: Place herbs, nuts or spices in a saucepan with the desired oil and heat to 140°C and hold for about 10 mins. Cool and pour into airtight sterilised bottles or containers and seal.
7. Herbs can be left in the oil or strained off before bottling.
8. Ensure herbs are submerged below the oil line.
9. These oils can be safely stored for a few months in a cool place away from sunlight, but should be stored under refrigeration once opened and consumed with two weeks.

Freshly made herb oils (cold infused) especially with 'soft' herbs such as basil, parsley, tarragon and dill, can be made with little prior preparation, albeit treated the same as any salad item; washed and lightly dried. They should, however, be consumed immediately or stored for no more than three days in a refrigerator.

Flavoured vinegar recipes, as with oils can be found in abundance in cookery books and on the internet. Not only herbs and spices lend themselves well to pickling but also do some fruits.

Recipes vary in there method, but usually the vinegar is either added whilst hot or cold. More importantly the type of vinegar chosen, will determine the final flavour; apple cider, white balsamic, rice wine, or white wine are ideal.

Infusion times vary and are dependent upon the herb, spice or fruit being used, though the average time is about two weeks. Raspberries, redcurrant, cherries, damson, blackcurrant and lavender all make good flavoured vinegars.

Drying
This method involves removal of water by evaporation which inhibits the growth of bacteria. Like curing, it has been practiced since ancient times to preserve foods.

Types of drying are: air-drying, sun-drying, smoke-drying and freeze-drying. Commercially dried products like milk powder and instant mashed potato are either spray or drum dried.

Unfortunately the climate in the United Kingdom does not lend itself well to natural sun-drying of food, because there is insufficient continuous sunshine, warmth and low humidity even during the summer months.

The drying of fresh herbs and certain other foods is possible, given a warm dry atmosphere such as an airing cupboard or similar.

Electric food dehydrators have become popular and are now used by chefs and cooks to dry all manner of items from fresh herbs, fruits and vegetables to meringues, fruit leather and jerky.

Smoking
Is a process of flavouring, cooking or preserving food by exposing it to the smoke from burning or smouldering plant materials, usually wood. It is also a preservation method used in combination with other forms of food preservation i.e. salt curing or drying.

- Hot smoking: a process where the food is actually cooked and smoked at the same time and is generally shorter than that for cold smoking. Food is cooked thoroughly, at temperatures between 52°C and 85°C, enabling food spoilage and food poisoning bacteria to be destroyed.
- Cold smoking: entails a longer process, requiring specialist equipment. Because low temperatures are involved, the smoking chamber and the source of the smoke must be separate.
  Cold smoked salmon, for example, is smoked for 2 to 3 days at temperatures between 20° and 32°C and is always cured prior to smoking, which is why it tastes salty.

The characteristics of wood give smoke antimicrobial and antioxidant properties. When wood is burned the following reactions take place:
- Cellulose and hemicellulose molecules caramelise on burning which provides colour and sweet, flowery and fruity aromas.
- At very high temperature phenols are released by the wood and at lower temperatures carbonyls both adhere to food surface to give colour and flavour.

- Nitrogen dioxide & carbon monoxide- diffuse into food to give the distinctive smoke ring.
- Formaldehyde and acids adhere to the food, slowing bacterial growth by lowering the pH and, along with creosote, react with proteins to toughen the foods surface.

TIPS on smoking:
Different materials used for smoking produce differing intensities and flavours of smoke, so some experimentation is necessary to arrive at the desired amount of smokiness. Various hard woods are available: alder, apple, beech, cherry, hickory, maple, oak, and these are produced in dust, chip and chunk form. Some herbs and spices can also be added to the smoking material to give additional flavours.

Foods must be relatively dry before smoking in order for the chemicals in the smoke to adhere to the surface, during which the pellicle (firm, brown skin or film) is formed.

Salting food before smoking removes some of the water and makes the smoke flavour more profound, but the excess should be rinsed off before smoking.

With hot smoking, the wood, should be glowing/smouldering with no visible signs of black smoke, otherwise this can overpower the taste of the food.

Too much fat or liquid on the food can drip onto the fire and cause 'flare ups' which in turn produces black smoke, resulting in a tainted flavour.

When using smoking boxes, controlling the amount of smoke in the box is important, leaving the lid on for long periods can impart too much smoke to the food. In most cases the food smoked this way is not cooked through thoroughly and will need further cooking in the oven.

Jams and marmalades

This is purely an over view of jam and marmalade making in order to highlight the key points.

Home jam making is just one method of food preservation and is still one that is highly valued today, not only by the maker but also the consumer. It is a great way of preserving fruit and vegetables during a particular season where they are plentiful, are of prime quality and usually cheaper to buy. The resulting produce can therefore be enjoyed at any time of the year.

Fruit preserves, conserves and marmalades are not that difficult to make, but a number of factors need to be observed to be assured of success.

There is a profusion of recipes for jams, conserves, marmalades and jellies available through the usual sources and while their ingredient content may vary, the process or method for making them, remains very similar.

Principles

Levels of pectin and natural acids vary from fruit to fruit and seasons, variety and ripeness of the fruit also impact on the setting properties of the end product.

Fruits high in pectin: blackcurrants, cooking apples, gooseberries and damsons. Low pectin content fruits such as cherries, pears, rhubarb and strawberries are also made into jam but usually need additional pectin. Citrus fruits, such as oranges, lemons, limes and grapefruit contain good levels of pectin and therefore are ideal for making marmalade.

Where there is a requirement to make a jam using fruit with low pectin, then additional pectin from alternatives fruits must be added.

The process begins with boiling the fruit slowly; this breaks down the cell wall structures and frees the pectin allowing it to act as the setting agent when the fruit pulp cools. With low acidic fruits (strawberries, cherries and pears), it is necessary to add extra acid, this can be in the form of lemon juice, citric or tartaric acid.

Before the sugar is added, a pectin test can be carried out to establish if the fruit pulp has high enough pectin content to afford setting. If the resulting set is very soft, then the pulp should be simmered for a further length of time and retested. If, again, there is little improvement in the set then extra pectin should be added.

Sugar gives the jam body and flavour and enables setting by developing gel formation through attracting water and preventing the pectin chains from remaining separate. Most jam and marmalade recipes use a ratio of 1:1 fruit to sugar. A useful guideline is that the final sugar content of jam should be between 65-69%.

A further important aspect in ensuring a good set is the pH of the jam. Acids are important in aiding pectin setting. The ideal pH range of the jam should be between *2.8* and *3.3*. Inexpensive digital pH meters can be purchased and these are far more accurate than using traditional litmus paper tests.

The addition of the required amount of sugar coupled with the correct pH (acidity) and the required temperature, allows the pectin chains to bind to each other, forming a gel. The temperature of the 'setting point' needs to be accurate if the pectin is to set and this is within a very narrow margin of between 104 and 105°C. Once this has been established, the jam can be allowed to cool, and the gel network 'traps' the water content of the jam, leading to setting.

Jars for bottling the finished jam should have a tight fitting lid, so that air is excluded. Jars and lids must be sterilized before use; this is achieved by either boiling them for about ten minutes or placing in a cool oven at about 150°C and then filled while still hot with the hot jam. Lids should not be screwed on or tightened up until the contents are cold, some advocate placing waxed paper discs on the jam surface prior to covering with a lid. The purpose of the waxed disc is to make an additional seal. By placing the disc onto the surface of the jam whilst still hot, the wax melts forming a thin protective skin; this hardens when the jam is cool.

Pectin test:
Method 1

1. Take one teaspoon of boiling fruit juice/pulp and drop into a cold glass or cup, allow it to cool for a minute and then add three teaspoons of methylated spirit and swirl it around or gently shake.
2. If a large clot forms from the juice/pulp, adequate pectin for a good set has been extracted and the sugar may be added to the fruit and juice.
3. If there is only a medium amount of pectin, several small clots will form.
4. If there is very little pectin content it will break into small pieces. Place the fruit pulp back into a clean pan and gently simmer for about a further 10mins. Redo the pectin test. If the result is similar additional pectin will need to be added.

Method 2 (wrinkle test)
1. Place a small spoonful of jam/marmalade and pour it onto a plate or similar.
2. Put the plate in the freezer for about 5mins.
3. If the jam has formed a skin and wrinkles when pressed it is ready.

Faults and tips:
1. Soft fruits can be macerated overnight in sugar and a little lemon juice; this will help them stay firmer during boiling.
2. Scum forms during boiling: Don't remove this, when the jam has reached setting point stir in a small amount of butter, this will remix the scum back into the jam.
3. Cook to 104°C and hold for 1-2 mins. Do not allow the temperature to increase above this or the jam will begin to discolour.
4. Poor set: Insufficient pectin, this could be due to the type of fruit, the lack of ripeness or not cooking to the correct temperature. Too much or too little sugar can also be to blame.

Remove from the jar and gently reboil for about 3-5mins, do a pectin test, if set is firmer re-pot into a clean jar. If it is still too runny, add extra lemon juice or pectin.
5. Fruit or zest floats: Bottled too early, next time allow the preserve to cool for 10-15mins.and stir to distribute the fruit, and then bottle.
6. Mould or fermentation: Ineffective sterilising of jars, seals or lids. Ensure lids form an airtight seal, and fill jars fully; leaving a large gap between the lid and the surface of the jam can develop mould formation.
7. Looses set during storage: pectin set preserves can break down during prolonged storage. Unopened jars should be stored in a cool dark place, opened jars can be stored in the refrigerator to extend shelf life.

As in nearly all situations of food storage there are extrinsic factors contributing to food spoilage that can be controlled and thereby prolong the shelf life and quality of the food item:

Freezing and refrigeration
Freezing: food is stored between -12° and -18°C for period up to 1 year, depending on the food and the freezer. Bacterial growth and multiplication is slowed down and some types of bacteria are destroyed in small numbers.

Freezing does cause some damage to food, if stored incorrectly or for prolonged periods, although the damage does not make the food unsafe for consumption.

Refrigeration: storing food between 5°C and above 0°C for a period of a few hours to days, depending on the food type. It prolongs the shelf life and eating quality, but is not suitable for some fresh foods (i.e. bananas and pineapples).

TIPS on chilled food storage:
1. Be aware of use by dates, foods begin to deteriorate after these dates and can be a health hazard if consumed.
   Food requiring chilled storage should be kept at temperatures between 5C and 0°C to prevent bacterial growth and deterioration of food quality. The governments Food Standards Agency recommend that opened bottles of ketchups, sauces, dressings and condiments such as mustards should also be stored under refrigeration regardless of their high content of sugar, acid or salt.
2. Check the refrigerator temperature on a regular basis, at least once a week, it may be that the temperature is above the minimum

temperature of 5°C. The door seal should also be checked occasionally to make sure it is keeping the cold in and the warm out.
3. Don't overfill the refrigerator compartment, allow for air circulation around food.

Frozen storage:
1. Prolonged storage and food not adequately wrapped can become freezer burnt. This is noticeable by a change in colour and texture of the surface of the food. This happens as the moisture content of the food evaporates leaving a cardboard like appearance, it is perfectly harmless, but the texture and flavours are compromised. To avoid this wrap food well and store for minimum amount of time.

Confit

From French *'confire'* meaning to preserve, it generally refers to foods which are cooked for long periods at low temperature in fat or oil, then preserved in that fat.

The British equivalent to this method of food preservation is that of 'potting', where cooked fish or meat, which is usually minced or pureed, is placed in a container and then covered with a layer of fat', a popular example of this are potted beef and salmon.

Food items for confit can be salted then cooked before being canned; this is done if the contents are to be stored for any length of time.

Modern confits are prepared, not so much for their preservative qualities, but to add a contrast in texture and flavour to a particular dish (e.g. pan fried duck breast with leg confit). Game and poultry legs, pork belly, fruits and condiments such as garlic and onion can all be treated in this manner.

While cooking times and temperatures are adequate enough to render food safe from food spoilage and poisoning microbes, the final process of sealing the confit in its own fat must be the total exclusion of air. If air is not totally excluded then the food could become contaminated making it unsafe for consumption. The nature of confits requires that they should be stored under refrigeration or frozen.

Fruit curds (aka cheese)

Yet a further type of preserved food is fruit curds or cheeses. Lemon curd is perhaps the first flavour that springs to mind, but curds can be made from other fruits. They are readily available in shops, although are generally easy to prepare, requiring little cooking time. Most recipes are based on citrus fruits because their tart acidity balances the richness of the butter and egg yolk, though passion fruit, cherry, apricot, gooseberry, rhubarb or quince can be used.

Technically they are all gelled emulsions consisting of butter fat, sugar, egg (usually yolk) and fruit flavour in the form of juice, pulp or flavour essence, and many commercially manufactured curds contain pectin to stabilise the mixture.

The fruits natural acid (chiefly citric), in conjunction with the heating process denatures the egg proteins thus giving the curd its typical texture and mouth feel, as well as its gelling and setting properties.

Citric acid lowers the pH of the curd and by doing so, prevents the growth of many microorganisms such as Salmonella which are found in eggs.

The sugar content not only provides sweetness but raises the coagulation point of the egg proteins and protects them from premature coagulation with the citric acid.

Almost all recipes are similar in terms of ratios of ingredient; however some use only the yolk while others, the whole egg. There are also differing views on the method used to prepare curds. While it suggested in some recipes, that all ingredients are first mixed together then cooked gently in a pan over direct heat, others say to mix, and cook the egg, sugar and fruit juice/pulp together first, then incorporate the butter afterwards.

However as the fat content acts as a prevention against over denaturation of the egg proteins during heating, it is more likely that, without the fat content, overheating of the mixture could lead to an over cooked or 'scrambled' result, especially if this is done over open heat. The correct application of heat in preparing curds is thus important. Cooking the mixture in a bain-marie (container over simmering water) affords greater control of the amount of heat than cooking over direct heat, and therefore poses a lesser risk of overcooking the curd. The drawback of using the bain-marie method is that it is extremely slow, and therefore the confident cook will probably opt for the much quicker method of cooking with direct heat.

Whichever method is adopted, the end result appears to be very similar in consistency and texture, although there may be some variations in characteristics due to the type of fruit used.

Note:
Aluminium pan should not be used to prepare fruit curds as the natural fruit acids can react with the egg yolks and turn the mixture a green colour.

Chapter 10

FATS, CARBOHYDRATES AND PROTEINS – AN OVERVIEW

Fats and oils

Lipid is a term used when referring to fats, oils, sterols and waxes. They are a group of naturally occurring organic compounds and are made up of the same elements as carbohydrates (carbon, hydrogen and oxygen). The bonds involved in lipids are covalent non-polar, which means they are fat soluble and will not dissolve (immiscible) in water.

The simplest classification is that fats are solid at room temperature, while oils remain liquid. Further general differences are that fats are derived from animal sources and oils from plants, though coconut and palm oil are two exceptions.

Fats are made from building blocks called fatty acids of which there are saturated and unsaturated and these are derived from triglycerides and phospholipids.

In unsaturated fats two or more carbon atoms are joined together by double bonds but only one hydrogen and in the case of monounsaturated, just two carbon atoms are double bonded. Polyunsaturated have several pairs of carbon atoms double bonded. The difference between fats and oils is the way in which the molecular strands pack together. In saturates they pack tightly and so are solid at room temperature, the opposite exists with unsaturated so they tend to be liquid at room temperature.

Oxidation is one of the causes of rancidity of lipids, when fats are exposed to heat or light, the more unsaturated the fatty acid, the greater is its susceptibility to oxidative rancidity.

Hydrolysis, a further cause of rancidity in fats, is the reaction of a lipid with water resulting in the formation of free fatty acids and salts of free fatty acids i.e. in butter, the saturated fats undergo hydrolysis because of the water content thus imparting a undesirable rancid odour and taste especially if stored for a long period in warm conditions.

Saturated fats include butter, meat and cocoa butter.

Unsaturated fats are vegetable oils such as canola oil, olive oil, peanut oil and sunflower oil.

Polyunsaturated fats include soybean oil, corn oil and fatty fish such as mackerel and herring (omega 3 fish oils), linseed and walnut oil (omega 6 oils).

Margarine contains a mix of mono and polyunsaturated fats and like butter is water in fat emulsion; the fat content must be at least 10% but no more than 90%.

Hydrogenation of vegetable oils is a commercial process in which hydrogen molecules are added to liquid oils to reduce the number of double bonds. This hardens the fat and improves cooking properties; it also aids in the reduction of rancidity thus improving storage capabilities.

Carbohydrates

Sugars, starches, and non-starch polysaccharides (NSPs or fibre).

Carbohydrates are compounds (organic) made up of carbon, hydrogen and oxygen atoms. The number of the different atoms (elements) and their configuration denotes the nature of the carbohydrate (CHO). For instance the single sugars glucose and fructose (monosaccharides) are both molecules made up of six atoms carbon, twelve atoms of hydrogen and six oxygen atoms. However, their structures are slightly different from each other because of the formation of their component atoms.

Complex CHOs are made up of many molecules bonded together and form long chains or polymers. Starches and cellulose are both classed as complex or polysaccharides because they are made up of many glucose units linked/bonded together.

Heteropolysaccharides are similar to polysaccharides in that they consist of long chains of monosaccharides, the difference being that they are formed of at least two or more different types of single sugars, pectin being one example.

Sugar or saccharides are classed as single or monosaccharides, disaccharides and oligosaccharides.

Glucose, which is made from water and carbon dioxide during photosynthesis is present in many plants, it is a single sugar (monosaccharide) and is one of the main building block of disaccharides. Glucose exists in more than one form but the D–glucose is one that is naturally occurring in nature. D-glucose has two variants: Alpha-glucose is the building block of starch and beta-glucose that of cellulose.

A further monosaccharide is fructose which is found in fruits and vegetables. Galactose forms with glucose to make lactose or the sugar found in milk.

Disaccharides consist of two single sugars bonded together and these include sucrose (table sugar) a glucose molecule bonded to a fructose molecule; lactose (milk sugar) a molecule of glucose bonded to a molecule of galactose and maltose (malt sugar), two molecules of glucose bonded together.

Oligosaccharides consist of a small number of monosaccharide units usually between 2 and 10 linked together and are found in vegetables such as broccoli, leeks, asparagus, onions and chicory.

Natural sugars extracted from sugar cane and beet are exactly the same as sugar found in fruit and vegetables, i.e. glucose, fructose and sucrose. It is these intrinsic compounds which give ripened fruit its sweetness as the plant starch is converted to sugar during ripening.

What makes sugars differ from each other is due mainly to the manner in which they are processed and it is their individual characteristics that make one sugar more suitable for a culinary use than another.

Sugars perform many functional roles in cooking, baking and confectionary; they are also added to processed foods and drinks to provide additional sweetness.

Starch is the energy reserve found in many plant tubers and in the endosperm of seeds where it forms granules of different size and shapes, wheat for example consists of both large and small granules

Chemically, starches are polysaccharides that consist of repeating alpha-glucose units. Starch molecules have one of two molecular structures: a linear structure, known as amylose; and a branched structure, known as amylopectin. Amylose and amylopectin, both of which are starch polymers, associate through hydrogen bonding and arrange themselves radially in layers to form granules. All starches are made up of differing amounts of amylose and amylopectin and ratios vary among the different plant sources. For example, grains such as rice have higher amylose content than tuberous plants such as potatoes. In general the ratio of amylose to amylopectin in native starch is: 20-25% amylose and 75-80% amylopectin.

Non-starch polysaccharides

These are complex carbohydrates, other than starches, found in foods. They contribute fibre to the diet but are not digested and are non-caloric; cellulose, pectins and gums are examples of NSPs.

Cellulose is a polysaccharide of many beta-glucose units or molecules linked together. Cellulose gives plants structural support which is formed in the cell walls. Cooking, unlike starch, does not affect cellulose fibres and the bonds cannot be broken down by the human body so pass through the digestive tract as fibre.

Hemicellulose and pectin are also formed in the cell walls of the plant and are enmeshed within the cellulose structural matrix. Both these substances are softened with heat, which leads to the softening of fruits and vegetables during cooking. Both hemicellulose and pectin are partially soluble in water.

Proteins
Proteins are highly complex organic structures found in animals and plants. They are the main constituents of meat and fish flesh and are found in smaller amounts in grains, nuts, pulses, vegetables and fruits.

Proteins are the building blocks of cells- growth and repair and maintenance, they are large molecules made of hundreds or thousands of small building blocks called amino acids joined together by peptide linkages. There are over 20 amino acids in food. They form protein molecules by joining together a nitrogen of one amino acid and the carbon of another amino acid. This, with the combination of other properties: 'R' side chain, determines the ultimate shape of the protein and therefore its behaviour in groups or in reactions with other compounds.

Proteins provide structure in living organisms such as muscle, skin and bones and we utilize all of these to different degrees in cooking. Enzymes are also proteins. These are catalysts and are involved in speeding up chemical reactions that take place in living animal tissue and plants. They do not, however, become part of the end product of the chemical reaction.

Meat protein: Meat is the flesh of a mammal or bird that is eaten as food. It can be skeletal muscle or animal offal; organs such as liver, kidneys, heart and tongue.

Meat is mainly composed of water (75%), protein (20%) and fat (2.5%) plus small amounts of other substances such as minerals and vitamins.

Meat is classified as red or white, depending upon the levels of myoglobin (red pigment) present. Whilst lamb, mutton and beef are considered as red meat, there is some debate as to whether pork is one or the other.

The colour of meat of different parts of an animal is also dependent on the use of muscles; regular use of muscles in poultry produces leg meat which is always darker than breast meat because these muscles are used frequently i.e. to stand on or run. Game meat such as hare, venison and wild boar, is always dark in colour because these animals are continually active.

Myosin and actin are the two most important types of protein in muscle tissue or meat. They are both classed as myofibrils (long threads in contractile muscle) and make up about two thirds of proteins in fish and animals. Both these protein fibres (filaments) are involved in muscle contraction. In young animals they are thin, becoming thicker with ageing.

It is the application of heat during cooking which brings about changes in both muscle and connective tissue proteins, the result of which is either meat that is tough and dry or tender and moist.

Below shows the effects of a gradual increase in temperature upon meat proteins
- 40°C - raw, soft to touch, collagen intact.
- 50°C - first juices, protein myosin coagulates.
- 60°C - begins to shrink, loss of juices, increased toughness, 66-73°C actin denatures.
- 70°C – continues to shrink, little juices left, collagen begins to dissolve.

Collagen and gelatine

The main structural protein in connective tissue is found throughout an animal in varying amounts; muscle, ligaments, tendons, bones and skin all contain collagen. It could be said that collagen along with elastin holds an animal together.

At about 70°C collagen begins breaks down to form gelatine, though the protein elastin which is also a component of connective tissue does not break down. The breakdown of collagen is through hydrolysis (through heat and moisture), which results in the reduction of protein fibres into peptides; this process is not reversible.

Gelatine is also produced commercially from collagen. It is an effective hydrocolloid used as a gelling/setting agent, stabilizer and thickener in food processing and cookery. It has a setting point of 15°C but is firmest at 4°C and has a melting point of 35°C.

Meat tenderness:

The breed of animal, gender, pre-slaughter stress, pH value of meat muscle, post-slaughter storage and ageing are all factors that can affect the quality of meat.

Pre slaughter stress also, ultimately, impacts the quality of the meat. If an animal suffers stress before and during slaughter glycogen (type of glucose stored as energy in muscle) is used up and levels of lactic acid are reduced, resulting in poor quality meat. In stress free and rested animals, glycogen levels remain high. Post slaughter lactic acid is produced and this produces meat of good quality in terms of taste, tenderness, colour and keeping.

Stress can be brought on by a number of factors; noise, different surroundings, transportation, cold weather etc. The period prior to slaughter when stresses occur, manifest in differing characteristics of post slaughter meat.

During post mortem (after death), the muscle fibres contract as the lactic acid content increases. This is known as rigor mortis and this occurrence causes muscle to shorten. Muscle shortening gives rise to muscle toughening, thus making the meat less tender, this being particularly the case in young cattle.

Meat 'ageing' or 'hanging' is more directly applied to beef and game. Its purpose is to make meat more tender by allowing natural enzymes to break down connective tissue in the muscle. Secondly, through the reduction of moisture content in the meat, flavours become more concentrated.

Lamb and pork however are both inherently tender and are slaughtered while young animals, so are not submitted to the ageing process.

Fortunately, with modern breeding, cattle transportation and slaughter techniques the chances of buying a tough joint of meat today is small. Also, advancements in the storage and ageing processes of beef have meant a better quality of meat in terms of tenderness and flavour.

Fish protein

The buoyant environment of water makes fish almost weightless, so their muscles are very different from meat. Not unlike meat, their muscle fibres are joined together by connective tissue but in much smaller amounts. The blocks of muscle (myomers) form the shape of the fish and are connected to the skin and the backbone. Fish muscle fibres are much shorter than those of meat. They are also weaker because the collagen contains less structure-reinforcing proteins than meat. Fish tissue acts as an energy store, built up and broken down as opposed to an animal which is reinforced with age. The muscle structure of fish species varies, from delicate small muscle fibres (flakes) as in plaice and sole to large coarse fibres such as tuna. These differences are determined by the fish's lifestyle and environment.

Fish protein content is about 15 to 20% and the amino acid content compares similarly to the makeup of meat protein.

Connective tissue (myoceptum) begins to quickly break down between 50 and 55°C and turns to a soft jelly-like substance, forming those instantly recognisable flakes that can be seen in cooked fish. It is at this stage that fish is at its moistest. The whole process is very quick and that is why fish can be so easily over cooked.

There are similarities between the structure and composition of shellfish muscle (meat fibres) and connective tissue and that of wet fish (any fish excluding shellfish). Because of this likeness shell fish should be given the same considerations in terms of cooking times and temperatures, as those for wet fish.

Fish proteins are more sensitive to heat than meat. Below shows the effects of a gradual increase in temperature upon meat proteins:
- 20°C - soft flesh, connective tissue begins to weaken.
- 40°C - protein myosin begins to de-nature, juices begin to run.

- 50°C - protein coagulated, continues to shrink, max juices.
- 60°C – continues to shrink, little juices left, gelatine forms.
- 70°C – becomes stiff and dry.

Dairy proteins

Egg proteins: are globular, these tend to be round, that is they are folded and curled into a spherical shape i.e. albumin in eggs. Eggs contain at least thirteen different proteins in varying amounts and each one coagulates at a different temperature. The average protein content of a whole egg is about 13%

Below are the temperature ranges for egg protein coagulation or when the egg begins to cook:
- Pasteurisation - 57°C for 75mins or 61°C for 3.5mins.
- Egg white — begins at 60°C and becomes firm at 65°C
- Egg yolk — begins at 65°C and becomes firm at 70°C
- Whole egg — begins at 68°C

As heat is applied to eggs the protein bonds begin to break, in doing so the curled proteins unfurl and form new bonds with other proteins, water is also trapped during this process. Continued heating promotes further bonding and this results in an overcooked rubbery texture.

Eggs have many functional properties and it is these that are make them such a versatile commodity in cooking and bakery

Cheese protein

Acids and enzymes denature milk proteins in the process of cheese making. Bacteria cultures added to the milk feed on the lactose (milk sugar), during this lactic acid is produced which in turn curdles the milk or precipitates the casein micelles forming a soft curd. Rennet, an enzyme (from ruminants' stomach) is added which further denatures the milk proteins and further liquid is expelled as whey.

Flour protein

About 95% of all wheat produced is common wheat or bread wheat (Triticum Aestivum)and is the most commonly used of all cereal grain flours in baking and cooking.

Durum wheat flour (Triticum turgidum), also a popular wheat flour is used extensively for the preparation of many types of pasta, pizza and bread dough.

Choosing the right type of flour is particularly important in baking, and whilst flexibility is permitted in situations where the flour is to be used as a thickening agent and cooking in general, the correct choice of flour for specific baking needs must be observed.

All cereal flours contain proteins; wheat, barley, rye and oats, but not all contain gluten; cornflour, arrowroot, buckwheat, tapioca, millet, potato and bean flours are gluten free, unless contaminated during growing, harvesting, milling or storage.

Gluten
The main constituents of gluten are the proteins glutenin and gliadin; both of these are present in almost equal amounts. The solubility of gliadin makes it essential for the giving dough the ability to rise during baking.

It is this component of flour that is of the most important in terms of uses in bakery; high gluten content flour is necessary to produce bread dough, laminated products such as puff pastry croissants and Danish pastries. Without this gluten content many baked goods would not be as we have come to accept and expect. Contrary to this many baked staples like cakes, sponges, and scones are made from flours with lower gluten content which renders their texture much softer and shorter than bread.

When flour is mixed with water, gluten begins to form an elastic and plastic network of coiled proteins, the higher the gluten content of the flour the more elastic or the more resistant to stretching it becomes. It is the manual development of gluten with the entrapment of air and carbon dioxide bubbles from the fermenting yeast that gives bread dough its shape and texture. Starch, which is present in much larger amounts in flour also serves to give bread its volume as well as associating with the gluten structure to make the dough more tender and less elastic.

Fruit and Vegetable proteins
In the plant world, soya has the highest protein content of 13% whilst other edible plants contain far less.

In cooking, the protein content of vegetables is not an issue and is of little concern to most of us unless it is totally relied upon in the diet to provide the essential amino acids as is the case with vegetarians.

Suffice to say that cooking and changes in pH does impact on plant proteins in similar ways to animal protein; native conformation and biological activities are changed.

The main objectives of cooking vegetables are to soften the texture of the plant tissue in order to make them tenderer to eat and digest and in many cases more flavoursome. Starchy vegetables are also cooked to soften the plant cell fibres and to transform raw starch into a soluble gelatinised, digestible form e.g. potatoes, parsnips and squash

Nuts, seeds and pulses also contain varying amounts of proteins.

Chapter 11

KITCHEN EQUIPMENT, UTENSILS AND GADGETS

Kitchen gadgets are supposedly designed to make the cook's life easier, or at least to remove some of the routine drudgery. There must be a lot of people who buy these or receive them as presents only to find that, within a short period of time, their new kitchen aid has been relegated from pride of place on the work surface to the dark and hardly ventured realms of the back of a kitchen cupboard, only to be remembered during a spring clean or prior to a visit to a car boot sale or charity shop. Thus said, many items of cookware are, without doubt, indispensible to the cook. For those who are just starting out on purchasing kitchen equipment, or maybe wish to know a little more about the essentials and none essentials, the recommended and the not so recommended, read on……..

Knives and sharpeners

Knives come in all shapes and sizes, makes, and price range, so choosing a knife or knives can be a minefield. Many knives will perform a range of tasks, while others are designed more specifically for one purpose; a filleting knife has a very flexible blade and is used for filleting and skinning fish, whereas a boning knife has a short yet sturdy blade for boning out meat and poultry.

Spending a fortune on knives is unnecessary, so too is buying a whole range of different ones, the likelihood of which is many will be never or rarely used.

Buying a good quality knife doesn't mean it has to be expensive; there are many good reasonably priced brands available in cooks shops and on the various websites.

My advice is, when buying knives for the first time, shop around, it is important that you take the opportunity to handle different knife brands as they all differ. Buy one knife and if you feel comfortable using it then you will be more likely to buy another of the same make.

Branded, Japanese-Western style knives have become increasingly popular, and understandably so, many are beautifully made and more a work of art than a purposeful cutting tool. Again, prices vary greatly depending upon the materials used, for a top of the range knife with a walnut handle and Damask steel blade expect to pay a considerable amount of money.

But regardless of the amount of money spent on buying knives, the lack of ability to maintain and sharpen a knife correctly renders the value of any knife to little or of no use. What is crucial? The knowledge of how to use them safely and proficiently and to be able to sharpen them effectively.

On many occasions I have seen students and chefs spend a fortune on buying the latest and most expensive knives, yet they haven't mastered even the basic technique of how to sharpen a knife correctly.

What to look for:
1. You may already have a knife that is your favourite and this is probably because it feels good to hold and has a good blade. When choosing a new knife, hold it in your hand, it should feel comfortable. A knife should be looked upon as an extension of the arm. Some knife handles are not ergonomically designed; this is an important issue, especially if you spend a lot of time cooking.
2. It doesn't matter if the handle is made of plastic, metal, composite or wood although wooden handles do need a little more maintenance.
3. There are knives for specific jobs such as filleting fish, boning knife for meat and poultry, serrated knife for cutting bread, cakes etc.
4. Knives can be bought singularly or in sets, the advantage of buying knives individually is that you can decide which brand of knife suits you best and you don't end up with one or two knives that you don't like or are never used.
5. Ceramic knives became popular a few years ago, but they break easily when dropped or even when an amount of pressure is exerted on them, so their rise to fame is short lived.

The following is a list of knives and their general uses. There are other more specialised knives available but this basic selection is ideal for most jobs around the kitchen.
a. Cooks/chef's knife for slicing, shredding and chopping, and blade lengths vary from between 16cm and 26cm.
b. Vegetable or paring knives for general preparation work, with a blade about 8cm long.
c. Utility knife with a blade about 14cm in length, again for general preparation jobs.
d. Serrated edge knife (optional) average blade length of 24-30cm, cutting bread and cakes.
e. Carving knife (optional) average blade length between 22 and 30cm, carving/slicing cooked meat, some fish.
f. Palette knife, average length 24cm, not a knife as such; useful for spreading filling and cream on cakes/gateaux, lifting and turning food when shallow frying.

Knife parts:
Tang: end of the knife blade that extends into the handle
Butt: the end of the handle
Spine: the top part of the knife running from the handle to the tip of the knife
Edge: blade of the knife
Tip: point of the knife
Heel: the thickest part of the knife blade next to the handle
Bolster: the thick band of the blade between the handle and the heel. It protects the hand from the top part of the knife edge.

Sharpeners

Sharpening a knife correctly in order to produce a sharp working edge is crucial, but achieving this can be easier said than done. It is not so much as what implement is used to sharpen a knife, but the technique involved which many cooks and chefs find difficult to master and this usually culminates in a blunt or partially blunt knife.

Again, the types and range of knife sharpeners available can be daunting. There are basically two types used to sharpen knives:

Steels

These are generally used for quick sharpening or honing a blade, but for really blunt knives they need to be sharpened on wet stones. Steels, as you would imagine, are made from hardened steel and are graded form coarse to smooth. There are also ceramic and diamond encrusted sharpening sticks available.

Regardless of type, they all perform a similar role; sharpen knives. I have used all types throughout my career and never really favoured one over the other, although diamond sharpeners I found disappointing in that they didn't last as long as the manufacturers guarantee.

Stones (wet stones, whetstones)

The only real way to successfully renew the edge on a knife blade is with the use of a whetstone. They are called whetstones because water is used during the sharpening process. Like knives sharpening stones come in many guises, not only in the materials they are made from but also cost.

Without going into too much detail, stones are available in natural and manmade materials. Natural stones are more expensive but produce a higher quality knife edge finish. Belgium Coticule and Blue whetstones are examples of good quality sharpening stones. In choosing a suitable whetstone, the grit (grain) concentration is perhaps the most important feature. Grain content range from 200 to over 8,000; low numbers indicate a very coarse stone and are extremely abrasive, at the opposite end stones with very high grain content are very smooth.

The general consensus is that stones between 700 and 1200 grain are an ideal choice for knife sharpening with a minimum size stone of 17x70cm. Combination stones, consisting of two differing grains bonded together, are also a good investment.

It is important to have some knowhow when it comes to sharpening a knife. A sharp knife means safer, faster and more accurate cutting. Cuts to fingers are less likely because less pressure is required with a sharp knife than with a blunt one. If you are new to knife sharpening, use an inexpensive one to practice on until the correct technique is acquired. Finally, there are some useful websites that give practical advice on buying and sharpening knives.

Electric sharpeners should be avoided, they remove far more metal from a knife and if used regularly the knife blade will be much narrower and the balance will be compromised.

Chopping boards
I was brought up with wooden chopping boards both at home and while working in the catering industry. Granted the condition of some of the wooden boards I came across during my time was in many cases appalling and they should have been disposed of there and then. Sometime during the 1960s someone invented the plastic board made from polyethylene, its marketing selling point was that it was easier to clean and therefore more sanitary. This claim has been questioned on several occasions by research studies ('Nordic Wood Project-Wood in Food' and the University of Michigan to name but two). The counter claims are that plastic-type chopping boards are no more hygienic to use than wooden chopping boards used under similar conditions. Out of all the wooden boards tested during these studies, oak wood proved to be the most hygienic and this was due primarily to natural bactericidal polyphenol substances present in the wood.

At the end of the day, it really depends on how well either of these cutting surfaces are treated and how they are looked after in terms of cleaning and sanitising. It is an accepted fact that wooden chopping boards are kinder to knife edges, allowing knives to stay sharp for longer than alternative surfaces such as plastic or glass.

Pans
The choice of pan/pans is dependent upon the quantities, type and method of cooking involved. But I have provided some general points on choosing and using pans to suit different requirements:

Traditional tinned copper pans, whilst look fantastic when polished, are impractical for the domestic kitchen. Though very good at conducting heat, they are very heavy and are not suited to high temperature cooking, such as stir-frying, because of the low melting point (232°C) of the tin lining.

Bare copper pan surfaces exposed to ingredients that are alkaline or acidic are reactive and should not be used as they can give food a metallic taste. There are, however, some good quality bonded dual metal pans, constructed of copper and stainless steel, that are very efficient and can be used on most cooking surfaces, they are far more durable and are non-reactive with alkaline or acidic foods. The down side is they need a little more maintenance if they are to look good.

Cast iron cookware is durable, but needs regular seasoning, or many foods will stick, especially when shallow-frying or searing. Non-enamelled cast-iron is reactive with some acidic foods, and rusts easily if not dried thoroughly.

Aluminium is a good conductor of heat, unfortunately pans made from this material damage easily and like cast-iron are reactive with acidic foods. However anodized aluminium pans are a good choice as they are stronger than traditional aluminium pans and are not reactive with foods.

Non-stick pans such as Teflon coating:
There is growing concern about the safety of using such cookware and much research has been carried out recently to establish the validity of these concerns. The main worry is the ability of non-stick materials to break down due to excessive heat and in the process giving off toxic chemical emissions.

The consensus at present is that this cookware is safe providing that temperatures above 260°C are NOT exceeded. Guidelines also suggest that any pans whose non-stick coating is damaged or scratched should not be used.

For further information regarding choice of cook ware: www.goodhousekeeping.co.uk/institute/product-reviews/buying-guides/how-to-buy-the-best-pots-and-pans

Graters
'Microplane' graters/zesters are by far the best product on the market. They are manufactured in a range to suit various jobs from fine for grating to citrus fruit zest to coarse for grating cheese or hard fruit and vegetables.

Peppermills
Mills that have metal grinding mechanisms last much longer than those constructed of nylon. Porsche make a very good mill, if a little pricey.

Baking mats and moulds
Silicone mats and moulds are, in many ways, now the preferred material for all things baking. They are a little more expensive than the traditional tin variety, but have similar advantages to metal non-stick bake ware; they do not need greasing prior to use, they bake products evenly, will not rust and cleaning is very simple and, because of their flexibility, they allow for easy removal of items from the mould. Because silicone moulds are a little flimsy, they need the support of a metal baking tray.

Temperature probes
A very useful kitchen aid, they take the guess work out of establishing temperatures of foods during cooking. They are inexpensive, easy to use, highly accurate and easy to maintain.

Combination liquidiser-cooker, soup maker, all-in-one cooker processor
These are sold using various descriptions, but the advantage of these electrical gadgets is that two and more processes can be done in the same appliance: cooking, blending, mixing, mincing, whipping and liquidising.

Stick-blenders *(hand held liquidisers)*
Are a good investment, they are good at liquidising small amounts of liquids quickly, such as soups and sauces.

Digital scales
A must for every kitchen especially for baking, they are far more accurate than the old counter balance type.

pH meter *(acid/alkaline)*
Very useful for the avid jam and marmalade maker.

Jam/sugar thermometer
Most kitchens where preserves are made on a regular basis will have one of these, and some are also useful for measuring the temperatures of the various stages of sugar boiling.

Smoking gun
These have gained popularity, with occasional appearances on TV cookery programmes. Their principle is simple; they deliver small amounts of cold smoke to food.

Shaped like a gun, the chosen wood dust is loaded into the chamber where it is then lit, a small fan blows the wood smoke along a flexible hose into a dome which is positioned over the food. The dome is left in place for a determined period of time, thus giving the food the desired intensity and flavour of smoke flavour. These however are not suitable for large scale cold smoking.

Water baths and thermal circulators
Used as an integral piece of equipment in 'sous vide' cooking, there is really nothing technical about how these devices work; water baths are nothing more than thermostatically controlled water tanks, thermal circulators do the same job but also stir the water around to ensure consistency of heat throughout the water.

Smaller sized water baths have been designed to suit the domestic market and, while there operation is easy enough, the overall principle of cooking food 'sous vide' is somewhat complex. An understanding and knowledge of the processes involved is necessary if foods cooked by this method are to be prepared safely and not pose a health threat to the consumer.

Vacuum packers
These are now manufactured with the domestic cook in mind. These compact table top machines operate by removing air from special plastic food grade bags and then heat sealing them so they remain airtight.

They are a handy tool in a kitchen arsenal, especially for those who do a lot of freezing, but are also good for packaging food for refrigeration. The removal of air means that vacuum packed foods can be stored for longer and if they remain sealed, they are less lightly to become contaminated. Raw foods are vacuum packed prior to cooking by sous vide in a water bath and cooked foods can also be reheated in the bags.

Induction hobs
Work on an electromagnetic induction principle, rather than radiant heat, as is the case of ceramic hobs. There has been much advancement since the early days of their development in the seventies and while still more expensive than traditional cooking appliances, have now become a little more affordable.

Induction tops have the advantage of heating cookware faster (up to 50%) and distribute heat more evenly than conventional cookers. They are also more accurate in terms of temperature control. Induction hobs are very energy efficient, up to 70% more than conventional gas and electric, as they only work when contact is made with the cookware; so pan on energy on, pan off, energy off.

Disadvantages are that aluminium, copper, glass and some stainless steel cookware cannot be used on them. However, some stainless steel cookware is induction capable and cast iron pans work well.

Warning: induction cookers should not be operated by people who have medical devices such as pacemakers or insulin pumps, electromagnetism emitted from these appliances can interfere with their function.

Many kitchens have a number of utensils that are essential for the preparation and cooking of food, and many dishes and meals could not be prepared and cooked without them. There are also the countless so called labour saving devices and gadgets; garlic peelers and crushers, herb choppers, onion choppers, avocado and banana slicers, asparagus peelers to name but a few, many of which I am not convinced actually do save the cook that much more time. All I can say is, why not just use a trusty knife?

And finally, if you're looking for a new utensil or a piece of kitchen equipment, don't forget about charity shops, you can pick up something for a fraction of the retail cost. More importantly, any electrical equipment they sell must be PAT tested; this also applies to care boot sales, but I am sure not many people are aware of that.

Chapter 12

Food safety and hygiene

Every now and then we read or hear about incidents or outbreaks of food poisoning associated with a food or meal consumed at a restaurant, café, take away or hotel, and on rare occasions the culprit is a shop. It is estimated that there are, in fact, more than one million cases of food poisoning each year in the UK, and this figure is probably far greater if those that go unreported are also taken in to account.

In all aspects of the food industry, employees who handle food must have food safety training at a level which is relevant to their job role. Whilst a recognised qualification is not compulsory many food workers actually are qualified and a food handler or establishment can be prosecuted if found guilty of breaching Food safety regulations. For the cook at home, no such requirement exists, so those involved in cooking, whether for family, friends, relations etc, can freely prepare and cook food which may not be as 'wholesome' as they may think, in fact the number of reported food poisoning cases of illness occurring in the home gives good reason for concern. Recent reports suggest that up to 30% of all reported food borne illness is caused by dinning at home rather than out.

In view of this, I thought it may be useful to highlight some of the important aspects of food safety, especially in the home environment.

Food safety is about prevention, preventing food from being contaminated, storing food safely, preparing and cooking food to make it safe to eat, because when unsound food is eaten, it is too late.

Bacteria and some viruses are the biggest cause of food- borne related sickness and some are more responsible than others. I am sure the reader has heard about Campylobacter, E.Coli and Salmonella at some time. These pathogenic bacteria are present on many foods and in varying numbers. Raw meat and fish and vegetables are contaminated with large numbers and therefore have the potential to cause harm, conversely, cooked foods contain very little if any, and therefore are not a concern unless they later become contaminated.

Viruses are different to bacteria in that they need living tissue on which to survive (bacteria don't) so these tend to be present in seafood and infected food handlers.

It is the control or reduction of these microbes that forms the crux of 'food safety'.

The four key concepts of food safety are:
- A. Food storage
- B. Food preparation
- C. Cooking
- D. Cleaning

A. FOOD STORAGE
The "Danger Zone"

This is a nationally recognised temperature scale and its purpose is to easily show safe and unsafe temperatures for storing raw and cooked food.

The scale or 'zone' ranges from 5°c up to 63°C. Between these temperatures, food poisoning microbes grow and multiply best, the optimum temperature for growth and reproduction is around 37°C (human body temperature). When raw or cooked food is held in this zone, bacteria present on the food can grow and multiply. Food stored under refrigeration therefore, must be kept at a maximum of 5°C or ideally, slightly lower. If cooked food is to be held hot for any length of time, then it must be kept at a minimum of 63°C.

It is important to remember that while heat kills most bacteria and viruses chilling and freezing does not. Microbe growth and reproduction is merely slowed down or halted, only to resume when temperatures are more favourable.

To summarise; storing foods below 5°C slows down both food spoilage and food poisoning bacteria, at above 5°C bacteria start to grow and multiply, and this continues as the temperature rises. At 63°C and above, many food poisoning microbes are destroyed. The correct storage temperature of foods hot or cold is therefore crucial.

Foods can be categorised as 'high risk' and 'low risk'. High risk foods are those that considerable amounts of moisture; this includes raw and cooked meats, poultry, fish, and dairy products. Leftover cooked foods can also become potential food hazards, gravies, custard, and cooked meats can all be susceptible to recontamination. Foods in this category should be stored under refrigeration or frozen. Low risk foods such as bread, biscuits, and cereals; dried goods such as pasta, rice and nuts can be safely stored in an ambient environment.

The three types of food storage are:
- A. Ambient is normally taken to mean room temperature that is within a range of between 15°C and 25°C. However further conditions can also include; dry, well-ventilated, and out of direct sunlight. This is ideal for storing un-opened bottles, tins and all dry goods.
- B. Refrigerated storage is more crucial as not only does storing foods at the correct temperature prolongs shelf life, but it also reduces the growth of bacteria, in particular on raw foods such as meat, poultry

and fish. Foods should be stored at a temperature of 5°C or below, though ideally the closer to 1°C the better. This raises an important point; many fridges however are not fitted with thermometers but usually with a dial with a numerical scale of 0 to 5. Whilst we know that turning the dial one way or the other, decreases or increases the fridge temperature there is no clear way of determining the actual working temperature of the cabinet. This important issue can be easily resolved by using a refrigerator thermometer; these are readily available and are cheap to buy. Site the thermometer towards the back and top of the fridge compartment and check the temperature on a regular basis; you can then adjust the temperature dial accordingly.

Raw meats and fish should also be stored at the lowest part of the fridge to avoid dripping onto cooked foods. Cover all foods to prevent cross contamination. Air should be allowed to circulate around a fridge compartment, so food should not be packed too tightly, as opposed to frozen storage where freezers should be packed well; this improves the efficiency of the freezer.

C. Frozen food should be ideally stored at -18°C or below in order to maintain the quality and safety of the food. Many domestic freezers actually operate at temperatures lower than this.

Summary:
i. Check fridge and freezer temperature on a regular basis:
Fridge= 1-5°C, Freezer = minus 18°C (though many freezers operate at lower temperatures which allows foods to be stored for a longer time). Where a refrigerator is not 'frost- free', it will be necessary to defrost occasionally so that the compartment can be cleaned. Regular defrosting, especially when there is a thick build up of ice, will help the refrigerator run more efficiently.
ii. All foods should be covered before putting into the fridge.
iii. Do NOT put hot food into a fridge or freezer; it will increase its internal temperature.
iv. Raw meat, poultry and fish should be stored at the lowest part of the fridge.
v. Left over foods should be consumed or discarded after three days.
vi. Wipe out the refrigerator with a surface sanitizer regularly.
vii. Use by dates are provided for a reason, equally as important is to store food at the correct temperature indicated on the packaging.

B. FOOD PREPARATION

'Cross-contamination' of cooked with raw food can easily happen during food preparation, raw meat and vegetables contain high levels of bacteria.

Cross contamination can happen through the use of equipment, contact with work surfaces, handling and storage.

1. Equipment and utensils such as knives and chopping boards can transfer bacteria to cooked foods if not cleaned thoroughly after preparing raw meat, fish or vegetables. Kitchen work surfaces and chopping boards not thoroughly washed after food preparation can be contaminated with bacteria from raw foods. If possible, set aside a chopping board solely for the use of preparing raw foods, this will also help to reduce the chances of cross contamination.
2. Hands are another vehicle for cross contamination, so regular washing of hands is good practice, especially after handling raw foods, handling waste, blowing the nose, and using the toilet. Any cuts and sores should be covered with a waterproof dressing or plaster.
3. Dish cloths, when used to wipe down work surfaces after preparing raw meat, fish and vegetables should be changed or sanitized straight away. Boiling the dishcloth or washing it the washing machine are effective ways to kill any bacteria present. Disposable clothes such as 'J cloths' are even better.
4. Tea towels are used for drying utensils and pots and pans, the same cloth that is used to dry hands can also become contaminated with microbes, so regular changing of tea towels is essential.
5. Meat and poultry, in particular, should never be washed, splashing water from washing spreads bacteria onto hands, work surfaces, clothing and utensils.
6. Soil contains bacteria; excessive soil from home grown vegetables should be removed before bringing into the kitchen. All vegetables should be washed before peeling and washed again before cooking.
7. Almost all foods come in outer packaging, which in many cases has been exposed to all forms of possible contamination. This, therefore, should be removed before placing foods in the fridge or freezer.
8. Frozen food, especially meat, fish and poultry, should be thoroughly de-frosted before cooking. This should be done by placing the food in a tray on the bottom of the fridge, any melting ice can be collected in the tray, thereby reducing contamination.

C. COOKING

Apart from cooking food to make it easier to eat or more digestible, food is cooked to make it safe. Cooking food kills almost all bacteria and virus, and this is why reaching the correct temperature and for the appropriate length of time is important.

All raw meats can carry harmful bacteria on the surface, and it is this part of the meat that is exposed to heat first, fortunately this results in nearly all bacteria being destroyed. This is partly why beef joints and steak can be served rare or under done. The inner bulk part of uncut meat is not contaminated, and it is only when the meat or poultry is cut, boned, chopped or minced, or has undergone other similar methods of preparation that the bacteria are then combined with the flesh of the meat or poultry. Beef burgers are a good example of meat that can be contaminated throughout with bacteria.

While visual appearance of the surface allows us to decide whether food is cooked and therefore safe to eat, establishing the core temperature of foods is not as easy and is dependent on the food that is being cooked, the method involved and length of cooking time. Roasted poultry can, for example, be deemed cooked when the juices running out of the bird don't contain any signs of blood (i.e. they run clear).

Thorough defrosting of frozen meat, in particular poultry is also vital, as partially frozen areas of a bird can mean that the meat does not reach a high enough temperature to destroy bacteria. In situations such as these the use of a thermometer guarantees accurate temperature measurement. Digital temperature probes are inexpensive and easy to use, they are very accurate and most read degrees in centigrade and Fahrenheit. They also require little maintenance except for a wipe with a sanitised cloth before and after use. Probes can be used at any time during the cooking process, but care should be taken not to puncture roasted meats too often as too allow juices to be lost.

Probes are also very useful for testing the internal temperature of reheated foods. Even a small dish of lasagne or cottage pie can take a surprising length of time to heat through thoroughly in an oven, especially if taken straight from the fridge or freezer.

Depending upon the size and thickness of the food, there can be a difference of up to $30°C$ or more between the edges and the centre. By using a probe the food can be tested to ensure it reaches the minimum core temperature of $75°C$ recommended for reheated foods, it also prevents serving cold or luke warm food.

(See temperatures for roasting meats in Chapter 1 Dry Methods of Cooking)

D. CLEANING

Another crucial aspect of ensuring food safety is maintaining cleanliness in and around the kitchen area.

The purpose of cleaning is to remove food particles, grease and dirt, and, equally as important, to kill harmful microbes such as bacteria and viruses.

Wipe and clean as you go; surfaces and equipment that come in contact with raw foods, can become contaminated. Chopping boards, knives and hands must be washed thoroughly before moving on to other tasks, in particular if preparing cooked food. Chopping boards are particularly effective at harbouring bacteria, food lodged in cracks and grooves caused by cutting and chopping can support bacterial growth, so scrubbing and sanitising is essential.

Detergents are chemicals that dissolve grease and remove food debris from surfaces but most are not effective at killing bacteria.

Disinfectants will kill harmful microbes, but are not effective detergents. Disinfectants also tend to have strong odours and can taint food so are unsuitable for use on food surfaces or in close contact with foods. Very hot water 82°C and above makes a very effective disinfectant and, because of the high temperature, disinfected utensils and equipment etc can be left to air dry, rather than by using a tea towel which could cause recontamination.

Sanitizers are both detergents and disinfectants in one, so will clean and disinfect at the same time. However, sanitizers need to be in contact with the surface for a period of time for them to be effective.

To summarise:
The main causes of food poisoning are:
  a) Preparing food too far in advance and leaving it within the danger zone for long periods (over two hours). Leftover food is kept in a warm room and not chilled.
  b) Not cooking or reheating food to the correct temperature.
  c) Cross contamination of cooked food with microbes from raw foods, transferred by equipment, hands or in contact with each other.
  d) Not thawing frozen poultry sufficiently.

Some relevant facts
Campylobacter is the most common cause of food poisoning in the UK and affects about 280,000 consumers each year. It is found mainly in raw poultry. Fortunately, it is readily destroyed with thorough cooking. The next most common cause of bacterial food poisoning is caused by Clostridium perfringens, and is usually found in poorly prepared and cooked meat and poultry.

Norovirus is usually transmitted through contaminated food or water; it is also linked to infected seafood such as oysters.

Salmonella is the pathogen that causes the most hospital admissions, it is commonly found on meat, poultry and vegetables, and in eggs and milk.

E.Coli is found in the human gut and is therefore transmitted to foods through poor standards of hygiene.

Poultry is responsible for the highest number of food poisoning cases, with over 240,000 reported.

Vegetables, fruit, nuts and seeds, caused the second highest number of cases of illness, with beef and lamb next

It is interesting to note that food poisoning incidents and outbreaks peak during the Christmas period and summer months. There are a number of reasons for the rise at Christmas. More poultry is consumed at this time of the year than any other, turkey especially. A large percentage of people wash their turkeys, which increases the risk of spreading bacteria around kitchen surfaces. Furthermore frozen birds are not defrosted hygienically or adequately or they are not cooked to the correct temperature. Leftover foods are not refrigerated and left out in a warm atmosphere for too long.

Peaks during spring and summer months occur because the weather is generally warmer and more humid, so providing ideal conditions to support the rapid growth and multiplication of harmful bacteria.

Outside activities increase, such as barbecuing, picnics, fairs and fetes, where appropriate hygienic provision is lacking, such as refrigeration and sanitation.

Food allergies – just when you thought it was safe to eat!

In December 2014 new EU regulations came into force requiring all food outlets; restaurants, cafes, pubs, takeaways, delis, bakeries to provide clear information about the food allergens contained in their menu items.

The allergens prescribed in the new EU FIR 1169/2011 laws are:
1. Gluten containing cereals
2. Crustaceans
3. Molluscs
4. Fish
5. Peanuts
6. Lupin
7. Tree Nuts (such as walnut, hazelnut, almond etc.)
8. Soya
9. Eggs
10. Milk
11. Celery
12. Mustard
13. Sesame

14. Sulphur dioxide

Estimates show that nearly 50% of the UK population suffer from food intolerance and 2% of adults have been diagnosed with a food allergy.

According to 'Allergy UK' over one million people have a food allergy, about one in every hundred Briton is allergic to peanuts alone and this is just one of 14 foods identified by the new EU legislation as food allergy causative agents.

With the ever expanding use of new ingredients from around the world, modern recipes and cooking techniques and along with an ever increasing population, it is unfortunately inevitable that cases of food related allergies will continue to rise.

For further details visit: Food Standards Agency www.food.gov.uk

Temperature conversions

Celsius °	Fahrenheit°	Gas mark	Description
-18 C	- 0.4 F	-	Frozen storage
0 C	32 F	-	Freezing point water
5 C	40 F	-	Max. fridge temp
100 C	212 F	-	Boiling point water
110 C	225 F	¼	Very cool/slow oven
130 C	250 F	½	" "
140 C	275 F	1	Cool/slow oven
150 C	300 F	2	" "
160 C	325 F	3	Cool – moderate
180 C	350 F	4	Moderate
190 C	375 F	5	Moderate
200 C	400 F	6	Moderate – hot
220 C	425 F	7	Hot
230 C	450 F	8	Hot – very hot
250 C	480 F	9	Very hot
260 C	500 F	10	Extremely hot

Please note these are approximate conversion figures

RECIPES

Basic stock

makes about 2 litres stock

1k raw chicken carcass, beef bones or lamb bones
2 litres water
1 medium carrot, 1 leek, 1-2 sticks celery and 1 medium onion, all left whole
2 bay leaves
Sprig fresh thyme or level teaspoon dried
2 cloves garlic
10 peppercorns, crushed
Method:
1. For brown stock: place the carcasses or bones and vegetables in a roasting tray, drizzle with a little oil and roast until golden brown, turning them occasionally to brown evenly.
2. Place the carcasses or bones (roasted or not) into a pan and cover with the water.
3. Remove roasted vegetables and put aside. Swill out roasting pan with a little water and add to the bones.
4. Bring up to the boil and turn down heat to a simmer. It is important to remove any scum that forms on the surface, if not removed this will make the stock cloudy and taste a little bitter.
5. After about 1 hour add the vegetables and skim again when necessary. Add the herbs.
6. Continue skimming until no more scum is formed. Water will need to be added occasionally to replace loss through evaporation.
7. Cooking times: chicken stock = 2.5hrs, lamb = 4hours, beef = 6 hours It is important that the stock does not boil during the cooking period.
   Cooking times are dependent upon the size of bones, for smaller pieces of bones; cooking times may be reduced slightly.
8. Strain the stock and chill, keep refrigerated and use within three days or freeze.

Notes:
I. Vegetables with strong flavours such as parsnip, swede, artichoke and fennel should not be added, as they will overpower other flavours.

II. Potatoes should not be added as they will make stock cloudy.
III. Do not add salt to stocks, this is added later when using the stock in a recipe.
IV. Tomato peel and seeds, mushroom trimmings, cooked bones e.g. from roasts can be added to stocks.
V. For chicken and lamb stock rosemary and rosemary can be added.

Chicken stock

Raw chicken carcass and trimmings are ideal, with the inclusion of some leg meat to improve chicken flavour. Don't use the breast meat as this is too good and will work out expensive. Do not wash any raw chicken prior to use as this spreads food poisoning bacteria around the sink and adjacent areas. For brown stock sprinkle the chicken pieces with a little powdered milk (10g per 1kg chicken) before roasting, this will promote colouring (see Maillard reaction) and give the stock a more appealing pale golden brown colour. The vegetables should be peeled, washed and kept in large pieces, browning the vegetables by frying or roasting will add further colour to the stock, but too much browning of bones and vegetables can result in a stock that is too dark, as chicken stock should be a pale golden brown.

Consommé (basic recipe)

4 portions

200g minced beef/chicken/fish
1 egg white and shell
1 litre brown beef/chicken or white fish stock; must be COLD
100g (total weight) equal amounts of finely chopped or minced carrot, onion, leek and celery
20g tomato puree (except for fish stock)
Pinch thyme
Bay leaf
8 peppercorns, crushed
1 clove garlic, roughly chopped
Mushroom trimmings - optional
Pinch salt
Method:
1. Mix all ingredients together well, add the cold stock and mix well again.
2. Place in a pan on the heat and slowly bring to the simmer, stirring occasionally.
3. As the liquid nears simmering point, the solid ingredients will begin to from a crust or clarification on the top. Once this happens, stirring must stop altogether.
4. DO NOT allow to BOIL, simmer very gently for about 30-40 mins. If necessary, move the pan to the side of the heat source to enable gentle simmering. DO NOT STIR again.
5. Carefully remove from the heat, press a small ladle down the side of the crust/clarification and scoop out a ladleful at a time, straining it carefully through a muslin cloth.
6. Remove surface grease with kitchen paper, check seasoning, and reboil. Chilling the consommé solidifies any surface fat making it easier to remove.
7. A measure of sherry or Madeira may be added to the consommé.
8. Consommé should be kept chilled and consumed within three days, it also freezes well

For further information see Chapter 4 – Stock, Soups and Sauces

Potato and watercress soup (basic recipe)

serves 2

20g butter
50g onion, finely chopped
200g potato, peeled, roughly chopped
400ml vegetable stock
2bunches (about 100g) watercress, leaves picked from stalks, washed and roughly chopped seasoning.

1) Heat the butter in a small saucepan over a medium-low heat, add the onion and seat without colour. Add the potato, watercress stalks and stock, bring to the boil and simmer for about 30mins or until the vegetables are soft.
2) Meanwhile, prepare a large bowl of iced water. Bring a large pan of water to the boil and plunge in the watercress leaves to wilt (about 15 seconds), reserving a few leaves to garnish. Quickly remove and put into the bowl of iced-water (refresh).
3) Squeeze the cooled watercress out and add to the pan. Liquidise the soup well, pass through a sieve, and check seasoning. Reheat carefully, don't allow the soup to boil or stand on the heat for any length of time to retain the bright green colour.

NOTE: For broccoli soup, remove the flower heads and treat as the watercress leaves, using broccoli stalks instead of the potatoes

Cured and pan fried mackerel, apple and fennel salad, cucumber mayonnaise

serves 2-4

Ingredients:
cured mackerel:

1 tsp dill, chopped
½ tsp horseradish, grated
5ml fresh lemon juice
Pinch sea salt
Pinch sugar
2 small mackerel fillets, trimmed, pin boned and sliced
little oil

apple and fennel salad:
50g apple julienne
75g fennel bulb julienne
salt and freshly ground black pepper
Little oil for frying

¼ cucumber, cut into small dice
3 tsp mayonnaise
little lemon and lime juice
Little dill, chopped
35ml double cream
salt and freshly ground black pepper

Method:
1. To cure the mackerel, place the dill, horseradish, salt and sugar, lemon and lime juice into a bowl and blend together. Place one mackerel fillet onto a tray and pour the blended mixture over the top, sprinkle over a little oil. Leave to cure for two hours in the fridge.
2. For the cucumber and mayonnaise; place all ingredients into a bowl and mix together, check seasoning, refrigerate.
3. For the salad: mix the apple and fennel together, gently mix in dressing.
4. For the pan fried mackerel; cut one fillet in half, bring a little olive oil to up to heat in a frying pan and add the fillets skin side down, cook for about two minutes or until just cooked through.
5. To serve, spoon the fennel and apple salad onto the serving dishes, place the pan fried mackerel on top, arrange cured fillets around and finish with a little chopped dill.

Open seafood lasagne, English asparagus, Prosecco and dill sauce

serves 2-4

Fresh pasta dough
{
- 120g '00' flour
- 1 egg, 1 egg yolk
- 10ml olive oil
- Large pinch salt
- Olive oil
}

8 asparagus spears
10g Shallots, finely chopped
25g butter
16 mussels, cleaned- discard any mussels with open or damaged shells
4 fresh scallops, removed from shell and cleaned, cut into 1cm cubes
200g fresh salmon, cut into 1cm cubes
4 tiger or Mediterranean prawns, trimmed and cut in half
60ml Prosecco or dry white wine
Fresh parsley
Fresh dill, finely chopped
150ml double cream
Sea salt and mill pepper

Method:
Pasta dough:
1. Sieve the flour and salt into a basin, make a well. Beat the eggs with the oil and water and pour into the well.
2. Mix together well, turn out onto a clean work surface and knead well until the dough becomes silky and not sticky, this should take about 10mins. If the dough is still sticky, add a little more flour, too dry, add a little water.
3. Wrap in film and leave in a cool place for about 30mins.
4. Roll out the pasta through a pasta machine and cut out 4 x 100cm circles

Filling:
1. Place half shallots into a saucepan with the mussels and prawns, parsley stalks and half the wine, cover with a lid, bring to simmer until shells open, remove from heat. Remove mussels and prawns; decant cooking liquor, leaving gritty sediment behind
2. Cook the asparagus in boiling salted water for about 5mins, keep crisp, refresh in cold water and drain.

3. Lightly season salmon and sear quickly in a hot frying pan with a little oil, remove keep warm, repeat the process with the scallops. Remove excess fat, add the remainder of shallots and butter and sweat off, add remainder of wine, reduce, add the mussel liquor, add the cream, reduce to a sauce consistency and check seasoning, add the dill.
4. Place mussels and prawns in a buttered dish, cover and warm in a moderate oven.
5. In simmering salted water add the lasagne and cook to al dente, remove carefully and drain.
6. Place a little sauce in the bottom of a pre-heated serving dish and place a sheet of lasagne on top.
7. Place salmon on top and a couple of mussels, spoon over a little sauce followed by a further sheet of lasagne.
8. Place a large prawn, remainder of the salmon and a scallop on top followed by a final sheet of lasagne and a spoonful of sauce.

Garnish with the remainder of the fish, decorate with dill
Any fresh or frozen fish can be used in this dish e.g. tuna, plaice, sea bass, pollock, cockles

For tips on boiling pasta please see Chapter 2 Boiling and Poaching

Tagliatelli Aribiata

serves 2

120g tagliatelli pasta
20ml olive oil
50g onion, peeled, finely chopped
½ red chilli, finely chopped
1-2 cloves garlic, crushed
40ml red wine
½ tsp tomato puree
150g fresh vine tomatoes, cut in half and roughly chopped
Salt and freshly ground black pepper
1 tbsp extra virgin olive oil
3 fresh basil leaves, to serve

Method:
1. For the aribiata sauce, heat the oil in a frying pan over a medium heat. Sweat the onions and garlic for 3-4 minutes, or until softened.
2. Add the wine and reduce. Add the chilli, tomato puree and tomatoes and continue to cook for 5-6 minutes, or until the tomatoes have begun to collapse. Season to taste with salt and freshly ground black pepper.
3. Boil the pasta in boiling salted water for about 5-8mins, drain, and add to sauce.
4. Place into serving dishes, drizzle with oil and garnish with basil leaves.
5. Accompany with freshly grated parmesan cheese.

Note; tinned plum tomatoes can be substituted for fresh.
For tips on boiling pasta please see Chapter 2 Boiling and Poaching

Paella

Serves 2

30ml olive oil
100g chorizo
4 pieces chicken, leg and breast
1 red pepper, skinned
50g onions, finely chopped
1 clove garlic, crushed
125g Valencia, Bomba, Bahia, Senia or Calasparra rice
250ml chicken stock
Small pinch saffron
100g squid rings-optional
150g fresh mussels, frozen will do
100g tomato, peeled, deseeded cut into small dice
1 bay leaf
100g prawns, large raw
50g frozen peas
Flat leaf parsley

Method:
1. Cut the chorizo into 1cm cubes and fry quickly in hot oil, remove from the pan.
2. Season the chicken and fry quickly in the same fat, remove and place with the chorizo.
3. Add the pepper, onion, garlic and rice to the oil, (a little more oil may be necessary) and sweat for 2-3min.
4. Add the saffron to the stock and bring to the boil, allow to infuse for 2-3 minutes. Add the stock to the rice and bring back to the boil, add the chicken and chorizo, cover and cook gently for about 10min stirring once or twice. Check seasoning.
5. Add the prawns, squid and mussels and cook for a further 3-4min with a lid or cover. Add the peas and cook for a further 2-3min.
6. Finish with chopped parsley

Note: it is important not to overcook the rice

For further information on rice grains see Chapter 2 Methods of Cooking – Boiling

Steak with Thai green risotto, shitake mushrooms

(serves 2)

2 fillet, rump or sirloin steaks, trimmed	Risotto:
30ml soy sauce	25g shopped shallots
40ml rice wine or white wine	15ml vegetable oil
5g sugar	50g Arborio rice
1 clove garlic, crushed	100ml chicken or vegetable stock
1tsp grated or finely chopped ginger	¼ lime zest and juice
Large pinch ground fennel	1 tsp Thai green curry paste
50ml vegetable of beef stock	65ml coconut cream
½ tsp corn flour	small sprig fresh coriander
100g shitake mushrooms	

Method:
1. Mix the soy sauce, wine, sugar, garlic, ginger, fennel and corn flour together, place in steaks and marinade for about 2 hours.
2. Risotto: sweat the shallots in butter without colour, add the rice, lime zest and curry paste.
3. Add the stock a ladleful at a time, stirring continuously and simmering gently until nearly all the stock has been absorbed. Add ginger, lime juice and coconut cream, finish with chopped coriander leaves, and check seasoning.
4. Heat a frying pan, add a little oil, and fry the shitake mushroom for 2 to 3mins, remove from the pan and keep warm.
5. Remove the steaks from the marinade and in the same pan fry the steaks to your liking, remove and pour the marinade into the pan bring to boil and reduce to a thin sauce consistency.
6. To serve: place a spoonful of risotto on warm serving dishes, place a steak on top, garnish with shitake mushroom, drizzle sauce around, decorate with coriander leaves.

For tips on cooking risotto see Chapter 2 Moist methods of Cooking – Boiling

Strawberry parfait

400ml double cream
100g of caster sugar
60ml of water
6 egg yolks
20mls water, crème de fraises or white wine
250ml strawberry purée

1. Whip the cream to soft peak and refrigerate.
2. Place the sugar and water in a saucepan and bring to the boil, continue to simmer until a temperature of 121°C is reached, remove from the heat.
3. Whisk the egg yolks in a bowl with the water, wine or strawberry liqueur until pale and frothy.
4. While the sugar syrup is still hot, slowly pour it onto the egg yolk mixture, whisking continually; the mixture should become thicker and increase in volume.
5. Once cool, fold in the strawberry purée and then fold in the whipped cream until the mixture is smooth and even.
6. Place in a suitable mould lined with cling film and freeze for about 24 hours to set.
7. To serve: Parfaits freeze very hard, so they need to be tempered before serving; remove from the freezer and allow to soften slightly (not melt), this will depend upon the temperature of the frozen parfait and the room and the size or thickness e.g. individual portions will soften quicker than a large block of parfait.

Make sure the serving dish is cold. Arrange accompaniments, garnishes and decoration on the plate first and finally place on the parfait.

For further information about parfaits please see Chapter 5 Desserts and Puddings

Amaretto panna cotta, mixed berry compote

serves four

450ml	double
80ml	milk
45g	sugar
8g	gelatine
55ml	Amaretto liqueur
40g	blueberries
40g	cranberries
40g	blueberries
25g	raspberries
50g	sugar
1	lemon-juice

Method:

1. Soak the gelatine leaves in cold water until soft.
2. Pour the cream and milk into a saucepan and bring to the simmer.
3. Squeeze the water from the gelatine.
4. Add the gelatine and sugar to the milk and cream, stir until dissolved.
5. Add the Amaretto and allow to cool, strain into four individual serving dishes.
6. Put the berries, sugar and lemon juice into a saucepan and heat gently.
7. Gently poach the berries until soft but still whole, cool and chill.
8. When the panna cotta is set, spoon the berry compote on top.
9. Serve with tuile or shortbread biscuits.

For tips on making panna cotta please see Chapter 5 – Desserts and Puddings

Basic Ice cream recipe – vanilla

1 vanilla pod
420g double cream
320ml skimmed milk
50g milk powder
140g sugar
78g egg yolk

Method:
1. Split the vanilla pod length ways and remove seeds.
2. Mix the milk powder with the milk and cream until dissolved. Add the vanilla pod and seeds.
3. Heat the liquid in a saucepan and simmer gently for about 5mins.
4. Place the egg yolks and sugar into a bowl and whisk until the mixture becomes pale white.
5. Whisk the boiled milk and cream onto the egg yolk mix, stir well and return to a clean pan.
6. Return to the heat and stir continually until the liquid reaches a temperature of 72°C and begins to thicken slightly. Hold this temperature for about 10mins, trying not to go above 72°C, when done remove from the heat.
7. Place the bowl into ice water and stir the mix, cooling the mixture down quickly.
8. Cover the mixture and refrigerate for about 24 hours.
9. Strain the mixture through a sieve, the mixture is now ready for churning.
10. Place ice cream containers in the freezer in preparation for transferring the ice cream from the machine to the freezer.

Lemon curd ice cream:

400g lemon curd
1 lemon, finely grated zest

Method:
1. Soften the lemon curd by beating with a spatula or whisk and add to the ice cream mixture, continue mixing until there are no lumps, if necessary strain through a sieve.
2. The mixture is now ready for churning.

Short crust pastry:

200g plain soft flour
50g margarine or butter (not chilled)
50g lard or vegetable fat (not chilled)
Pinch salt
35 - 50ml tablespoons cold water

Method:
1. Sieve the flour and salt. Mix both fats together; do not allow them to become too soft. This can be done using a spatula or in an electric mixer.
2. Rub the fat into the flour (by hand or by using a mixer) until a sandy texture is achieved. It is important to make sure there are no lumps of fat.
3. Make a well in the centre add nearly all the water, gently mix to a smooth paste, if still a little dry add the remainder of the water. Do NOT over handle.
4. Wrap in film and refrigerate for 30mins. before use.

Sugar (sweet) paste

1 egg
50g caster sugar
125g butter or ½ butter and ½ margarine
200g plain flour with a pinch salt

Method:
1. To make rubbing-in easier, make sure the fat is not too cold/firm.
2. Using the finger tips or paddle on a food mixer rub the fat into the salt and flour until an even sandy texture, making sure there are no lumps of fat.
3. Add the sugar to the flour.
4. Beat the egg a little and add to the flour and sugar. Gently mix in until smooth, do NOT over handle. The pastry will seem very soft, so it will need refrigerating to firm up.
5. Wrap in cling film and chill well before use.
6. If the pastry will become very firm, remove from the fried about 20mins. before using.
7. Ensure rolling surface and pin have a thin dredging of flour. Handle little as possible; the heat from hands can may the pastry very soft and difficult to roll.

Note: for a richer [pastry use egg yolks instead of whole eggs.

Choux pastry

250ml/½ pt
Pinch salt and sugar
100g/4ozs butter or margarine or half and half
125g/5ozs strong flour, sifted
3-4 eggs, beaten

Method:
1. In a saucepan, bring water, salt, sugar and fat to the boil; simmer until all the fat has melted. Remove from the heat.
2. Add the flour all at once to the water and beat vigorously to a smooth texture. It may appear lumpy at first, but will become smooth with continual beating.
3. Return to the heat and keep mixing until the mixture leaves the sides of the pan, remove from the heat and allow to cool, although it does not have to be cold. The eggs must not be added while the mix is still hot, if this happens, the eggs will begin to cook before they can be incorporated into the flour mixture.
4. Mix in the beaten eggs gradually until smooth.
5. The mixture should be quite firm, if it is too soft, it may be difficult to pipe out.

Nut brittle

100g sugar
100g nuts: mixed or single type, coarsely chopped or sliced

Method:
1. Put the sugar into a saucepan and place onto a low heat.
2. Shake the pan a little as it starts to melt. The sugar starts to clump together, and then goes slightly translucent, then it will start to colour.
3. Once it reaches between 149 to 154°C remove from heat and add nuts and quickly stir in.
4. Pour onto a silicone mat or baking tray lined with greaseproof paper. Leave to cool.
5. Once cold it will have set as hard as rock. Break into shards.

Caramels

180 ml double cream
1/2 teaspoon vanilla bean paste
160g light corn or golden syrup
200g granulated sugar
60 g salted butter, cut into pieces, at room temperature

Method:
1. Line a 9-inch (23 cm) shallow baking sheet with foil and lightly oil.
2. Heat the cream with 30g of the butter in a small saucepan with the vanilla and 1/4 teaspoon sea salt until the mixture begins to boil. Remove from heat, cover, and keep warm.
3. In a heavy duty saucepan heat the corn or golden syrup, with the sugar, and cook, stirring gently, ensuring the sugar melts smoothly. Stir occasionally to maintain an even temperature throughout the mix.
4. Cook until the syrup reaches 155°C.
5. Check the temperature.
6. Turn off the heat and stir in the warm cream mixture, until smooth.
7. Return to the heat and cook the mixture to 127°C.
8. Remove the pan from the heat, remove the thermometer, and stir in the pieces of butter, until melted and the mixture smooth.
9. Pour the mixture into the prepared tin. After about ten minutes, sprinkle the sea salt over the top. Set on a cool rack and let cool completely. Once cool, lift out the foil with the caramel, peel away the foil, and slice the bar of caramel with a long, sharp knife into squares or rectangles.

Fudge

100g caster sugar
60g evaporated milk
18g butter
100g golden syrup
Little vanilla

Method:
1. Line an 8cm square tin with baking paper.
2. Combine all the ingredients in a large saucepan. Place over a low heat and gently melt the ingredients together.
3. When the mixture is smooth, increase the heat and cook until the mixture reaches 116°C on a sugar thermometer.
4. Once the temperature is reached, remove from the heat and leave to cool slightly before beating with a wooden spoon until it loses its shine.
5. Pour into the lined tin and place in the fridge to set for at least 1 hour. Once set, cut into squares to serve.

Chocolate brownie

200g dark chocolate
100g unsalted butter, very soft
250g caster sugar
4 large free range eggs, beaten to mix
1tsp vanilla essence or vanilla bean paste
60g plain flour
60g cocoa powder
15cm square brownie tin or baking tin greased and base-lined
Method:
1. Heat the oven to 180C, gas 4. Break up the dark chocolate. Put into a heatproof bowl and melt gently in a pan over simmering water, making sure the water doesn't touch the base of the bowl. Remove the bowl from the heat and leave to cool until needed.
2. Put the butter and sugar into the bowl of a food mixer and beat until fluffy. Gradually beat in the eggs, beating well after each addition. Beat in the vanilla essence or paste.
3. Spoon the cooled melted chocolate onto the mixture then mix in thoroughly. Sift the flour and cocoa powder onto the mixture and gently stir in.
4. When completely combined, spoon the mixture into the prepared tin and spread evenly.
5. Bake in the heated oven for about 20 mins. until firm to the touch but still a bit fudgy. The chocolate will continue to cook slightly for a few minutes after coming out of the oven.
6. Remove the tin from the oven and set on a wire cooling rack. Leave the chocolate brownies to cool completely before cutting into pieces.

For tips on making brownies please see Chapter 6 – Pastry and baked Goods

Fondue

Ingredients:
150g Gruyere, Emmental or Jarlsberg cheese or a combination of
3g corn flour
½ clove garlic
80ml white wine
3ml lemon juice
Pinch English mustard powder
Pinch of nutmeg

The use of a double boiler or bain-marie allows for better control of the heat source so that the fondue will never get hot enough to break. The crucial point with fondue is keeping the temperature low once the cheese is added. The perfect temperature range is between 65 and 66^{0}C which is the melting point of the cheeses

Method:
1. Rub the inside of the pan with a cut clove of garlic. Add the wine and heat gently.
2. Grate the cheese into a bowl; add the corn flour and mustard powder.
3. Add the corn flour coated cheese shreds a handful at a time, mixing it into the hot wine, allowing the cheese to melt before adding more.
4. Once all the cheese is added, the consistency should be a smooth sauce.
5. Add the lemon juice. Check the seasoning.
6. Serve with toasted croutons, savoury crackers or sticks of crisp vegetables.

Fondue will thicken and set rapidly as it begins to cool just a little. If it is too hot the proteins will press into each other, causing the fondue to break; too cool and it will thicken and set. If the fondue becomes too stiff, add a little wine, stirring in until the fondue has loosened.

Wine is important, it goes beyond just flavour: the natural tartaric acid in wine prevents the cheese's casein proteins from clumping together and turning the fondue into a stringy, broken mix.

Citric acid has the same effect as tartaric acid; lemon juice helps the fondue's stability, because, and like wine, it also adds flavour. (Citric acid is one of the original key ingredients in Kraft cheese slices). Use a dry white wine, the more acidic the wine the better.

Passion fruit curd

180ml passion fruit juice
4 medium egg yolks
155g caster sugar
125g butter

The amount of juice from a fresh passion fruit varies slightly, but on average about 30mls of liquid including the seeds and 15mls strained. Passion fruit pulp/puree can also be bought from specialist suppliers; this is advisable if larger amounts are required. Some recipes include pectin or corn flour which help to stabilise the mixture during keeping, though neither are essential

Method:
1. In a stainless steel or glass bowl, mix the egg yolks, passion fruit juice and sugar together.
2. When the sugar has dissolved, strain to remove the chalazae and any shell.
3. Place the bowl over a pan of simmering water and stir.
4. When the mixture is warm, add the butter in small chunks and continue stirring.
5. Check the temperature now and again with a probe, continue heating and stirring until a temperature of 82°C has been reached, at this temperature the curd should be quite thick. Remove from the heat; continue to stir for a further two or three minutes, as the mixture cools the curd will become thicker.
6. While still warm and viscous, pour into sterilised jar, when cold cover tightly with lids.

For further tips and advice on making curds please see Chapter 9 on Food Preservation

Basic Cold set vanilla cheese cake recipe

For both cheesecakes use a 18cm loose bottom/spring form cake tin or a deep flan ring lined with greaseproof paper.

250g of mascarpone
250g of cream cheese
200ml of whipping cream
1 lemon juice
1 vanilla pod or 8g vanilla bean paste
75g of caster sugar
2 leaves gelatine

1. Soak the gelatine leaves in cold water until soft.
2. Mix the cream cheese, mascarpone and vanilla together until smooth, and then fold in the cream.
3. Squeeze out the gelatine and place in a saucepan with the lemon juice.
4. Heat the lemon and gelatine until melted, add the sugar and stir until dissolved.
5. Pour the gelatine mix into the cream cheese mixture and mix well.
6. Pour the cheese cake mix on top of the biscuit base, level with the back of a spoon or palette knife. Refrigerate for at least twelve hours.

Biscuit base:
200g digestive biscuits
75g of butter

Method:
1. Break the biscuits into a crumb. Place into a plastic bag and break with a rolling pin or blitz in a food processor.
2. Melt the butter in a saucepan, add the biscuit crumb and mix until combined.
3. Place into the base of the lined flan ring or dish, pressing down to form an even and firm base, chill well.

Basic baked vanilla cheesecake recipe (starch less)

175g of caster sugar
3 eggs, lightly beaten

2 tsp vanilla bean paste
675g of cream cheese
100ml of double cream

Method:
1. Bake the biscuit base in the oven at 180°C for about 10mins. or until light golden brown.
2. In a bowl, beat the cream cheese, vanilla and sugar together; add the cream and the eggs.
3. Gently mix until smooth, do not beat to vigorously, too much air will spoil the surface of the cheesecake.
4. Pour the mixture onto the biscuit base and cook at 160°C for about 45mins. The top should still have a slight wobble, with a little colouring around the edge.
5. Turn the oven off but leave the cheese cake inside with the door open for about 30mins.
6. Allow to go cold before removing from the tin.

For tips on making cheesecakes please see Chapter 5 Desserts and Puddings.

Orange marmalade

makes about 6 x 450g jars
1k oranges
1 lemon
2 litres water
1.5k granulated sugar

Method:
Preparation: sterilise jars/bottle: wash thoroughly, rinse and place on a tray in the oven at about 160°C for about 15mins, alternately boil jars and lids for about 20mins.
1. Wash the fruit, remove some or all of the zest/peel, and cut into strips to a thickness of your liking. Make sure the peel is cut into a uniform shape. Some recipes suggest soaking the peel overnight to soften before boiling.
2. Cut the fruit in half. Drape a large piece of muslin of a pan or bowl and squeeze the juice into it. Add the water and orange peel into a pan with the juice.
3. Put all the squeezed orange halves and pips into the muslin and tie up into a loose bag.
4. Place the muslin bag into the saucepan with the water, juice and peel and bring to the boil.
5. Continue to simmer until the peel is soft and translucent. This can take between about forty and ninety minutes, depending upon the thickness of the peel. The liquid should also be reduced by about half at this stage.
6. Remove the muslin bag, and when cool, squeeze the juice into the pan. It is crucial that as much liquid as possible is squeezed out, as this contains large amounts of pectin.
7. A pectin test can be carried out now to establish if the pectin levels are high enough to set the marmalade.
8. Add the sugar and stir until it is totally dissolved, before gradually bringing up to a rolling boil.
9. Remove any scum that appears and continue to boil and cook to 104^0C.
10. Pour into prepared jars, and fill to 3mm below the rim, cover immediately with waxed paper, place the lids on when cold.

NOTES:

Use Seville oranges where possible, they are packed with pectin. When using juicing oranges it may be necessary to add additional pectin or use jam sugar (contains pectin).

Granulated sugar gives a clearer, brighter finish to marmalade; brown sugars and treacle give a darker colour.

Warming the sugar before adding to the fruit juice, reduces the boiling time which results in a more natural orange colour and flavour.

For clearer, translucent preserves, the scum must be removed from the surface of the marmalade as it continues to boil.

Adding a small amount of butter at the end of the cooking time helps re-introduce the scum to the marmalade.

Bottling: the jars and marmalade should be at the same temperature.

Levels of pectin vary from fruit to fruit. Citrus fruit; blackberries, apples, redcurrants, have high pectin levels. Others are low in pectin such as strawberries, lemon juice is added to strawberry jam to help the set. Pectin test:

This will determine pectin content and setting quality
1. Take one teaspoon of clear boiling fruit juice/pulp and drop into a cold glass or cup, allow it to cool for a minute and then add three teaspoons of methylated spirit and swirl it around or gently shake.
2. If the juice/pulp forms a large clot, then there is sufficient pectin to produce a good set. The sugar may be added.
3. If there is only a medium amount of pectin, several small clots will form. It is unlikely that this will form a good set. Reboil the juice for a further 10mins.
4. If there is very little pectin content it will break into small pieces. Place the fruit pulp back into a clean pan and gently simmer for about a further 10mins. Redo the pectin test. If the result is similar additional pectin will need to be added.

For further information on making preserves please see Chapter 9 on Food preservation

Resources and useful contacts

BOOKS

McGee, H. *On Food and Cooking* – Hodder & Stoughton 2004
(Considered by many as the 'bible' of food science and related topics, great for reference)

Gu *Gu Chocolate Cookbook* – Harper Collins 2012

Hermé, *Pierre Chocolate desserts* 2002

Davies, J *Hammonds Cooking Explained* – Longman 4th edition 1997

MAFF, *Home Preservation of Fruit and Vegetables* – HMSO 1989

WEBSITES

Meat and dairy

Agriculture and Horticulture Development Board
www.ahdb.org.uk
All matters relating to farming and food production. Information about meat and butchery, learning resources

Meat and fish marinating, grilling, smoking and barbecuing
www.amazingribs.com

Seafood

Seafish
www.seafish.co.uk
All matters related to fish and shell fish. Types, purchasing, fish cuts, recipes

Marine Stewardship Council
www.msc.org
Regulatory body for the UK fishing industry

Chocolate
www.callebaut.com/uken/homepage
All things chocolate: history, types chocolate, recipes and techniques

Gluten free information

Gf Jules
www.gfjules.com

Coeliac organisation
www.coeliac.org.uk/home

Cooking equipment suppliers

Nisbets
www.nisbets.co.uk/Catering/Online
Good for all sorts of small and large kitchen/dinning equipment mail order

Continental Catering Supplies
www.chefs.net
Kitchen and dining equipment

Specialised ingredient suppliers
MSK
www.msk-ingredients.com
Highly specialised ingredient and some equipment suppliers

Sous Chef
www.souschef.co.uk
Non-specialised and specialised ingredient suppliers

Chefs' techniques
Chefs steps
www.chefsteps.com
Very professional website and forum covering cooking techniques, access to lots of recipes

General
Good Housekeeping Institute
www.goodhousekeeping.co.uk/institute

Serious eats
www.seriouseats.com
Ingredients, techniques, cuisines

Seasoned advice
www.cooking.stackexchange.com
Question/answer site for professional chefs and amateur cooks

Food safety/hygiene

Food Standards Agency
www.food.gov.uk

GLOSSARY

Acid: opposite to a base. Any class of compounds that form hydrogen ions when dissolved in water. On a pH scale acids are identified as 6 to 0, 6 being very slightly acidic, 0 very acidic.
Natural occurring acids are: citric (citrus fruits), malic (apples), acetic (vinegar), tartaric (grapes), and lactic (yoghurt). All foods are classed as being acidic, neutral or base.
Actin: a protein found in meat filaments and with myosin is involved in contraction and relaxation of muscles.
Agar: substance obtained from algae used as a setting agent. It is used as a vegetarian option to gelatine and because of its high gel melting point is ideal for use in hot climates.
To incorporate agar it must be boiled for about two minutes and will begin to form a gel at about 32°C and will remain firm up to about 65°C, however to melt the formed gel it must be reheated to 85°C. Agar can be purchased in powder, flakes and liquid form, though liquid is the easier to use Agar is also used in the manufacture of ice cream and is used in the brewing industry
Al dente: (Italian meaning 'to the tooth') describes how rice and pasta dishes are cooked so that the centre is still quite firm.
Alkali: opposite of an acid. An aqueous solution with a pH value between 7 and 13 on the pH scale.
Allergen (food): any food or drink which causes an allergic reaction in a person and can be life threatening. Food intolerance is a sensitivity to food or drink causing some reactions, not normally life threatening.
Amylose: one of two components that make up starch (with amylopectin). It is a strait chained polymer of a-glucose units. It is found in lesser amounts than amylopectin in starch foods such rice and potatoes and is more soluble in water than amylopectin
Amylopectin: one of two components that make up starch (with amylose). It forms branched chain polymer units. It is found in greater amounts than amylose in starch foods such as rice and potatoes and is less soluble in water than amylose
Arrowroot: the dried ground starch from the rhizome of the Maranta genus of plants, used as a thickener. It is less starchy than corn flour and gives a light texture, neutral flavour and sets almost clear on forming a gel. Ideal for thickening fruit sauces
Aspic: a savoury jelly made from meat, fish or vegetable stock, fortified with gelatine. It was used extensively in cold buffet work in the past to coat various items in order to prevent drying out and produce an appetising shine. Aspic was also used in conjunction with chaud-froid (hot-cold);

velouté sauce which was used as a coating for cold buffet items as a 'canvas' for decoration before finishing with aspic

Classic dishes include – poached eggs in aspic (Oeufs en gelée)

Au gratin: of food sprinkled with grated cheese or breadcrumbs and browned in the oven or under a grill e.g cauliflower au gratin

Bake blind: prebaking of pastry cases prior to be filled with a filling not requiring cooking e.g fruit flan. The walls and base of the raw pastry are usually supported in its baking case or tin with the use of baking beans

Baking powder: a chemical form of aerating agent used in cake and scone making. Consists of bi-carbonate (base) of soda and cream of tartare or other acids. When mixed with water and exposed to heat give off carbon dioxide. Double acting baking powder functions when cold and hot, most powders today are 'slow acting'

Bard: to lay strips of fat or fat bacon over poultry and game bird breasts prior to roasting to keep the meat moist.

Base: refers to a substance that is alkaline not acid

Baste: to pour liquid or melted fat over meat as it cooks-roasts to add moisture

Béchamel: or basic white sauce, one of Escoffier's 'mother sauces', used as a foundation for sauces such as: cheese (Mornay), parsley, mustard, egg and anchovy. Thin, less viscous béchamel can be added to a soup in place of cream

Betalains: class of water soluble red and yellow plant pigments, they are found in flowers and roots. The colour of beetroot and chard is an example of a betalains

Blanching: a) partially cooking vegetables (particularly green) in boiling water or steam to denature enzyme activity which can otherwise lead to colour loss.

b) Cooking deep fried potatoes (French fries) at low temperatures without colour, they are then plunged into hotter fat to crisp and add colour

Bloom: final shape of bread after proving and before baking. To soak or soften gelatine in cold water. Bloom test: test to measure strength of gelatine or a gel

Bouquet garni: a bunch of herbs; usually parsley, thyme, bay leaf and peppercorns enclosed in a leek leaf or muslin bag for flavouring stocks, soups, stews or braises

Bromelain: enzyme found in pineapples. It has proteolytic properties i.e breaks down proteins and is used as a meat tenderiser

Carbon dioxide (CO_2): a colourless and odourless gas and makes up a small percentage of earth's atmosphere. In cooking is produced by yeast during the baking and brewing processes, it is also produced by a chemical reaction in baking powder. It acts as an aerating gas that makes cakes and bread rise **(leaven).**

Carbohydrate (CHO): biological molecule. Includes sugars, starches, and cellulose

Carotenoids: fat soluble plant pigment giving fruit and vegetables yellow/orange colour

Cartouche: a) a piece of greased paper placed on top of and in contact with the surface of a sauce or soup to prevent skin formation
b) a piece of greased paper placed on top of food items to reduce evaporation e.g. on top of poached fruits

Catalyst: substance that increases the rate of a chemical reaction, without taking part in the reaction, i.e. enzymes

Cellulose: most abundant organic substance on earth, found in plants, shrubs and trees and forms the structure of plant cell walls. It is a polymer, forming straight chains of (100-1,000s) of glucose units linked by glycosidic bonds. In food and cooking terms it is 'dietary fibre'

Chlorophyll: is the most common and familiar pigment family found in plant stems and leaves and are an important component involved in plant photosynthesis. Chlorophyll gives green vegetables and fruits their colour, it is easily destroyed by heat and acids. When chlorophyll is heated the magnesium atom in the molecule is replaced by a hydrogen one, when this occurs, chlorophyll changes to pheophytin; the colour of the vegetable changes from bright green to olive-gray.
Cooking times therefore should be kept to a minimum and cooking water should be slightly base to avoid discolouration. Prolonged storage of green vegetables also results in a breakdown of the pigments

Citric acid: found in a number of fruits; oranges, limes, lemon and grapefruit. Used as a flavouring and preservative. Delays the onset of enzymatic browning in cut fruit and prevents crystallisation of sucrose

Civet (jugged hare): a classical French stew of furred game usually hare or rabbit

Coagulation: (of proteins when heated) interchangeable with 'denaturation'

Coalesce: in context of emulsion sauces: the consolidation of minute or small droplets of oil forming larger drops which happens when mayonnaise or hollandaise sauce curdles or splits

Collagen and elastin: proteins that make up connective tissue. They are present in tendons and ligaments; connecting muscle to bone and bone to bone respectively.
Connective tissue is found in larger amounts in aged meat and in the muscles of animals that have been used regularly during their life
Collagen breaks down during cooking and forms gelatine. Elastin, a highly elastic substance does not break down regardless of the amount of heat applied.

Colloid: a homogeneous substance consisting of dispersed, small or minute insoluble particles suspended throughout another substance. Gels, sols, and emulsions, where particles do not settle out are classed as colloids. Milk (fat globules suspended in water), whipped cream (foam- air in water) are good examples.

Conduction: a process where heat is transmitted directly through a substance by molecular friction. Heat is conducted along a metal pan handle causing it to get hot

Convection: the transmission of heat by circulation or movement of hotter area of a liquid or gas to a cooler area, this usually happens by heated areas rising and cooler ones sinking to replace them

Core temperature: internal temperature of foods. This should be taken at the thickest part of the meat or dish and in large volumes of cooked foods, probing should be done in three or four different places to obtain correct readings. Probing of refrigerated foods is good practice to ensure the correct storage temperature.

Cornflour: (corn starch) the dried starch obtained from corn (maize), it is used as a thickener for soups and sauces and can be added to batters to produce lighter textures, it is also used in the manufacture of corn syrup. Cornflour is incorporated into a soup or sauce by being mixed with a cold liquid (slurry) and then stirred into the boiling liquid

Dashi: a soup or stock made from various ingredients, including kombu (kelp), fermented tuna and fungi and originates from Japanese cuisine.

Deglacer: French culinary term meaning to swill the concentrated juices and sediment in a pan that meat or fish have been fried or roasted. This is usually done with alcohol such as wine, brandy or sherry, stock or cream depending on the intended sauce

Demi-glace: meaning half-glaze in classical French cuisine, rarely made or used today in its original form, now produced as convenience product in powder/granule. It was made by reducing equal quantities of brown beef or veal stock with espagnole by half and formed the foundation for many 'small brown sauces' such as Bordelaise, Chasseur, Piquant and Bercy.

Denature: as in proteins subjected to heat, acids, alcohol, alkali, or mechanical stress; involves the breaking down or altering of some protein structures and by doing so changes their native state whereby they become no longer functional; this process is not reversible.

Examples of protein denature: by mincing meat (mechanical stress), application of heat-cooking, addition of acid-ceviche (citric acid), addition of alkali- bcarbonate of soda to tenderise meat, alcohol – red wine in a marinade and enzyme action – during hanging of meat or the addition of fruit enzymes, from pineapple (bromelain) or pawpaw (papain) .

Dripping: saturated beef fat that has been rendered (melted) down and solidified on cooling. It has lost popularity in cooking because it is characteristically a saturated fat.

Drupe fruit: soft fruit containing one stone or pit e.g. peach, apricot, cherry, plum, damson, sloe.

Emulsifier: substance that enables and stabilises an emulsion i.e. prevents liquids from separating out e.g. oil and vinegar (water) in mayonnaise. Lecithin in egg yolk is an emulsifier. Lecithin extracted from soya is used extensively in the food industry as an emulsifier.

Emulsion: dispersion of minute droplets of one liquid in another in which it does not mix or dissolve e.g. mayonnaise, hollandaise, beurre blanc.

Espagnole (Spanish sauce): a basic brown meat sauce usually of beef or veal. It was used as a base for a numerous repertoire of 'small brown' sauces such as Madeira, bordelaise (red wine), chasseur, piquant. One of the 'mother sauces' created by Escoffier.

Estouffade: a brown meat stock or a brown meat braise in modern usage.

Flavour enhancer: food additives used to bring out the flavour in a wide range of foods without adding a flavour of their own. e.g. monosodium glutamate. Salt, though not an additive brings out the flavours of foods.

Freezer burn (by sublimation): refers to food being damaged by oxidation or dehydration and can be seen as discolouration and cardboard like texture of the food surface. Sublimation: transition of ice to a vapour without passing through the water stage

Fructose or fruit sugar: is a monosaccharide found in plants and when bonded to glucose forms the disaccharide sucrose (table sugar.

Ganache: a mixture of melted chocolate mixed with cream used. It can be used as a spread or filling for cakes and as a base for chocolate truffles, its consistency is determined by adjusting the ratio of chocolate to cream.

Gel: a solid or semi solid, jelly like substance that consists of a cross-linked system which gives the gel its structure.

Gelatine: the result of the breakdown of collagen (protein with elastin, found in connective tissue, skin ligaments, bones and meat that has been subjected to prolonged moist heat.

It is a hydrocolloid, used as a setting agent and used in jellies and cold desserts. Gelatine sets when cold at about 15°C and melts at between 25°C-40°C . Gelatine can be purchased in powder/granule or sheet/leaf form, though leaf gelatine is easier to use.

Glacé (vegetables): to cook vegetables in a minimum amount of water with sugar, salt and butter. As the vegetables cook the water is driven off, leaving a glaze of butter and sugar. Peas, beans, carrots, swede and turnips can be cooked by this method.

Glucose: simple sugar or monosaccharide and most important in human metabolism. Glucose exists in two forms of D-glucose and these constitute the building blocks of starch as alpha-glucose and cellulose as beta-glucose units.

Glutenin and gliadin: both are proteins found almost in equal amounts in wheat flour and are the main components of gluten. Strong flours such as bread and pasta contain higher amounts of gluten than soft or cake flours. The correct choice of flour is all important when used in baking and cookery

Gluten free: foods or food products that do not contain gluten or are contaminated with gluten. Gluten is one of 14 recognised food allergens introduced into legislation in the UK in December 2014, the legislation originates from the European parliament.

Gravlax (gravad lax): Nordic dish consisting of raw salmon (or other oily fish) cured in salt, sugar and dill. It is usually served sliced thinly as a starter or as part of a smorgasbord.

Guar gum: Is extracted from the seed of bean-like plant the Indian tree. It is used in food processing as an emulsifier and stabilizer. It has eight times the thickening power as cornstarch and is used as in baked goods to increase dough yield and improve texture and shelf life. Further uses include preventing syneresis in pastry fillings and as a binder for meat products.

Hemicellulose: related to cellulose but differs in that is made up of several different single sugars or monosaccharides. It forms shorter branched chains (500-3,000 sugar units) than cellulose, and like cellulose provides supporting material in the cell wal.

Hermetic: sealed or closed, airtight to prevent air entering or escaping a container.

Hydrocolloid: a substance that forms a gel in the presence of water. They remain as a 'sol' in liquid form and a 'gel' when solid. Gelatine is a very effective hydrocolloid. Savoury and fruit jellies are examples of this.

Hydrophobic and hydrophilic: hydrophobic meaning water (hydro) phobic (fearing). Hydrophilic: water loving. Emulsifiers have two facets, one attracted to water and the other to oil so they act as a bridge and hold two liquids together which otherwise would be immiscible; mayonnaise, hollandaise.

Immiscible: of liquids not capable of mixing together i.e. oil and water.

Jus: translated from French means juice. Mainly used to describe gravy or well reduced meat stock served as a sauce or gravy. e.g Jus rôti (roast gravy).

Kham: a type of aerobic yeast that thrives in the presence of lactic acid. It can form a white film on the surface of fermented vegetables during pickling, it is not harmful.

Knead: to work firmly with the hands, as in bread making to work the dough to develop the gluten.
Lard: saturated pork fat that has been rendered down (melted), used in cooking and as a shortener in pastry making.
Lactose or milk sugar, is a disaccharide (two sugars) of glucose and galactose.
Leaven: to cause to raise or rise as in cakes and bread with the action of yeast or baking powder.
Lecithin: a phospholipid found in animal and plants such as soya. Is capable of attracting both water and fatty substances and is therefore used as an emulsifier. Egg yolk used in mayonnaise and hollandaise sauce contains lecithin.
Legume: an edible plant pod enclosing a seed or seeds.
Lycopene: bright red fat soluble carotenoid pigments found in tomatoes, watermelon and papaya. Because of its water insolubility is stable in cooking.
Maillard reactions: a chemical reaction between amino acids and reducing sugars which gives food a distinctive brown colour during cooking at high temperatures.
Miso: Japanese seasoning made from fermented soy beans and other ingredients. Used in soups; mixed with dashi (broth/fish stock) to make miso soup, sauces and pickles.
Muslin: cotton fabric with a plain weave used for cheesecloth, filtering wine and port and consommé.
Myoglobin: oxygen carrying protein pigment found in muscle tissue responsible for giving meat its red colour. Prolonged storage or heat changes the meat to a grey colour, metmyoglobin is formed.
Myosin: protein fibre in meat and fish that works with **actin** in muscle contraction and relaxation.
Osmosis: diffusion of a liquid (water) through a semi permeable membrane from a solution of low concentration (more dilute) to a solution with high concentration (more concentrated) e.g brining (salting) meat and pickling vegetables.
Oxidative enzymatic browning: is a chemical reaction involving polyphenol oxidase, enzymes and oxygen which creates brown pigments (melainins) in fruits and vegetables. The reaction occurs when fruit and vegetable cells are cut or damaged exposing them to the air
pH: (potential or concentration of hydrogen).
Is a measurement of the acidity or alkalinity of a substance is. It ranges from 0 to 14. Neutral being 7 i.e. it is neither acid nor base (alkaline). Above 7 the substance is said to be alkaline and grows in alkalinity the higher up the scale. Acids have a pH that is less than 7 and become more acid lower down the scale

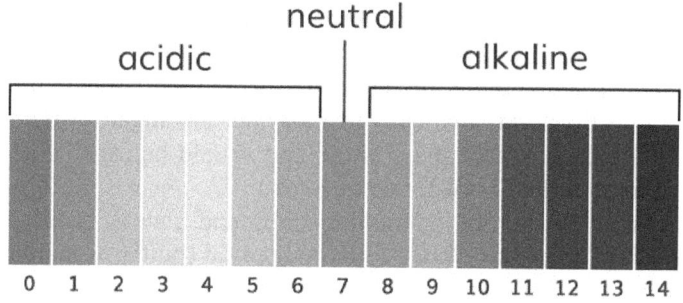

(Courtesy of of Alexey Bezrodny)

Every type of food has a pH value; animal proteins, grains and coffee are acidic, in particular vinegar. Vegetables tend to be alkaline, whereas sugar, flour and butter are neutral

Pathogen: a microbe: bacteria, virus or other microorganism capable of causing disease as opposed to a commensal which does not cause illness

Pectin: complex polysaccharide found in the cell walls of plants and helps bind cells together. It is extracted from fruits during jam and marmalade making causing the fruit mixture to set on cooling

Phytochemical: natural chemical compounds found in plants. Over 4,000 identified, some provide plants with colour (lycopene in tomatoes, chlorophyll in green vegetables) others act as anti-oxidants, others have therapeutic and disease preventative properties.

Pluche: small sprig of fresh herbs.

Polymer: a molecular structure built from a large number of the same or similar units (molecules) bonded together. Starch is a polymer of repeated glucose units bonded together.

Polyphenol: a structural class of natural, synthetic and organic chemicals found in abundance in tannins.

Polysaccharide: a carbohydrate such as starch or cellulose. Consist of three or more simple (monsaccharide) sugars bonded together.

Precipitate: causing solids to clump together to form a solid in a liquid e.g. casein proteins in milk precipitate when rennet is added in cheese making..

Proteolytic: enzymes which break down proteins into peptides or amino acids, see bromelain.

Proof, prove: to cause to swell or raise dough during preparation of fermented bread products.

Pulse: the dried seeds of various plants used in cooking, examples are beans, chickpeas, peas and lentils.

Purge (drip loss): loss of free water from meat cuts.

Pyrolysis: a decomposition of organic material brought about by high temperatures in the absence of oxygen. Example: caramelisation of sugar.
Rechauffe: reheated leftover food, a reheated dish e.g. cottage pie.
Ribbon stage: the point at which whisked eggs and sugar form a firm trail or ribbon on the surface of the mixture and should be capable of holding the pattern for a minute or two. See sabayon.
Roux: classical thickening agent for soups and sauces based on equal quantities of fat and flour. White roux: melted fat (butter or margarine)and flour used to make béchamel. Blonde/faun roux: flour lightly coloured in the fat (butter or margarine) for veloute sauces and soups. Brown roux: flour browned in fat (lard or dripping) used in basic brown sauce (**espagnole**) and brown soups.
Sabayon: whole egg whisked over heat to a ribbon stage and the first step in making genoise sponge. Zabaglione; an Italian dessert of egg yolks, sugar and wine whisked over heat to a form a thick foam.
Shortener: term used in bakery for fats which keep pastry short. Fats are rubbed into flour to act as a barrier to water to reduce gluten development as in short crust pastry.
Slurry: a combination of flour, corn flour or arrowroot mixed with a small amount of liquid to a thin paste to enable smooth incorporation of the thickener into a hot liquid e.g. custard powder mixed with cold milk, stirred into boiled milk to make custard.
Sous vide (under vacuum): method of cooking food in vacuum sealed packs at lower temperatures than conventional methods of cookery, cooking times can also be prolonged depending on the food type.
Stabiliser: food additive helps preserve structures of processed foods. Used in emulsions such as salad dressings to prevent separating out. Agar, cellulose, gelatine, pectin and xanthan gum are all examples of stabilisers.
Starch: polysaccharide, carbohydrate found in seeds, fruits, tubers, roots and stems of plants. Potatoes, rice, tapioca, flour are good sources of starch.

Modified starch or starch derivatives are prepared by physically, enzymatically, or chemically treating native starch to change their properties. They are used in practically all starch applications, i.e. as a thickener, stabilizer, and emulsifier and are modified to enhance performance in different applications and increase stability against excessive heat, acid, shear, time, cooling, or freezing. They are also used to change food texture and to decrease or increase viscosity.
Sucralose: (E995) a heat stable sugar sweetener. Can be used in bakery as a sugar substitute on a one for one basis. Brand names: Splenda.
Sugar: sweet, soluble carbohydrate, sourced from sugar cane and beet. Simple/single sugars are glucose, fructose an galactose. Di-saccharides are two single sugars bonded together: sucrose, maltose and lactose.

Sugar substitutes: natural or synthetically produced food additives providing a sweet taste.

Suspension: a substance dispersed in a liquid in clusters or particles in which the solids will eventually settle out; starch in water, dust in the air.

Sweating (of vegetables and rice): to cook or partly cook in fat (butter, oil or margarine) without colouring in order to soften and release flavour and aroma compounds. Sweating rice for a risotto to seal the starch within the grain.

Syneresis: release of moisture from a gel structure due to high or low temperatures. Examples are expulsion of water in over cooked scrambled egg, liquid weeping form lemon pie filling. Hydrocolloid gums such as xanthan and guar and modified starches are used extensively in food processing to prevent syneresis.

Trivet: a bed of bones or vegetables upon which meat is placed for roasting. The trivet prevents over cooking of the meat surface in contact with the roasting tray.

Velouté (meaning velvet): one of 5 mother sauces (Escoffier) or soup made with chicken, fish or veal stock and thickened with a blonde **roux**.

Viscosity: is a measure of a fluids resistance to gradual deformation by shear stress or tensile stress. Correspondingly it refers to the thickness, for example, water has a lower viscosity to that of cream

Yeast: is a living organism. It respires and with moisture and sugar produces carbon dioxide.

Xanthan gum: is a polysaccharide made by fermenting corn sugar with a microbial called Xanthomonas campestris. It is used extensively in food processing to make products thicker (i.e salad cream), as a stabilizer (prevent ingredients from separating) and in gluten free products which gives dough or batter a "stickiness" that would otherwise be achieved with gluten.

Bibliography

H. McGee, Hodder and Stoughton 2004 On Food and Cooking
V. Vaclavik, Springer 4th edition Essentials of Food Science
H. This, Columbia University Press 2007 Kitchen Mysteries
A. Davis, Oxford University press 1999 Oxford Companion to Food
M. Bilet and N. Myhrvold 2011 Modernist Cuisine, the Art and Science of Cooking
P. Gayler, Kyle Cathie Ltd, 2008 Sauce Book
P. Barham, Springer 2001 The Science of Cooking
Hanneman.L.J. Butterworth Heinmann 1995 Patisserie
Campbell, J. Fosket, D. Ceserani, V. Hodder Education Practical Cookery 11th edition

Thanks to:
Agriculture and Horticulture development Board
Livestrong.com
National Cattlemen's Beef Association

Illustrations:
Cuts of meat UK – 'Counterfeit_ua' iStock
pH scale – 'Alexey Bezrodny' iStock
Plant cell components – 'colematt' iStock

Robert Stordy

Robert Stordys' career began after successfully achieving professional catering qualifications at Hollings College in Manchester. Since then he has worked a chef for over forty years, working in some of the most prestigious hotels such as the Savoy Hotel and Claridges in London, and Gleneagles in Scotland. He has also worked in the Channel Islands, Italy and Dubai.

During his academic career, Robert has taught in both Further and Higher Education. As a lecturer at the University of Derby he delivered both kitchen based studies as well as taking a lead role in introducing Food Science studies to Culinary Arts programmes. Further qualifications were achieved in the Science of Gastronomy after studying with the University of Hong Kong.

As a chef, Robert has won numerous awards and accolades including North West Chef of the Year, University Chef of the Year and Best in Show and Gold medal at TUCO competitions held in 2014, 2015 and 2016.

Robert is a judge for international professional culinary competitions held at Hospitality shows in London and Birmingham and is a judge for the annual Derbyshire Life Magazine Food and Drink Awards.

He is a Fellow of the World master Chefs Society, a Master craftsman with the Craft Guild of Chefs, and holds a Licentiateship from City and Guilds of London Institute.

INDEX

Acrylamide, **150**
Actin, **148, 172, 173**
Agar, **108, 109**
Amylopectin, **90, 91, 143**
Amylose, **90, 91, 143**
Apple, **93, 95, 98**
Arrowroot, **65,144**

Babas, **132**
Bacteria, **138,154, 155, 185-90**
Baking, **34, 119-134**
Bard, **223**
Bavarois, **110**
Béarnaise, **69**
Béchamel, **62-65**
Beef, **22-25, 29,30, 32, 40-42, 152**
Beetroot, **83, 88**
Blanching, **15, 86, 87**
Boiling, **37, 45, 46, 85-87**
Braising, **37-39**
Brûlée, **100**
Beurre blanc, **71**
Beurre fondue, **72**
Butter, **71, 126**

Cakes, **129-134**
Caramelisation, **142**
Carbohydrates, **170-171**
Carrots, **88**
Carry over cooking, **140**
Cartouche, **66**
Carving, **33**
Celery, **89**
Cellulose, **170-171, 224**
Cheese, **175**
Chicken, **18-21**
Chocolate, **104,**
Choux paste, **119**
Collagen, **23, 148, 173**

Conduction, **34, 87, 137**
Confit, **167**
Connective tissue, **172-174**
Consommé, **58**
Convection, **137-138**
Cornflour, **65, 144**
Coulis, **99**
Crackling, **30**
Cream,**102-104, 114**
Curds, **167**
Curdling, **73, 100**
Curing, **157**
Custard, **73, 100**

Danger Zone, **186**
Deep – Frying, **16**
Denaturation, **147**
Dressings, **78**
Drying, **162**
Duck, **19**
Durum wheat, **49**

Eggs, **48, 50, 51, 67**
Elastin, **23, 148**
Emulsion, **66**
Enzymes, **141, 147, 155**

Fat, **30, 126, 169**
Fish, **11, 152, 174**
Flour, **48, 127, 128**
Freezing, **166, 186-87**
Fruits, **51, 92-99**
Frying, **7-10, 12, 15-17**

Game, **21-22**
Gelatine, **108, 148, 173**
Gelatinisation, **143, 148**
Genoese, **129**
Gliadin, **144, 176**
Glucose, **170**

Gluten, **128, 175, 176**
Glutenin, **13, 178**
Gravy, **74**
Grilling, **17**

Herbs, **55, 79**
Hollandaise, **69**
Hot water crust, **125**

Jam, **148, 164, 165**
Jus, **74**

Knives, **177-178**

Lamb, **22, 33, 43, 55, 174**

Maillard, **7, 8, 142, 143, 149**
Marmalade, **149**
Mayonnaise, **68**
Meringue, **101**
Mould, **155**
Mousse, **111**
Myoglobin, **30**
Myosin, **148, 172-174**
Non-enzymatic browning, **142**
Oils, **8, 14, 17, 126, 160, 169**
Onions, **89**
Ovens, **34**

Pancakes, **12**
Panna cotta, **110**
Pasta, **47, 48**
Pasteurisation, **149**
Pectin, **97, 149, 164, 165**
pH, **158, 164**
Phospholipid, **30, 67, 169**
Pickling, **158**
Pilaf, **47**
Poaching, **45, 50, 197**
Pork, **22-29, 31, 32, 43**
Potatoes, **90**
Pot-roast, **37**
Poultry, **18**

Pressure cooking, **46**
Protein, **172-176**
Puff pastry, **123**
Pyrolysis, **142**

Radiation, **139**
Refrigeration, **166, 186-167**
Retrogradation, **143, 146**
Rice, **47, 48, 171**
Risotto, **47**
Roasting, **18-28**
Rough puff paste, **123**
Roux, **64**

Sauce, **62-79**
Sauté, **13**
Savarin, **132**
Shallots, **89**
Short crust paste, **120**
Shortbread, **126**
Shortening, **127**
Slow cooking, **39, 98**
Smoking, **162**
Soufflés *(hot)*, **107**, *(cold)* **110**
Soups, **57-61**
Sous vide, **44**
Sponge, **129**
Starch, **143-145**
Steaks, **10**
Steaming, **51**
Sterilisation **137, 149**
Stewing, **37, 38**
Stir-frying, **14**
Stocks, **53-57**
Suet paste, **122**
Sugar, **115 170**
Sweating, **13**
Sweet pastry, **120**
Swiss roll, **129**
Syneresis, **146**

Tarte tatin, **124**
Ttemperature probe, **20**

Tenderising, **148**
Tuile, **125**
Turkey, **19-21**

Vanilla, **73**
Veal, **25**
Vegetables, **80-92**
Venison, **33**

Vinaigrette, **66-68**
Vinegar, **68-69**, **158-160**

Yeast, **132**, **155**
Yorkshire pudding, **34**

Lightning Source UK Ltd.
Milton Keynes UK
UKHW02f0622280218
318621UK00007B/190/P